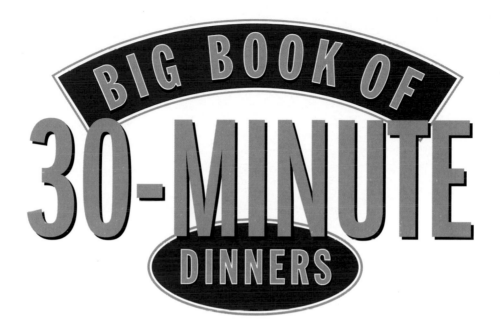

BIG BOOK OF 30-MINUTE DINNERS

BARNES
&NOBLE
BOOKS
NEW YORK

Pictured on front cover:

Bow Ties with Sausage and Sweet Peppers (see recipe, page 41)

Pictured on back cover:

Top Left: Sausage-Vegetable Soup (see recipe, page 144)

Top Right: Margarita Chicken (see recipe, page 60)

Bottom Left: Easy Sweet-and-Sour Chicken (see recipe, page 216)

Bottom Right: Gingered Peach and Pear Crisp (see recipe, page 281)

Previously published as
Better Homes and Gardens® Big Book of 30-Minute Dinners

Copyright 2003, 2000 by Meredith Corporation, Des Moines, Iowa. First Edition.

This edition published for Barnes & Noble, Inc., by Meredith Books

Printed in China

ISBN: 0-7607-5573-6

04 05 06 07 M 9 8 7 6 5 4 3 2 1

Preparing a home-cooked meal for your family is a pleasure to be cherished. With the **Big Book of 30-Minute Dinners,** it's easy to fit wholesome, family-pleasing home cooking into your busy schedule. Filled with more than 275 time-saving recipes, this enticing collection of fresh-tasting main dishes, soups, side dishes, and desserts gives you what you need to get dinner on the table in minutes. In addition, for health-conscious cooking, you'll find dishes that are low in fat marked with a ♥ symbol. What's more, there are dozens of helpful hints and a special section of kids' favorites. Don't wait any longer—select a couple of these full-flavored dishes and cook a satisfying meal for your family tonight.

TABLE OF CONTENTS

3

Bow Ties with Sausage and Sweet Peppers
See recipe, page 41

beef, pork, & lamb

tenderloins with rosemary and mushrooms

Serve these savory steaks with a packaged salad mix, steamed asparagus spears, and purchased dinner rolls for a speedy yet elegant meal.

INGREDIENTS

- 1 tablespoon margarine or butter
- 1 tablespoon cooking oil
- 4 beef tenderloin steaks, cut 1 inch thick
- 2 cups sliced fresh mushrooms
- 2 green onions, sliced (¼ cup)
- 1 tablespoon snipped fresh rosemary or 1 teaspoon dried rosemary, crushed
- ½ teaspoon bottled minced garlic or 1 clove garlic, minced
- ¼ teaspoon pepper
- ⅓ cup dry sherry, dry red wine, or beef broth
- Fresh rosemary sprigs (optional)

Sliced green onion adds a colorful accent to just about any dish.
When cutting the onions, slice all of the white bulb and about an inch or so of the green stem. One green onion should give you about 2 tablespoons sliced onion.

Prep time: 15 minutes
Cooking time: 15 minutes

DIRECTIONS

1. In a large skillet melt margarine or butter. Stir in cooking oil. Trim any separable fat from steaks. Add steaks to skillet and cook over medium to medium-high heat for 10 to 12 minutes or to desired doneness, turning once. Transfer to a serving platter, reserving drippings in skillet. Keep steaks warm.

2. Stir mushrooms, green onions, rosemary, garlic, and pepper into reserved drippings. Cook and stir over medium-high heat for 3 to 4 minutes or until mushrooms are tender. Reduce heat.

3. Carefully stir in sherry, wine, or beef broth. Cook and stir about 1 minute more or until heated through. Spoon over steaks. If desired, garnish with fresh rosemary sprigs. Makes 4 servings.

NUTRITION FACTS PER SERVING:

249 calories
14 g total fat
4 g saturated fat
64 mg cholesterol
83 mg sodium
4 g carbohydrate
1 g fiber
23 g protein

beef tenderloins with wine sauce

Had a great day at work and feel like celebrating? Serve these richly sauced steaks for dinner.

INGREDIENTS

- 4 beef tenderloin steaks, cut 1 inch thick
- ½ teaspoon coarsely cracked black pepper
- 1 tablespoon margarine or butter
- ½ of a medium onion, chopped (¼ cup)
- ¼ cup beef broth
- ¼ cup dry red wine
- 1 teaspoon dried marjoram, crushed

Prep time: 10 minutes
Cooking time: 15 minutes

DIRECTIONS

1. Trim any separable fat from steaks. Press pepper onto both sides of steaks. In a large skillet cook steaks in hot margarine or butter over medium to medium-high heat for 10 to 12 minutes or to desired doneness, turning once. Transfer steaks to a serving platter, reserving drippings in skillet. Keep steaks warm while preparing the sauce.

2. For sauce, stir onion into reserved drippings in skillet. Cook for 3 to 4 minutes or until onion is tender. Remove from heat. Carefully add broth, wine, and marjoram to onion in skillet, stirring to scrape up any browned bits. Return to heat. Bring to boiling. Reduce heat. Boil gently, uncovered, about 2 minutes or until mixture is reduced to about ¼ cup. Serve sauce over steaks. Makes 4 servings.

NUTRITION FACTS PER SERVING:

315 calories
15 g total fat
5 g saturated fat
112 mg cholesterol
176 mg sodium
2 g carbohydrate
0 g fiber
38 g protein

7

herbed steak

Enjoy this delicious steak in the summertime. For optimal flavor, use a vine-ripened tomato and fresh herbs.

INGREDIENTS

- 2 beef top loin steaks, cut ¾ inch thick (about 1¼ pounds total)
- 1 tablespoon margarine or butter
- 3 green onions, sliced (about ⅓ cup)
- 1½ teaspoons snipped fresh thyme or basil or ½ teaspoon dried thyme or basil, crushed
- ¼ teaspoon salt
- ⅛ teaspoon pepper
- 1 medium tomato, chopped (⅔ cup)
  Fresh basil or thyme (optional)

Prep time: 10 minutes
Cooking time: 12 minutes

DIRECTIONS

1. Trim any separable fat from steaks. Cut each steak in half. In a large heavy skillet cook steaks in hot margarine or butter over medium heat about 10 minutes or to desired doneness, turning once.

2. Remove steaks, reserving drippings in skillet. Keep steaks warm. Cook green onions, snipped or crushed thyme or basil, salt, and pepper in drippings for 1 to 2 minutes or until green onions are tender. Stir in tomato. Heat through. Spoon over steaks. If desired, garnish with additional fresh basil or thyme. Makes 4 servings.

NUTRITION FACTS PER SERVING:

207 calories
9 g total fat
3 g saturated fat
81 mg cholesterol
230 mg sodium
2 g carbohydrate
0 g fiber
28 g protein

sautéed sirloin and mushrooms

Bottled hoisin sauce, traditionally an Oriental condiment, gives the mushroom glaze a subtle, sweet-and-tangy flavor. Look for hoisin sauce with the Oriental products in your grocery store or in an Oriental market.

INGREDIENTS

- 1 to 1¼ pounds boneless beef sirloin steak, cut ½ inch thick
- ¾ teaspoon herb pepper or ¼ teaspoon garlic pepper
- 1 tablespoon margarine or butter
- ¾ cup beef broth
- 1 tablespoon hoisin sauce, teriyaki sauce, or Worcestershire sauce
- 1 small onion, cut into very thin wedges
- ½ of an 8-ounce package sliced fresh mushrooms (about 1½ cups)

Prep time: 10 minutes
Cooking time: 20 minutes

DIRECTIONS

1. Cut steak into 4 serving-size pieces. Sprinkle with herb pepper or garlic pepper. In a 10-inch skillet cook steak in hot margarine or butter over medium heat for 8 to 10 minutes or to desired doneness, turning once. Remove steak from skillet. Keep steak warm.

2. For mushroom glaze, carefully add beef broth and hoisin, teriyaki, or Worcestershire sauce to skillet. Cook and stir until bubbly, scraping brown bits from the bottom of the pan. Stir in onion wedges and sliced mushrooms. Cook over medium-high heat about 8 minutes or until vegetables are tender and the glaze is reduced by half its volume (to 1 cup). Transfer warm steak to dinner plates and spoon glaze over. Makes 4 servings.

NUTRITION FACTS PER SERVING:

247 calories
13 g total fat
5 g saturated fat
76 mg cholesterol
410 mg sodium
3 g carbohydrate
1 g fiber
27 g protein

9

beef steak with red onion relish

A good steak can be part of a healthful diet. Choose a lean cut, such as sirloin, and trim off any separable fat.

INGREDIENTS

- 1 **pound boneless beef sirloin steak, cut ¾ inch thick**
- ¼ **to 1 teaspoon coarsely ground black pepper**
- 2 **teaspoons cooking oil**
- 1 **large red onion, thinly sliced and separated into rings**
- 1 **8½-ounce can tomatoes, cut up**
- ¼ **cup dry red wine**
- ½ **teaspoon dried sage, crushed**
- ¼ **teaspoon salt**

Dry red wine boosts the flavor of hearty beef dishes like this one. When selecting a wine to use, opt for a dry red dinner wine, such as red burgundy, cabernet sauvignon, or chianti. If you prefer not to add dry red wine to a dish, beef broth makes a good substitute.

Start to finish: 25 minutes

DIRECTIONS

1. Trim any separable fat from steak. Cut the steak into 4 serving-size pieces, and rub both sides with the pepper. In a large nonstick skillet heat oil over medium-high heat. Add the steaks and cook about 8 minutes or until medium doneness, turning once. Remove the steak from the skillet; reserve drippings. Keep steak warm.

2. In the skillet cook onion in drippings over medium heat for 5 to 7 minutes or until crisp-tender. Carefully add tomatoes, wine, sage, and salt. Bring to boiling. Cook 1 to 2 minutes or until most of the liquid is evaporated. Serve onion mixture with steak. Makes 4 servings.

NUTRITION FACTS PER SERVING:

246 calories
12 g total fat
4 g saturated fat
76 mg cholesterol
200 mg sodium
3 g carbohydrate
1 g fiber
26 g protein

INGREDIENTS

1   14½-ounce can Mexican-style
    stewed tomatoes
1¾ cups water
    Several dashes bottled hot
    pepper sauce
1¼ cups long grain rice
1   to 1¼ pounds beef flank steak
1   teaspoon chili powder
½   teaspoon salt

¼   teaspoon ground cumin
¼   teaspoon ground black pepper
    Dash ground cinnamon
    Snipped fresh cilantro or parsley
    (optional)

flank steak with spanish rice

Summertime, or anytime, you can grill the flank steak instead of broiling it. Cook the meat directly over medium coals for 18 to 22 minutes total for medium doneness, turning once. Flank steak is a lean cut of beef, so avoid overcooking it or it may become dry and tough.

Start to finish: 30 minutes

DIRECTIONS

1. In a 2-quart saucepan combine the stewed tomatoes, water, and hot pepper sauce. Bring to boiling. Stir in uncooked rice. Return to boiling; reduce heat. Cover and simmer for 20 minutes. Remove from heat; let stand for 5 minutes.

2. Meanwhile, trim any separable fat from steak. Combine chili powder, salt, cumin, black pepper, and cinnamon. Rub spice mixture into flank steak on both sides. Place steak on unheated rack of broiler pan. Broil steak 3 inches from the heat for 6 minutes. Turn and broil until desired doneness. (Allow 7 to 8 minutes more for medium-rare.)

3. To serve, thinly slice flank steak diagonally across the grain. Fluff rice with a fork. Serve steak slices over rice. If desired, sprinkle with cilantro or parsley. Makes 4 to 6 servings.

NUTRITION FACTS PER SERVING:

 409 calories
9 g total fat
4 g saturated fat
53 mg cholesterol
698 mg sodium
54 g carbohydrate
1 g fiber
27 g protein

beef-vegetable ragoût

The earthy, elegant, and traditionally long-simmered French stew called ragoût gets an update in taste and reduced preparation time. This version, flavored with port wine and filled with crisp, bright vegetables, can be on the table in 30 minutes.

INGREDIENTS

- ¾ pound beef tenderloin, cut into ¾-inch pieces
- 1 tablespoon olive oil or cooking oil
- 1½ cups sliced fresh shiitake or button mushrooms (about 4 ounces)
- 1 medium onion, chopped (½ cup)
- 1 teaspoon bottled minced garlic or 2 cloves garlic, minced
- 3 tablespoons all-purpose flour
- ½ teaspoon salt
- ¼ teaspoon pepper
- 1 14½-ounce can beef broth
- ¼ cup port wine or dry sherry
- 2 cups sugar snap peas or one 10-ounce package frozen sugar snap peas, thawed
- 1 cup cherry tomatoes, halved
  Hot cooked wide noodles or bow-tie pasta (optional)

Casseroles and stews

are time-honored traditions at the table. Why? The main reason is these one-pot meals can stand alone, if necessary. All of the elements of the meal are in one place, so there aren't three pots to watch and wash. For casual entertaining, this hearty and flavorful ragoût can be made ahead and simply reheated while the noodles are cooking (just add the snap peas right before serving so they stay crisp and green). Serve with crusty bread and a salad, if you like, and your company fare is finished.

Start to finish: 30 minutes

DIRECTIONS

1. In a large nonstick skillet cook and stir meat in hot oil for 2 to 3 minutes or until meat is of desired doneness. Remove meat from skillet; reserve drippings. Keep meat warm.

2. In the same skillet cook mushrooms, onion, and garlic until tender.

3. Stir in flour, salt, and pepper. Add beef broth and wine or sherry. Cook and stir until thickened and bubbly. Stir in sugar snap peas; cook and stir for 2 to 3 minutes more or until peas are tender. Stir in meat and tomatoes; heat through. If desired, serve over noodles or pasta. Makes 4 servings.

NUTRITION FACTS PER SERVING:

- 252 calories
- 9 g total fat
- 3 g saturated fat
- 48 mg cholesterol
- 647 mg sodium
- 17 g carbohydrate
- 3 g fiber
- 21 g protein

stir-fried beef and noodles

INGREDIENTS

- 1 3-ounce package beef-flavor ramen noodles
- ½ pound beef sirloin steak, cut ¾ inch thick
- 1 tablespoon cooking oil
- 1 medium carrot, thinly sliced (½ cup)
- 1 stalk celery, bias-sliced (½ cup)
- 1 6-ounce package frozen pea pods, thawed
- ¼ cup water
- 1 tablespoon snipped fresh parsley
- 2 teaspoons teriyaki sauce
- ½ teaspoon ground ginger
- ¼ teaspoon crushed red pepper (optional)

Want a more Oriental flair? Substitute ¼ teaspoon five-spice powder for the ground ginger.

Start to finish: 30 minutes

DIRECTIONS

1. Cook ramen noodles according to package directions, except drain the noodles and reserve the seasoning package.

2. Meanwhile, trim any separable fat from the steak. Cut the steak into thin bite-size strips; set aside.

3. Pour cooking oil into a wok or large skillet. (Add more oil as necessary during cooking.) Preheat over medium-high heat. Add carrot and celery. Stir-fry for 2 to 3 minutes or until crisp-tender. Remove the vegetables from the wok or skillet.

4. Add the steak strips to the hot wok. Stir-fry for 2 to 3 minutes or to desired doneness. Return carrot and celery to the wok. Stir in noodles, reserved seasoning package, pea pods, water, parsley, teriyaki sauce, ginger, and, if desired, crushed red pepper. Cook over medium heat until heated through, stirring occasionally. Makes 3 servings.

NUTRITION FACTS PER SERVING:

621 calories
30 g total fat
3 g saturated fat
50 mg cholesterol
1,724 mg sodium
61 g carbohydrate
2 g fiber
30 g protein

southwest beef and linguine toss

A jar of picante sauce makes an easy yet flavor-packed sauce for this stir-fried dish.

INGREDIENTS

- 4 ounces packaged dried linguine
- ¾ pound beef top round steak
- 1 tablespoon cooking oil
- 2 teaspoons chili powder
- ½ teaspoon bottled minced garlic or 1 clove garlic, minced
- 1 small onion, sliced and separated into rings
- 1 red or green sweet pepper, cut into strips
- 1 10-ounce package frozen whole kernel corn
- ¼ cup picante sauce
  Fresh cilantro (optional)
  Chili powder (optional)

Start to finish: 25 minutes

DIRECTIONS

1. Cook linguine according to package directions. Drain. Rinse with warm water. Set aside.

2. Meanwhile, trim any separable fat from steak. Cut steak into thin, bite-size strips. Set aside.

3. Pour cooking oil into a wok or large skillet. (Add more oil as necessary during cooking.) Preheat over medium-high heat. Stir-fry the 2 teaspoons chili powder and garlic in hot oil for 15 seconds. Add onion; stir-fry for 1 minute. Add the red or green pepper; stir-fry for 1 to 2 minutes more or until vegetables are crisp-tender. Remove vegetables from wok.

4. Add the beef to the hot wok; stir-fry for 2 to 3 minutes or to desired doneness. Return vegetables to the wok. Stir in corn and picante sauce. Add the cooked linguine. Toss together to coat with sauce. Cook and stir until heated through. If desired, garnish with fresh cilantro and sprinkle with additional chili powder. Makes 4 servings.

NUTRITION FACTS PER SERVING:

- 351 calories
- 9 g total fat
- 2 g saturated fat
- 54 mg cholesterol
- 166 mg sodium
- 43 g carbohydrate
- 1 g fiber
- 27 g protein

spicy steak and ranch salad

INGREDIENTS

- ½ cup canned French-fried onions
- 1 pound boneless beef top sirloin steak, cut 1 inch thick
- 1 tablespoon Cajun seasoning or Homemade Cajun Seasoning (see recipe, page 121)
- 1 tablespoon lime juice
- ½ teaspoon bottled minced garlic or 1 clove garlic, minced
- 1 10-ounce package European-style salad greens (romaine, iceberg lettuce, radicchio, endive, and leaf lettuce)
- 2 carrots, cut into thin bite-size strips
- ½ cup thinly sliced radishes
- ½ cup bottled fat-free ranch salad dressing

Steak and onions as you've never seen them before! Sirloin is perked up by Cajun spices before slicing, then arranged on tossed greens and topped with a scattering of crispy French-fried onions. This innovative recipe has the makings of an instant classic.

Start to finish: 25 minutes

DIRECTIONS

1. In a large nonstick skillet cook French-fried onions over medium-high heat about 2 minutes or until browned, stirring occasionally. Set aside.

2. Meanwhile, trim any separable fat from steak. Combine Cajun seasoning, lime juice, and garlic; rub over both sides of steak. In the same skillet cook steak over medium heat to desired doneness, turning once. (Allow 6 to 8 minutes for medium-rare or 9 to 12 minutes for medium.) Remove skillet from heat; let stand for 10 minutes. Cut steak into thin bite-size slices. If desired, season with salt.

3. On a large serving platter toss together the salad greens, carrots, and radishes. Arrange steak strips over salad greens. Sprinkle with French-fried onions. Drizzle dressing over salad. Makes 4 servings.

Wide strips of carrot make this salad extra-colorful. To create the strips, cut a carrot in half crosswise with a knife. Then use a vegetable peeler to slice off lengthwise strips.

NUTRITION FACTS PER SERVING:

310 calories
13 g total fat
4 g saturated fat
76 mg cholesterol
557 mg sodium
16 g carbohydrate
3 g fiber
28 g protein

15

garlic-mustard steak sandwiches

Another time, skip the hoagie rolls and serve these zesty steak strips with fresh tomato slices, corn on the cob, and a tossed green salad.

INGREDIENTS

- 2 tablespoons Dijon-style mustard
- ½ teaspoon dried marjoram or thyme, crushed
- ½ teaspoon bottled minced garlic or 1 clove garlic, minced
- ¼ teaspoon coarsely ground black pepper
- 1 to 1½ pounds beef flank steak
- 4 to 6 hoagie rolls, split
  Dijon-style mustard (optional)

Coarsely ground pepper gives this hearty sandwich extra pizzazz. Look for it in the spice aisle of your supermarket. Or, grind whole black peppercorns with a pepper mill.

Prep time: 10 minutes
Broiling time: 12 minutes

DIRECTIONS

1. In a small mixing bowl combine the 2 tablespoons mustard, marjoram or thyme, garlic, and pepper. Trim any separable fat from the steak. Brush both sides of the steak with the mustard mixture.

2. Place the steak on the unheated rack of a broiler pan. Broil 4 to 5 inches from the heat for 12 to 17 minutes or to desired doneness, turning once. Thinly slice steak diagonally across the grain. Serve steak strips in hoagie rolls. If desired, pass additional mustard. Makes 4 to 6 servings.

NUTRITION FACTS PER SERVING:

176 calories
9 g total fat
3 g saturated fat
53 mg cholesterol
255 mg sodium
1 g carbohydrate
0 g fiber
22 g protein

hot italian beef salad

For a reduced-fat version of this flavorful salad, use a fat-free Italian salad dressing. You'll cut the fat per serving by a whopping 18 grams.

INGREDIENTS

¾ **pound beef flank steak or beef top round steak, cut 1 inch thick**

6 **cups packaged torn mixed salad greens**

3 **teaspoons olive oil or cooking oil**

1 **medium red or green sweet pepper, cut into bite-size strips**

½ **cup clear Italian salad dressing or red wine vinegar and oil salad dressing**

1 **tablespoon grated Parmesan cheese**

Coarsely ground black pepper

Start to finish: 20 minutes

DIRECTIONS

1. Trim any separable fat from steak. Cut steak into thin bite-size strips. Arrange the mixed salad greens on 4 salad plates.

2. In a large skillet heat 2 teaspoons of the oil. Add the sweet pepper; cook for 1 to 2 minutes or until nearly crisp-tender.

3. Add the remaining oil to the skillet. Add steak strips. Cook and stir for 2 to 3 minutes or to desired doneness. Add the salad dressing. Cook and stir until heated through.

4. Spoon the beef mixture over the salad greens. Sprinkle with Parmesan cheese and coarsely ground pepper. Serve immediately. Makes 4 servings.

NUTRITION FACTS PER SERVING:

318 calories
24 g total fat
5 g saturated fat
41 mg cholesterol
348 mg sodium
7 g carbohydrate
2 g fiber
19 g protein

Mixed salad greens can be any combination of greens that you like. A blend of textures, colors, and flavors makes for a more interesting salad. Iceberg, leaf, bibb, and romaine are all mild-flavored greens, while spinach, arugula, endive, chicory, escarole, and radicchio have a bit more bite. If you don't want to keep several kinds of greens on hand, look for packaged salad mixtures in the produce section of your supermarket. You'll find a variety of combos from a classic iceberg blend to more unusual French- or Italian-style mixtures.

basil-mozzarella cheeseburgers

Our Italian-style version of the perennially favorite outdoor hamburger uses 90-percent lean beef.

INGREDIENTS

- ¼ cup finely chopped onion
- 2 tablespoons fine dry bread crumbs
- 2 tablespoons finely chopped green sweet pepper (optional)
- 2 tablespoons catsup
- 1 tablespoon prepared horseradish
- 1 tablespoon prepared mustard
- ¼ teaspoon salt
- ¼ teaspoon ground black pepper
- 1 pound extra-lean ground beef
- 4 slices smoked or regular mozzarella cheese

- 4 whole wheat hamburger buns, split and toasted
- Fresh basil leaves
- ¼ cup Red Sweet Pepper Relish (see recipe, below)

Prep time: 15 minutes
Grilling time: 14 minutes

DIRECTIONS

1. In a medium mixing bowl combine onion, bread crumbs, and, if desired, green pepper. Add the catsup, horseradish, mustard, salt, and black pepper. Add ground beef; mix well. Shape the meat mixture into four ¾-inch-thick patties.

2. Grill patties on the rack of an uncovered grill directly over medium coals for 7 minutes. Turn burgers; grill 7 to 11 minutes more or until no pink remains, topping each burger with a slice of cheese for the last 2 minutes of grilling.

3. Serve burgers on toasted whole wheat buns with fresh basil leaves and the Red Sweet Pepper Relish. Makes 4 servings.

Red Sweet Pepper Relish: In a food processor bowl combine ½ cup purchased roasted red sweet pepper strips; 1 tablespoon finely chopped pitted ripe olives; 2 teaspoons olive oil; 2 teaspoons snipped fresh thyme or ½ teaspoon dried thyme, crushed; and ¼ teaspoon ground black pepper. Cover and process with several on-off turns until coarsely chopped. Cover and chill until ready to serve. Makes about ⅔ cup.

NUTRITION FACTS PER SERVING:

421 calories
20 g total fat
9 g saturated fat
93 mg cholesterol
702 mg sodium
28 g carbohydrate
2 g fiber
30 g protein

18

INGREDIENTS

- 1½ cups fresh mushrooms (such as crimini, porcini, morel, shiitake, or button), quartered, halved, or sliced
- 2 green onions, sliced (¼ cup)
- 4 teaspoons margarine or butter
- ½ pound veal leg round steak or veal sirloin steak or 2 skinless, boneless chicken breast halves (½ pound total)
- ⅛ teaspoon salt
- ⅛ teaspoon pepper
- ⅓ cup dry marsala or dry sherry
- ¼ cup chicken broth
- 1 tablespoon snipped fresh parsley

veal scaloppine with marsala skillet

Chicken breasts make an inexpensive substitute for traditional veal, if you prefer. Serve with steamed Italian flat beans or whole green beans.

Start to finish: 15 minutes

DIRECTIONS

1. In a 12-inch skillet cook mushrooms and green onions in 2 teaspoons of the hot margarine for 4 to 5 minutes or until tender. Remove from skillet, reserving drippings. Set aside.

2. Meanwhile, rinse veal or chicken and pat dry with paper towels. Cut veal into 2 serving-size pieces. Place each piece of veal or chicken breast half between 2 sheets of plastic wrap. Working from center to edges, pound lightly with the flat side of a meat mallet to about ⅛-inch thickness. Remove the plastic wrap.

3. Sprinkle meat with salt and pepper. In the same skillet cook veal or chicken in the remaining hot margarine over medium-high heat for 2 minutes or until no longer pink, turning once. Transfer to dinner plates. Keep warm.

4. Add marsala or sherry and chicken broth to drippings in skillet. Bring to boiling. Boil mixture gently, uncovered, about 1 minute, scraping up any browned bits. Return mushroom mixture to skillet; add parsley. Heat through. To serve, spoon the mushroom mixture over meat. Serve immediately. Makes 2 servings.

NUTRITION FACTS PER SERVING:

- 283 calories
- 12 g total fat
- 3 g saturated fat
- 92 mg cholesterol
- 384 mg sodium
- 6 g carbohydrate
- 1 g fiber
- 27 g protein

roast beef and red pepper sandwiches

For this hearty meat and vegetable sandwich, use leftover roast beef or beef from the deli.

INGREDIENTS

- ⅓ cup light mayonnaise dressing or mayonnaise
- ⅓ cup Dijon-style mustard
- 2 to 4 tablespoons prepared horseradish
- 6 6- or 7-inch Italian bread shells (Boboli) or Italian flatbreads (focaccia)
- ¾ pound thinly sliced cooked lean roast beef
- 1 12-ounce jar roasted red sweet peppers, drained and cut into ¼-inch-wide strips
- 6 ounces thinly sliced Monterey Jack cheese
- 2 cups fresh watercress
- 2 cups fresh spinach

On-call sandwiches are ideal for busy days because they're ready when you are. To make these robust beef sandwiches ahead, assemble the ingredients, wrap the sandwiches in plastic wrap, and store them in the refrigerator for up to 24 hours.

Start to finish: 25 minutes

DIRECTIONS

1. In a small bowl combine mayonnaise dressing, mustard, and horseradish. Slice bread shells in half horizontally. Spread bottom of each bread shell with mustard mixture; layer with roast beef, roasted red sweet peppers, Monterey Jack cheese, watercress, and spinach. Top with bread tops.

2. To serve, slice each sandwich in half. Makes 12 servings (half sandwich per serving).

NUTRITION FACTS PER SERVING:

303 calories
14 g total fat
4 g saturated fat
41 mg cholesterol
656 mg sodium
27 g carbohydrate
2 g fiber
20 g protein

INGREDIENTS

- ¼ cup mayonnaise or salad dressing
- 2 tablespoons chutney, chopped
- ½ teaspoon curry powder
- ¼ cup chunky peanut butter
- 8 slices whole grain bread or rye bread
- ½ pound thinly sliced, cooked lean roast beef or pork
- 8 thin slices tomato
- 4 lettuce leaves

curried roast beef sandwiches

Chutney adds to the East Indian flavor of this sandwich. Look for it in your supermarket's condiment aisle. Commercial chutneys come in a variety of flavors—they often contain mangoes, tamarinds, raisins, and spices, and can be spicy-hot.

Start to finish: 15 minutes

DIRECTIONS

1. In a small mixing bowl stir together the mayonnaise or salad dressing, chutney, and curry powder. Set aside.

2. Spread peanut butter on 4 of the bread slices. Top with roast beef or pork. Spoon curry mixture over meat; top with tomato, lettuce, and remaining bread slices. Makes 4 servings.

A pasta salad side dish comes together quickly if you remember to cook extra pasta whenever you fix it as a main course. Store cooked pasta in your refrigerator for 3 days. Toss it with a bottled dressing and chopped vegetables for a high-carbohydrate accompaniment to this sandwich.

NUTRITION FACTS PER SERVING:

467 calories
25 g total fat
5 g saturated fat
53 mg cholesterol
487 mg sodium
37 g carbohydrate
5 g fiber
28 g protein

tortellini alfredo with roasted peppers

Cheese-filled tortellini make a delicious substitution for the meat-filled tortellini.

INGREDIENTS

- 1 9-ounce package refrigerated meat-filled tortellini
- ½ of a 7-ounce jar roasted red sweet peppers (½ cup)
- ½ cup refrigerated light alfredo sauce
- ½ cup shredded fresh basil
- ¼ to ½ teaspoon coarsely ground black pepper

Shredding fresh basil is easy. Simply roll several leaves together loosely. Then, using a sharp knife, cut the roll crosswise into thin strips.

Start to finish: 25 minutes

DIRECTIONS

1. Cook the tortellini according to package directions; drain. Meanwhile, drain the roasted sweet peppers and cut into ½-inch-wide strips.

2. In a large saucepan heat the alfredo sauce. Add the cooked and drained tortellini. Reduce heat; add the sweet pepper strips. Simmer, uncovered, for 5 minutes, stirring often.

3. To serve, stir half of the basil into the pasta mixture. Spoon mixture into shallow pasta bowls or onto dinner plates. Sprinkle with ground black pepper and top with the remaining basil. Makes 3 servings.

NUTRITION FACTS PER SERVING:

  362 calories
12 g total fat
5 g saturated fat
61 mg cholesterol
710 mg sodium
50 g carbohydrate
1 g fiber
16 g protein

INGREDIENTS

4   boneless pork loin chops, cut
    ¾ inch thick

1   tablespoon herb-pepper
    seasoning

2   tablespoons olive oil

2   cups cut-up salad-bar vegetables
    (such as sweet peppers,
    carrots, mushrooms, onion,
    and/or broccoli)

1   14½-ounce can chicken broth

2   cups quick-cooking brown rice

¼   cup chopped roasted red sweet
    pepper
    Fresh herb sprigs (optional)

peppered pork chops and pilaf

Roasted red pepper comes in both mild and hot forms. For this recipe, be sure to select roasted red sweet pepper. Look for it in the produce section of your supermarket or in the canned vegetable aisle.

Start to finish: 25 minutes

DIRECTIONS

1. Sprinkle both sides of pork with 2 teaspoons of the herb-pepper seasoning. In a large skillet cook chops in 1 tablespoon of the olive oil for 5 minutes. Turn chops. Cook for 5 to 7 minutes more or until just slightly pink in centers and juices run clear.

2. Meanwhile, cut vegetables into bite-size pieces. In a saucepan heat the remaining olive oil. Add vegetables and cook for 2 minutes. Carefully add broth. Bring to boiling. Stir in uncooked rice, roasted sweet pepper, and remaining herb-pepper seasoning.

Return to boiling; reduce heat. Cover and simmer for 5 minutes. Remove from heat. Let stand 5 minutes. Serve chops with rice. If desired, garnish with fresh herb sprigs. Makes 4 servings.

NUTRITION FACTS PER SERVING:

431 calories
20 g total fat
5 g saturated fat
77 mg cholesterol
408 mg sodium
34 g carbohydrate
5 g fiber
31 g protein

If you don't have chicken broth on

hand, substitute chicken bouillon and water instead. To make the equivalent of a 14½-ounce can of broth, combine 2 teaspoons of bouillon granules or 2 bouillon cubes with 1¾ cups of boiling water.

23

apricot pork medallions

Tangy apricot sauce enhances the mild flavor of the fork-tender pork tenderloin slices.

INGREDIENTS

- 1 cup quick-cooking rice
- ¾ pound pork tenderloin
- 1 tablespoon margarine or butter
- 1 16-ounce can unpeeled apricot halves in light syrup
- 1 tablespoon cornstarch
- ¼ cup red plum jam or currant jelly
- 2 tablespoons white wine vinegar
- 2 green onions, sliced (about ¼ cup)

Start to finish: 20 minutes

24

DIRECTIONS

1. Cook rice according to package directions. Meanwhile, trim any separable fat from pork. Cut pork into ¾-inch slices. Place each piece of pork between 2 sheets of plastic wrap. Working from center to edges, pound lightly with flat side of meat mallet to ½-inch thickness. Remove plastic wrap.

2. In a large skillet cook pork in hot margarine or butter over medium-high heat for 4 to 6 minutes or until just slightly pink in centers and juices run clear, turning once. Remove pork from skillet. Keep warm.

3. Meanwhile, for sauce, drain apricots, reserving ⅔ cup of the juice. Set juice aside. Slice apricot pieces. In a small saucepan stir together reserved apricot juice and cornstarch. Stir in plum jam or currant jelly and vinegar. Cook and stir over medium heat until thickened and bubbly. Cook and stir for 2 minutes more. Stir in apricots. Heat through.

4. Divide rice among 4 dinner plates. Top with pork medallions. Spoon sauce over pork. Sprinkle with green onions. Makes 4 servings.

NUTRITION FACTS PER SERVING:

- 341 calories
- 6 g total fat
- 2 g saturated fat
- 60 mg cholesterol
- 85 mg sodium
- 50 g carbohydrate
- 2 g fiber
- 21 g protein

INGREDIENTS

- 2 medium fennel bulbs
- 4 boneless pork loin chops, cut 1½ inches thick (America's Cut)
- Salt
- Pepper
- 1 small onion, sliced
- 1 tablespoon olive oil
- ½ of a small head cabbage, coarsely chopped (about 2½ cups)
- ½ cup pear nectar or apple juice
- ¼ cup balsamic vinegar
- ½ teaspoon caraway seed
- ½ teaspoon dried thyme, crushed
- ¼ teaspoon salt
- ¼ teaspoon pepper
- ⅛ teaspoon ground nutmeg
- Pear nectar or apple juice
- 2 tablespoons cold water
- 1 tablespoon cornstarch
- 1 large pear, cored and sliced

pork with pear, fennel, and cabbage

Fennel bulbs are sold with stalks attached. The vegetable has a celerylike texture, and the stalks have feathery green tops or leaves. The stalks should be crisp, and the leaves, bright green and fresh-looking.

Start to finish: 30 minutes

DIRECTIONS

1. Trim fennel; cut into thin wedges. Trim any separable fat from pork. Season pork with salt and pepper. In a 10-inch skillet cook the chops and onion in hot oil about 8 minutes or until browned, turning once. Drain off fat.

2. Arrange the fennel and cabbage on top of meat. In a small bowl stir together the ½ cup pear nectar or apple juice, the vinegar, caraway seed, thyme, the ¼ teaspoon salt, ¼ teaspoon pepper, and the nutmeg; pour into skillet. Cover and simmer for 12 to 15 minutes or until tender. Use a slotted spoon to transfer the pork and vegetables to a serving platter. Keep warm.

3. For sauce, measure the pan juices. If necessary add enough additional pear nectar or apple juice to pan juices to make 1¼ cups liquid; return to skillet. Blend together the water and cornstarch; stir into juices. Cook and stir over medium heat until thickened and bubbly. Stir in pear slices; heat through. Spoon pear slices and sauce over pork and vegetables. Makes 4 servings.

To keep the chops and vegetables warm, cover the serving platter with foil. Or, if you prefer, use a heatproof platter and place the foil-covered platter in an oven on low heat.

NUTRITION FACTS PER SERVING:

334 calories
15 g total fat
4 g saturated fat
77 mg cholesterol
229 mg sodium
25 g carbohydrate
2 g fiber
26 g protein

25

pork chops with chili-apricot glaze

Chili sauce and brown mustard give this sweet fruit glaze a little bite.

INGREDIENTS

- ¼ cup apricot jam or preserves
- ¼ cup chili sauce
- 1 tablespoon sweet-hot mustard or brown mustard
- 1 tablespoon water
- 4 boneless pork top loin chops, cut 1 inch thick (about 1½ pounds total)

Make broiled Parmesan potatoes to

accompany the chops. Cut 2 medium potatoes into ¼-inch slices. Arrange potatoes on broiler pan next to meat; brush potatoes with melted margarine or butter seasoned with paprika, garlic powder, and pepper. Broil potatoes for 8 to 9 minutes; turn and sprinkle with Parmesan cheese. Broil 4 to 6 minutes more. If desired, broil strips of red or green sweet peppers, too.

Prep time: 5 minutes
Broiling time: 16 minutes

DIRECTIONS

1. For glaze, cut up any large pieces in apricot jam or preserves. In a small saucepan combine jam or preserves, chili sauce, mustard, and water. Cook and stir over medium-low heat until heated through. Remove from heat.

2. Trim any separable fat from pork chops. Place chops on unheated rack of broiler pan. Broil 4 to 5 inches from heat for 8 minutes.

3. Turn pork chops; brush generously with glaze. Broil 8 to 12 minutes more or until centers of chops are just slightly pink in centers and juices run clear. Spoon any remaining glaze over meat

before serving. Makes 4 servings.

Note: If you can't find boneless chops, purchase a 1-pound boneless pork loin roast and slice into 4 portions yourself.

NUTRITION FACTS PER SERVING:

244 calories
9 g total fat
3 g saturated fat
64 mg cholesterol
303 mg sodium
18 g carbohydrate
0 g fiber
21 g protein

INGREDIENTS

- 2 tablespoons dried mushrooms (such as shiitake or porcini)
- ¼ cup dried tomatoes (not oil packed)
- 6 ounces packaged dried trenne or bow ties
- 2 cups green beans cut into 1½-inch-long pieces
- 1 medium yellow summer squash, sliced (1¼ cups)
- 1 cup milk
- ¾ cup chicken broth
- 1 green onion, sliced
- 1 tablespoon cornstarch

- ½ teaspoon lemon-pepper seasoning
- ¼ teaspoon salt
- 1 pound boneless pork loin chops, cut ¾ to 1 inch thick
- 1 tablespoon olive oil

summer pasta with pork

This colorful dish marries all the elements of a delicious warm-weather dinner. Fresh-from-the-garden green beans and summer squash, combined with a few pantry foods like dried mushrooms and tomatoes, means dinner alfresco is just a few easy steps away.

Start to finish: 30 minutes

DIRECTIONS

1. Soak mushrooms and tomatoes for 5 minutes in enough boiling water to cover. Drain and snip, discarding mushroom stems. Set aside.

2. Cook pasta according to package directions, adding beans to the water with pasta. Add squash for the last 2 minutes of cooking. Drain. Keep warm.

3. Meanwhile, stir together the milk, chicken broth, green onion, cornstarch, lemon-pepper seasoning, and salt. Set aside.

4. Trim any separable fat from pork chops. Season pork lightly with additional salt and lemon-pepper seasoning. In a medium skillet cook pork in hot oil over medium heat for 10 to 12 minutes or until just slightly pink in centers and juices run clear, turning once. Remove pork from skillet; cut into thin, bite-size strips. Keep warm.

5. For sauce, drain fat from skillet. Pour cornstarch mixture into skillet. Cook and stir until thickened and bubbly, scraping up any brown bits from bottom of skillet. Reduce heat; cook for 2 minutes more. Stir in mushrooms and tomatoes.

6. Divide pasta mixture among 4 dinner plates. Top with pork; spoon sauce over all. Makes 4 servings.

NUTRITION FACTS PER SERVING:

453 calories
20 g total fat
8 g saturated fat
110 mg cholesterol
659 mg sodium
43 g carbohydrate
2 g fiber
26 g protein

27

peppered pork with chive sauce

For pork that is juicy and tender, cook it just until the center of the meat is slightly pink and the juices run clear. It is safe to eat slightly pink pork loin.

INGREDIENTS

- 4 boneless pork loin chops, cut ¾ inch thick
- 1 teaspoon coarsely ground tricolored peppercorns or coarsely ground black pepper
- 2 teaspoons cooking oil
- ¼ cup water
- 3 tablespoons dry sherry or chicken broth
- 1 3-ounce package cream cheese with chives, cut up

Snipped fresh chives (optional)

While the chops cook, steam or microwave quartered new potatoes and green beans, then drizzle with lemon juice. Serve glasses of apple cider with dinner.

Start to finish: 20 minutes

DIRECTIONS

1. Trim any separable fat from pork chops. Sprinkle both sides of pork chops with pepper, rubbing it lightly into the pork. In a 10-inch skillet cook pork in hot oil for 8 to 10 minutes or until just slightly pink in centers and juices run clear, turning once. Remove pork from skillet. Keep warm.

2. For sauce, carefully add the water to the hot skillet. Add sherry or broth to skillet and heat until bubbly. Add the cream cheese. Using a wire whisk, heat and whisk over medium heat until the cream cheese is melted. Serve sauce over pork. If desired, sprinkle with snipped chives. Makes 4 servings.

NUTRITION FACTS PER SERVING:

291 calories
20 g total fat
8 g saturated fat
92 mg cholesterol
117 mg sodium
2 g carbohydrate
0 g fiber
23 g protein

INGREDIENTS

- **1 pound pork tenderloin**
- **Salt**
- **Coarsely ground black pepper**
- **Nonstick cooking spray**
- **¾ cup cranberry juice or apple juice**
- **2 teaspoons spicy brown mustard**
- **1 teaspoon cornstarch**
- **1 cup sweet cherries (such as Rainier or Bing), halved and pitted, or 1 cup frozen unsweetened pitted dark sweet cherries, thawed**

pork medallions with cherry sauce

During the autumn months, pork is often prepared with fruit such as prunes or apples. These quick-seared medallions cloaked in a delightful sweet cherry sauce provide a whole new reason—and season—to pair pork with fruit. (Also shown on the cover.)

Start to finish: 20 minutes

DIRECTIONS

1. Trim any separable fat from pork. Cut pork crosswise into 1-inch slices.

Place each slice between 2 sheets of plastic wrap. With the heel of your hand, press each slice into a ½-inch-thick medallion. Remove plastic wrap. Sprinkle lightly with salt and coarsely ground black pepper.

2. Coat an unheated large nonstick skillet with cooking spray. Heat skillet over medium-high heat. Add pork; cook for 6 minutes or until just slightly pink in centers and juices run clear, turning once. Remove pork from skillet. Keep warm.

3. Combine cranberry or apple juice, mustard, and cornstarch; add to skillet. Cook and stir until thickened and bubbly. Cook and stir for 2 minutes more. Stir cherries into mixture in skillet. Serve over pork. Makes 4 servings.

Keep the pork medallions juicy by turning the pieces with tongs. Piercing them with a fork lets some of the scrumptious juices escape.

NUTRITION FACTS PER SERVING:

- 197 calories
- 5 g total fat
- 2 g saturated fat
- 81 mg cholesterol
- 127 mg sodium
- 12 g carbohydrate
- 0 g fiber
- 26 g protein

29

cumberland pork medallions

The key ingredients in the full-flavored sauce traditionally known as Cumberland sauce are currant jelly and wine.

INGREDIENTS

- 1 pound pork tenderloin, sliced crosswise into ¾-inch slices
- 1 tablespoon cooking oil or olive oil
- 2 green onions, sliced (¼ cup)
- ½ cup dry red or white wine or apple juice
- ½ cup chicken broth
- 2 tablespoons currant jelly
- 1 teaspoon Dijon-style mustard
- 1 tablespoon chicken broth or cold water
- 1 teaspoon cornstarch

For a satisfying side dish, try this easy rice dish. Before making the entrée, start a saucepan of quick-cooking brown rice (enough for 4 servings); during the last 5 minutes of cooking, add ½ cup frozen peas. Season to taste.

Start to finish: 25 minutes

DIRECTIONS

1. Trim any separable fat from pork slices. In a 10-inch skillet cook pork slices in hot oil over medium heat for 6 to 8 minutes or until just slightly pink in centers and juices run clear, turning once. Remove meat from skillet. Keep warm.

2. Add green onions to skillet; cook just until tender. Add wine or apple juice and the ½ cup broth. Boil gently over medium-high heat about 4 minutes or until reduced to about ½ cup. Add jelly and mustard, stirring until jelly is melted. Combine the 1 tablespoon broth or water and cornstarch; stir into skillet. Cook and stir over medium heat until thickened and bubbly. Cook and stir for 1 minute more. Serve sauce with the pork medallions. Makes 4 servings.

NUTRITION FACTS PER SERVING:

- 231 calories
- 8 g total fat
- 2 g saturated fat
- 81 mg cholesterol
- 220 mg sodium
- 8 g carbohydrate
- 0 g fiber
- 26 g protein

INGREDIENTS

- 1 **tablespoon water**
- 1 **tablespoon white wine Worcestershire sauce**
- 1 **teaspoon lemon juice**
- 1 **teaspoon Dijon-style mustard**
- 1 **pound boneless pork loin roast, cut into four ³⁄₄- to 1-inch slices**
- 1 **teaspoon lemon-pepper seasoning**
- 2 **tablespoons margarine or butter**
- 1 **tablespoon snipped fresh chives or parsley**

pork diane

For a dinner meat-and-potato lovers will relish, serve chive-buttered new potatoes (see tip, below) with this savory pork dish. End the meal with a light dessert of low-fat ice cream topped with fresh or frozen sliced strawberries.

Start to finish: 15 minutes

DIRECTIONS

1. For sauce, stir together the water, Worcestershire sauce, lemon juice, and mustard; set aside.

2. Trim any separable fat from pork slices. Sprinkle both sides of each slice with lemon-pepper seasoning. In a 10-inch skillet cook pork in hot margarine or butter over medium heat for 6 to 10 minutes or until just slightly pink in centers and juices run clear, turning once.

Remove meat from skillet. Keep warm. Remove skillet from heat.

3. Add sauce to skillet. Stir until well blended. Pour sauce over meat; sprinkle with chives or parsley. Makes 4 servings.

NUTRITION FACTS PER SERVING:

192 calories
13 g total fat
4 g saturated fat
51 mg cholesterol
441 mg sodium
1 g carbohydrate
0 g fiber
16 g protein

To make chive-buttered

new potatoes, simply quarter 8 to 10 new potatoes and cook, covered, in the microwave oven with 2 tablespoons water on 100% power (high) about 8 minutes or until tender. Drain. Dot potatoes with butter and snipped fresh chives.

italian pork sandwiches

For added pizzazz, cook the pork as directed, then cook some chopped onion and chopped green sweet pepper in the skillet. Stir in the Italian cooking sauce and continue as directed.

INGREDIENTS

- ¾ **pound pork tenderloin**
- ¼ **cup seasoned fine dry bread crumbs**
- 1 **tablespoon margarine or butter**
- ½ **cup Italian cooking sauce, spaghetti sauce, or pizza sauce**
- 4 **kaiser rolls or hamburger buns, split**
- 2 **tablespoons grated Parmesan cheese**

Toast the kaiser rolls or hamburger buns, if you like, by arranging the split rolls or buns, cut sides up, on the unheated rack of a broiler pan. Broil 4 inches from heat for 1 to 2 minutes or until cut surfaces are golden brown. Check the rolls often to prevent overbrowning.

Start to finish: 15 minutes

32

DIRECTIONS

1. Trim any separable fat from pork. Cut pork crosswise into 4 slices. Place each slice of pork between 2 sheets of plastic wrap. Working from center to edges, pound with the flat side of a meat mallet to ¼-inch thickness.

2. Place seasoned bread crumbs in a shallow bowl. Dip each pork slice into the bread crumbs, coating lightly.

3. In a large skillet cook 2 of the pork slices in hot margarine or butter for 6 to 8 minutes or until pork is no longer pink, turning once. Remove from skillet. Keep warm. Repeat with remaining pork, adding more margarine or butter, if necessary.

4. Add Italian cooking sauce, spaghetti sauce, or pizza sauce to skillet. Cook and stir until heated through. Place each pork slice on the bottom of a roll or bun. Spoon some sauce over each. Sprinkle each with Parmesan cheese; add tops of rolls or buns. Makes 4 servings.

NUTRITION FACTS PER SERVING:

805 calories
13 g total fat
4 g saturated fat
70 mg cholesterol
1,279 mg sodium
86 g carbohydrate
17 g fiber
34 g protein

INGREDIENTS

- ¾ **pound pork tenderloin**
- 1 **beaten egg**
- 1 **tablespoon milk**
- ½ **cup cornflake crumbs**
- ⅛ **teaspoon garlic powder**
- 2 **tablespoons margarine or butter**
- ¼ **cup water**
- ¼ **cup dry sherry, dry marsala, or water**
- 1 **teaspoon instant chicken bouillon granules**
- **Dash pepper**
- 1 **tablespoon snipped fresh parsley**

sherried pork

Just add steamed baby carrots and peas and a loaf of crusty French bread for an elegant dining experience.

Start to finish: 25 minutes

DIRECTIONS

1. Trim any separable fat from pork. Cut pork crosswise into 4 slices. Place each slice of pork between 2 sheets of plastic wrap. Working from center to edges, pound with the flat side of a meat mallet to ½-inch thickness.

2. In a shallow bowl combine egg and milk. In another bowl combine cornflake crumbs and garlic powder. Dip each pork slice into the egg mixture; then dip into the crumb mixture, coating well.

3. In a large skillet cook 2 of the pork slices in hot margarine or butter for about 8 minutes or until pork is no longer pink, turning once. Remove from skillet. Keep warm. Repeat with remaining pork, adding more margarine or butter, if necessary.

4. Stir the ¼ cup water; the ¼ cup sherry, marsala, or water; bouillon granules; and pepper into the drippings in the skillet, scraping up any browned bits. Bring to boiling. Boil rapidly for 2 to 3 minutes or until mixture thickens slightly. Serve over pork slices. Sprinkle with parsley. Makes 4 servings.

Look for cornflake crumbs near the dry bread crumbs at your supermarket. Or, if you prefer, crush your own by placing cornflakes in a self-sealing plastic bag and rolling over them with a rolling pin until fine crumbs form.

NUTRITION FACTS PER SERVING:

- 224 calories
- 10 g total fat
- 3 g saturated fat
- 114 mg cholesterol
- 416 mg sodium
- 7 g carbohydrate
- 0 g fiber
- 21 g protein

33

easy moo-shu-style pork

For an attractive garnish, save some of the shredded carrot from the coleslaw mix.

INGREDIENTS

- 8 7-inch flour tortillas
- 3 tablespoons cold water
- 2 tablespoons soy sauce
- 1 tablespoon cornstarch
- 2 teaspoons toasted sesame oil
- 1 teaspoon sugar
- ¼ teaspoon bottled minced garlic
- ¾ pound pork tenderloin or pork loin
- 1 tablespoon cooking oil
- 3 cups packaged shredded cabbage with carrot (coleslaw mix)
- ⅓ cup hoisin sauce
- Shredded carrot (optional)

Toasted sesame oil is a reddish-brown oil made from toasted sesame seeds. Look for it in the Oriental food section of the supermarket. Use it sparingly; a little goes a long way.

Start to finish: 20 minutes

DIRECTIONS

1. Wrap tortillas in foil. Warm in a 350° oven for 10 minutes. Meanwhile, for sauce, in a small mixing bowl stir together water, soy sauce, cornstarch, sesame oil, sugar, and garlic. Set aside.

2. Trim any separable fat from pork. Cut pork into thin bite-size strips. Pour cooking oil into a wok or large skillet. (Add more oil as necessary during cooking.) Preheat over medium-high heat. Add the pork strips and stir-fry for 2 to 3 minutes or until no longer pink.

3. Push meat from the center of the wok. Stir sauce; add to the center of the wok. Cook and stir until thickened and bubbly. Cook and stir for 2 minutes more. Add shredded cabbage with carrot to skillet. Stir to coat with sauce.

4. Spread one side of each warm tortilla with some of the hoisin sauce. Spoon about ½ cup of the pork mixture onto the center of each tortilla. Fold bottom edge up over filling. Fold sides to the center, overlapping edges. Secure with toothpicks. If desired, garnish with carrot. Makes 4 servings.

NUTRITION FACTS PER SERVING:

435 calories
14 g total fat
3 g saturated fat
60 mg cholesterol
2,266 mg sodium
49 g carbohydrate
1 g fiber
27 g protein

34

INGREDIENTS

- ¾ pound lean boneless pork
- 1 medium onion, chopped (½ cup)
- 1 tablespoon cooking oil
- 3 cups frozen loose-pack broccoli, cauliflower, and carrots
- 4 ounces packaged dried medium noodles or curly medium noodles (3 cups)
- 1 10¾-ounce can reduced-sodium condensed cream of celery soup
- 1 cup reduced-sodium chicken broth
- ¾ cup water
- ½ teaspoon dried marjoram or thyme, crushed
- ¼ teaspoon pepper

pork and noodle skillet dinner

Strips of boneless chicken breast or thighs taste equally delicious in this creamy one-dish meal.

Prep time: 15 minutes
Cooking time: 12 minutes

DIRECTIONS

1. Trim any separable fat from pork. Cut pork into thin bite-size strips. In a 12-inch skillet cook and stir pork and onion in hot oil over medium-high heat for 3 to 4 minutes or until pork is no longer pink.

2. Stir in frozen vegetables, uncooked noodles, soup, broth, water, marjoram or thyme, and pepper. Bring to boiling; reduce heat. Cover and simmer for 12 to 15 minutes or until noodles are tender, stirring occasionally. Makes 4 servings.

Reduced-sodium chicken broth is

available in cans. If you can't find it at your supermarket, substitute regular chicken broth. Keep in mind, however, the amount of sodium will increase by one-third.

NUTRITION FACTS PER SERVING:

- 317 calories
- 12 g total fat
- 3 g saturated fat
- 64 mg cholesterol
- 531 mg sodium
- 33 g carbohydrate
- 3 g fiber
- 19 g protein

35

thai cobb salad

Hit a home run with this refreshing mix of meat, cubed avocado, roasted peanuts, and spicy ginger-soy dressing. Leftover grilled meats work admirably, or deli-sliced meats can pinch-hit.

INGREDIENTS

½ cup bottled fat-free Italian salad dressing

1 tablespoon soy sauce

1 to 1½ teaspoons grated fresh ginger

¼ to ½ teaspoon crushed red pepper

8 cups torn mixed salad greens

1½ cups coarsely chopped cooked pork, beef, or chicken (8 ounces)

1 avocado, halved, seeded, peeled, and cut into ½-inch pieces

1 cup coarsely shredded carrots

¼ cup coarsely snipped fresh cilantro

2 green onions, thinly sliced (¼ cup)

¼ cup honey-roasted peanuts (optional)

To carry through with the Asian flavors, include Chinese cabbage as part of the mixed greens.

Start to finish: 25 minutes

DIRECTIONS

1. For dressing, in a large bowl combine salad dressing, soy sauce, fresh ginger, and crushed red pepper. Add salad greens; toss lightly to coat.

2. Divide salad greens among 4 dinner plates. Top each with meat, avocado, carrots, cilantro, green onions, and, if desired, peanuts. Makes 4 servings.

NUTRITION FACTS PER SERVING:

255 calories
15 g total fat
4 g saturated fat
52 mg cholesterol
743 mg sodium
11 g carbohydrate
4 g fiber
19 g protein

grilled ham-on-rye special

Serve in-season fruits—grapes or watermelon in the summer, apples or pears in the fall—as a fresh side to this hearty hot sandwich. Year-round, it will be a hit with your family. (Don't forget the chips and pickles, too.)

INGREDIENTS

- ¼ cup Thousand Island salad dressing
- 1 teaspoon prepared mustard
- 1 cup packaged shredded cabbage with carrot (coleslaw mix)
- 1 tablespoon margarine or butter
- 8 slices rye bread
- 4 ounces thinly sliced cooked ham
- 4 ounces thinly sliced Swiss cheese

Prep time: 15 minutes
Cooking time: 4 minutes

DIRECTIONS

1. In a small bowl stir together salad dressing and mustard. Stir in shredded cabbage with carrot; mix well.

2. Spread a thin layer of margarine or butter on one side of each bread slice; turn bread over. Top 4 of the bread slices with half of the ham. Spoon on cabbage mixture evenly; top with sliced cheese and remaining ham. Top with remaining bread slices, margarine side up.

3. Heat a large skillet or griddle. Place sandwiches in skillet or on griddle. Cook over medium-low heat for 2 to 3 minutes or until golden; turn sandwiches over. Cook 2 to 3 minutes more or until bread is golden and cheese starts to melt. Makes 4 servings.

NUTRITION FACTS PER SERVING:

409 calories
20 g total fat
8 g saturated fat
47 mg cholesterol
976 mg sodium
40 g carbohydrate
5 g fiber
19 g protein

For a change of pace, use marble rye or whole wheat bread and mozzarella, Monterey Jack, or Colby cheese in this meat-and-cheese sandwich.

curried fruit with ham steak

A can of tropical fruit salad jump-starts the tangy, sweet sauce.

INGREDIENTS

1. 1½-pound cooked center-cut ham slice, cut ¾ inch thick
1. 15¼-ounce can tropical fruit salad in light syrup or one 16-ounce can chunky mixed fruit in light syrup
1. small onion, chopped (⅓ cup)
½ to 1 teaspoon curry powder or ⅛ teaspoon ground nutmeg or ginger
1. tablespoon margarine or butter
2. teaspoons cornstarch
¼ cup unsweetened pineapple juice or orange juice

Plan several days' meals at once

so you can buy all your groceries in just one supermarket trip. After all, a trip to the pantry takes a lot less time than another trip to the store.

Start to finish: 20 minutes

DIRECTIONS

1. Trim any separable fat from ham. Place ham on the unheated rack of a broiler pan. Broil 4 to 5 inches from the heat for 12 to 14 minutes or until heated through, turning once.

2. Meanwhile, for sauce, drain fruit, reserving syrup. Set aside. In a small saucepan cook onion and curry powder, nutmeg, or ginger in margarine or butter over medium heat until onion is tender. Stir in cornstarch. Add pineapple juice or orange juice and reserved fruit syrup. Cook and stir over medium heat until thickened and bubbly. Cook and stir for 2 minutes more. Carefully stir in drained fruit. Heat through. Serve warm sauce over ham. Makes 6 servings.

NUTRITION FACTS PER SERVING:

232 calories
8 g total fat
2 g saturated fat
60 mg cholesterol
1,390 mg sodium
14 g carbohydrate
1 g fiber
24 g protein

ham and chutney pasta salad

If you have some extra time before serving, quick-chill the ham mixture in the freezer for 5 to 10 minutes.

INGREDIENTS

- 8 ounces packaged dried medium shell macaroni
- ½ cup chutney
- ½ cup mayonnaise or salad dressing
- 2 green onions, sliced (¼ cup)
- ⅛ teaspoon coarsely ground black pepper
- 1½ cups cubed cooked ham (8 ounces)
- 4 lettuce leaves
  Cherry tomato wedges (optional)

Start to finish: 25 minutes

DIRECTIONS

1. Cook macaroni according to package directions. Drain. Rinse with cold water. Drain again.

2. Meanwhile, cut up any large pieces of chutney. Stir together the chutney, mayonnaise or salad dressing, green onions, and pepper.

3. Toss together the chilled macaroni, chutney mixture, and ham. Line 4 salad plates with lettuce leaves. Serve ham mixture on lettuce-lined plates. If desired, garnish with cherry tomatoes. Makes 4 servings.

NUTRITION FACTS PER SERVING:

580 calories
26 g total fat
4 g saturated fat
46 mg cholesterol
850 mg sodium
66 g carbohydrate
2 g fiber
20 g protein

Organization is the key to getting meals ready quickly.

Arrange your kitchen so you can find things easily. Store utensils and groceries near the places you'll use them most often. (For example, store pots and pans near your stove.) Stock duplicates of often-used utensils to cut down on mid-recipe dishwashing. Turn labels on cans or boxes toward the front of your shelves so you can read them at a glance. Finally, read recipes through and assemble everything you need before starting.

39

sausage, beans, and greens

Escarole, a type of endive, typically is used in salads, but it makes a great addition to this one-pot dish.

INGREDIENTS

½   pound hot or mild Italian sausage links, bias-sliced into ½-inch pieces

1   medium onion, chopped (½ cup)

2   19-ounce cans white kidney beans (cannellini), rinsed and drained

¾   cup reduced-sodium chicken broth

¼   cup dry white wine or reduced-sodium chicken broth

2   tablespoons snipped fresh thyme or 1 teaspoon dried thyme, crushed

2   cups torn escarole or fresh spinach

¼   cup shredded Parmesan cheese (optional)

Cannellini beans
are white Italian kidney beans. They're found in the canned vegetable section of the supermarket or in the Italian food aisle. If you can't find them, substitute navy beans or Great Northern beans.

Start to finish: 25 minutes

DIRECTIONS

1. In a large saucepan cook sausage and onion over medium heat 5 minutes or until onion is tender. Drain off fat. Add beans, the ¾ cup chicken broth, the ¼ cup wine or chicken broth, and thyme. Bring to boiling; reduce heat. Cover and simmer for 5 minutes. Stir in escarole or fresh spinach; heat through.

2. To serve, ladle mixture into serving bowls. If desired, sprinkle with Parmesan cheese. Makes 4 servings.

NUTRITION FACTS PER SERVING:

309 calories
12 g total fat
4 g saturated fat
32 mg cholesterol
921 mg sodium
39 g carbohydrate
13 g fiber
24 g protein

INGREDIENTS

- 8 ounces packaged dried large bow tie pasta
- ¾ pound hot Italian sausage links
- 2 medium red sweet peppers, cut into ¾-inch pieces
- ½ cup vegetable broth or beef broth
- ¼ teaspoon coarsely ground black pepper
- ¼ cup snipped fresh Italian parsley

bow ties with sausage and sweet peppers

You will be amazed that so few ingredients generate so much flavor.

Start to finish: 25 minutes

DIRECTIONS

1. Cook pasta according to package directions; drain. Return pasta to saucepan.

2. Meanwhile, cut the sausage into 1-inch-thick pieces. In a large skillet cook sausage and sweet peppers over medium-high heat until sausage is no longer pink. Drain off fat.

3. Stir the broth and black pepper into skillet. Bring to boiling; reduce heat. Simmer, uncovered, for 5 minutes. Remove from heat. Pour over pasta; add parsley. Toss gently to coat. Transfer to a warm serving dish. Makes 4 servings.

If red sweet peppers aren't available, use yellow or green sweet peppers instead.

NUTRITION FACTS PER SERVING:

397 calories
18 g total fat
6 g saturated fat
94 mg cholesterol
713 mg sodium
38 g carbohydrate
3 g fiber
24 g protein

florentine pizza

Tailor this piled-high pizza to suit your taste by choosing hot Italian sausage or mild Italian or bulk pork sausage. If you purchase Italian sausage links, remove the casings, then cook the sausage.

INGREDIENTS

- ½ pound Italian sausage or bulk pork sausage
- 1 cup sliced fresh mushrooms
- 1 8-ounce can pizza sauce
- ½ of a 10-ounce package frozen chopped spinach, thawed and well drained
- 1 16-ounce package Italian bread shell (12-inch Boboli)
- 1 cup shredded mozzarella cheese (4 ounces)

Prep time: 15 minutes
Baking time: 13 minutes

To use half of a package of frozen

spinach, micro-cook the unwrapped spinach on 30% power (medium-low) for 2 to 4 minutes or until soft enough to cut in half with a sharp knife. Rewrap one half and return to the freezer. Continue to cook the remaining half on 30% power for 3 to 5 minutes or until thawed.

DIRECTIONS

1. In a large skillet cook sausage and mushrooms until meat is no longer pink. Drain off fat. Pat meat mixture with paper towels to remove excess fat. Stir in pizza sauce and spinach. Cook and stir until heated through.

2. Meanwhile, place bread shell on a lightly greased baking sheet. Bake in a 400° oven for 5 minutes. Top with meat mixture. Sprinkle with shredded cheese. Bake for 8 to 10 minutes more or until cheese melts and pizza is heated through. Makes 4 servings.

NUTRITION FACTS PER SERVING:

547 calories
23 g total fat
7 g saturated fat
54 mg cholesterol
1,483 mg sodium
58 g carbohydrate
2 g fiber
30 g protein

INGREDIENTS

- 4 fully cooked knockwurst or other mild-flavored sausage
- 1 12-ounce bottle dark beer
- 1 14½-ounce jar sauerkraut, rinsed and well drained
- 2 tablespoons apple cider or apple juice
- 2 teaspoons finely shredded orange peel
- ½ teaspoon ground cardamom
- 4 hoagie buns
   German-style or sweet-hot mustard

sauerkraut and sausage rolls

Apple cider, orange peel, and cardamom add new flavor surprises to this two-fisted sandwich, made extra-hearty with dark, full-bodied beer.

Start to finish: 25 minutes

DIRECTIONS

1. Use a fork to pierce each knockwurst 2 or 3 times. In a large saucepan heat beer until simmering; add knockwurst. Simmer, uncovered, about 10 minutes or until heated through.

2. Meanwhile, in a medium saucepan combine sauerkraut, apple cider or juice, orange peel, and cardamom. Heat through.

3. To serve, split buns, cutting each to within ½ inch of edge. If desired, toast buns under broiler. Spread bottom half of each bun with mustard. Drain knockwurst; place one in each bun. Divide sauerkraut mixture among buns. Makes 4 servings.

NUTRITION FACTS PER SERVING:

517 calories
13 g total fat
4 g saturated fat
19 mg cholesterol
1,749 mg sodium
82 g carbohydrate
6 g fiber
17 g protein

Whenever you're shredding citrus peel, go ahead and shred more than you need. Place any extra shredded peel in a small airtight container, then label and freeze. It's ready when you need it and is as fresh-tasting as the minute you shredded it. You can store shredded citrus peel in the freezer for up to 6 months.

skillet sausage and potatoes

Gung-ho outdoor lovers will opt for cooking breakfast over the coals. Indoor campers can follow the range-top directions. Before leaving for your trip, cook the potatoes ahead. You'll need about 2 pounds of potatoes for 5 cups of cubes.

INGREDIENTS

- 2 tablespoons olive oil or cooking oil
- 5 cups cubed cooked potatoes
- 2 medium onions, cut into thin wedges and/or chopped (1½ cups)
- ½ pound smoked turkey sausage, diagonally sliced ¼ inch thick
- 1 tablespoon olive oil or cooking oil
- 2 tablespoons snipped fresh thyme or 1 teaspoon dried thyme, crushed
- 1 to 1½ teaspoons cumin seed, slightly crushed
- ¼ teaspoon salt
- ¼ teaspoon pepper

Take the fixin's for this hearty dish camping. To tote the ingredients, pack everything except the sausage in a picnic basket or sturdy box. Keep the sausage on ice in a cooler.

Prep time: 10 minutes
Cooking time: 16 minutes

DIRECTIONS

1. Pour the 2 tablespoons oil into a heavy 12-inch ovenproof skillet. Place skillet directly over hot coals or on the range top. Lift and tilt to cover bottom of skillet with oil. Cook the potatoes and onions, uncovered, in hot oil over medium-high heat about 5 minutes or until onion is nearly tender, stirring occasionally.

2. Add sausage and the 1 tablespoon oil. Cook, uncovered, about 10 minutes more or until potatoes and onions are tender and slightly brown, stirring often. Stir in thyme, cumin seed, salt, and pepper; cook and stir for 1 minute more. Makes 6 servings.

Note: If you are cooking at a high altitude, prepare as directed, except increase the cooking times. Allow 15 to 20 minutes for potatoes and onions, 12 minutes after adding the sausage, and 2 to 3 minutes after adding the seasonings.

NUTRITION FACTS PER SERVING:

270 calories
10 g total fat
2 g saturated fat
24 mg cholesterol
419 mg sodium
36 g carbohydrate
2 g fiber
10 g protein

Skillet Sausage and Potatoes and Green Chili Muffins (see recipe, page 242)

44

nuevo pork 'n' beans

Add a Mexican accent to a knife-and-fork sandwich by corralling a can of refried beans, chorizo sausage, and cheese.

INGREDIENTS

- 6 ounces spicy chorizo or bulk Italian sausage
- 1 16-ounce can fat-free refried beans
- 1 4½-ounce can diced green chili peppers, drained
- 3 8-inch-long pieces baguette-style French bread, split lengthwise and toasted
- ½ of a medium red sweet pepper, cut into thin strips
- ½ of a medium green sweet pepper, cut into thin strips
- ½ cup shredded reduced-fat Monterey Jack cheese (2 ounces)

Prep time: 20 minutes
Broiling time: 1 minute

DIRECTIONS

1. Remove casings from sausage, if present. In a skillet crumble sausage; cook over medium heat until no longer pink. Drain sausage in colander; wipe skillet with paper towels. Return sausage to skillet.

2. Stir in refried beans and chili peppers; heat through. Spread sausage-bean mixture on bottom halves of bread; arrange bread on unheated rack of a broiler pan. Top with sweet pepper strips; sprinkle with cheese. Broil 4 inches from heat for 1 to 2 minutes or until cheese melts. Place toasted bread tops over filling; cut each portion in half crosswise. Makes 6 servings.

Chorizo is a spicy
Mexican pork sausage that's available in bulk or link form. Look for it in larger supermarkets or in Mexican specialty food shops.

NUTRITION FACTS PER SERVING:

311 calories
15 g total fat
6 g saturated fat
7 mg cholesterol
865 mg sodium
53 g carbohydrate
4 g fiber
20 g protein

hot apple and cheese sandwiches

Choose your favorite eating apple, such as a Golden Delicious or Granny Smith, for this flavorful sandwich.

INGREDIENTS

- 1 **medium apple**
- 4 **English muffins, split**
- 2 **tablespoons creamy Dijon-style mustard blend**
- 4 **slices Canadian-style bacon**
- 4 **slices process Swiss cheese**
- 1 **tablespoon margarine or butter**
  Apple chunks (optional)

For a quick coleslaw with a new twist, use broccoli coleslaw mix (a blend of broccoli, red cabbage, and carrot). Simply add some bottled ranch salad dressing, stir, and quick-chill in the freezer while the sandwiches cook.

Prep time: 15 minutes
Cooking time: 9 minutes

DIRECTIONS

1. Core apple and slice crosswise, forming rings. Spread cut sides of muffin halves with mustard blend.

2. To assemble, top 4 of the muffin halves with a slice of bacon, 1 or 2 apple rings, and a slice of cheese. Top with the remaining muffin halves, cut sides down. Spread margarine lightly on outside of each sandwich.

3. Heat a large skillet or griddle. Place sandwiches in skillet or on griddle. Cook over medium-low heat about 5 minutes or until golden; turn sandwiches over. Cook 4 to 5 minutes more or until golden and cheese starts to melt. Cut sandwiches in half. If desired, garnish each sandwich with an apple chunk. Makes 4 servings.

NUTRITION FACTS PER SERVING:

343 calories
15 g total fat
6 g saturated fat
39 mg cholesterol
837 mg sodium
33 g carbohydrate
1 g fiber
18 g protein

grilled canadian bacon pizza

INGREDIENTS

- 1 6-ounce jar marinated artichoke hearts
- 4 6-inch Italian bread shells (Boboli)
- ½ cup shredded fontina or mozzarella cheese (2 ounces)
- 4 slices Canadian-style bacon, cut into strips (2 ounces)
- 2 plum-shaped tomatoes, sliced
- 1 green onion, thinly sliced
- ¼ cup crumbled feta cheese (1 ounce)
- 2 teaspoons snipped fresh oregano or basil

Pizza—on the grill? You bet! The intense, direct heat of the grill approximates that of a wood-fired pizza oven, imparting the pie's veggies and cheese with a pleasing smoke flavor, the Canadian bacon with real sizzle, and the golden crust with a delightful crunch.

Prep time: 20 minutes
Grilling time: 8 minutes

DIRECTIONS

1. Drain artichoke hearts, reserving marinade. Halve artichoke hearts lengthwise; set aside.

2. Brush the top sides of bread shells with some of the reserved marinade. Sprinkle fontina or mozzarella cheese over shells. Divide artichoke hearts, Canadian-style bacon, tomatoes, and green onion among shells.

3. Transfer the bread shells to a large piece of double-thickness foil. In a grill with a cover, place foil with bread shells on the rack directly over medium heat. Cover and grill about 8 minutes or until cheese is melted and pizza is heated through. Sprinkle on feta cheese and oregano or basil. Makes 4 servings.

NUTRITION FACTS PER SERVING:

465 calories
19 g total fat
6 g saturated fat
44 mg cholesterol
1,264 mg sodium
56 g carbohydrate
2 g fiber
23 g protein

To save time, start the coals before preparing the pizza. Before grilling, test the coals for medium heat by holding your hand over the coals at the same height the pizza will be grilled and counting "one thousand one, one thousand two." If you can hold your hand over the coals for 4 seconds, the heat is medium.

b.l.t. with cheese

Take your choice of a cheese-topped B.L.T. or be adventurous and try the guacamole, turkey, or pesto variation.

INGREDIENTS

- ¼ cup mayonnaise or salad dressing
- 8 slices whole grain bread, toasted
- 12 slices bacon or turkey bacon, cooked, drained, and coarsely crumbled
- 2 medium tomatoes, halved and sliced
- 4 slices cheese (such as havarti with dill, white cheddar, or Jarlsburg)
- 4 to 8 leaf lettuce leaves or 8 to 12 fresh spinach leaves

Just about any deli salad goes well with a B.L.T. Pick up a pint of potato salad, coleslaw, or pasta salad at the grocery store. At home, lighten the deli salad by draining off any excess dressing. Stir in chopped broccoli, shredded cabbage, or shredded carrot to stretch the salad.

Start to finish: 25 minutes

DIRECTIONS

1. Spread mayonnaise or salad dressing on one side of each slice of toasted bread. For sandwiches, top 4 bread slices with bacon, tomato, and cheese. Top remaining bread slices with lettuce. Assemble sandwiches and cut in half to serve. Makes 4 servings.

B.L.T. : Prepare as above, except omit cheese.

B.L.T. with Guacamole: Prepare as above, except substitute frozen (thawed) guacamole for the mayonnaise or salad dressing and omit cheese.

B.L.T. with Turkey: Prepare as above, adding 1 or 2 thin slices cooked turkey breast to each sandwich (2 to 4 ounces total).

B.L.T. with Pesto: Prepare as above, except reduce mayonnaise or salad dressing to 3 tablespoons and stir in 2 tablespoons purchased pesto. Omit cheese.

NUTRITION FACTS PER SERVING:

473 calories
34 g total fat
5 g saturated fat
59 mg cholesterol
783 mg sodium
28 g carbohydrate
1 g fiber
18 g protein

INGREDIENTS

8   lamb loin chops, cut ½ inch thick

3   tablespoons orange marmalade

4   teaspoons Dijon-style mustard

mustard-orange lamb chops

You need only three ingredients for this delightful entrée.

Start to finish: 10 minutes

DIRECTIONS

1. Trim any separable fat from chops. Place chops on the unheated rack of a broiler pan. Broil 3 to 4 inches from the heat to desired doneness, turning once after half of the broiling time. (Allow 7 to 9 minutes for medium-rare to medium doneness.)

2. Meanwhile, in a small saucepan stir together the orange marmalade and mustard. Cook and stir over medium heat until heated through. Spoon over chops. Makes 4 servings.

NUTRITION FACTS PER SERVING:

 228 calories
9 g total fat
3 g saturated fat
80 mg cholesterol
199 mg sodium
11 g carbohydrate
1 g fiber
26 g protein

Eliminate grimy broiler pans. Line your broiler pan with foil and coat the unheated rack with nonstick cooking spray. Doing so makes cleanup a snap. Just wash the rack in hot soapy water. The nonstick spray reduces any need for scrubbing. And cleaning the pan is even easier. Simply remove the foil, wad it up, and throw it out.

tuscan lamb chop skillet

Tuscans, once disparaged by the rest of Italy as "bean eaters" because of their love of the legume, now wear that mantle with pride. Here healthful white beans are flavored with rosemary and garlic, then topped with lamb chops.

INGREDIENTS

- 8 lamb rib chops, cut 1 inch thick (1½ pounds total)
- 2 teaspoons olive oil
- 1½ teaspoons bottled minced garlic or 3 cloves garlic, minced
- 1 19-ounce can white kidney (cannellini) beans, rinsed and drained
- 1 8-ounce can Italian-style stewed tomatoes
- 1 tablespoon balsamic vinegar
- 2 teaspoons snipped fresh rosemary
- Fresh rosemary sprigs (optional)
- Snipped fresh rosemary (optional)

Balsamic vinegar is a sweet, dark brown vinegar made from the boiled-down juice of white grapes. Traditional balsamic vinegar labeled "aceto balsamico tradizionale" cannot contain any wine vinegar and must be aged at least 12 years. Look for it in larger supermarkets.

Start to finish: 18 minutes

DIRECTIONS

1. Trim any separable fat from chops. In a large skillet cook chops in hot oil over medium heat about 8 minutes for medium doneness, turning once. Remove from skillet. Keep warm.

2. Stir garlic into drippings in skillet. Cook and stir for 1 minute. Stir in beans, undrained tomatoes, vinegar, and 2 teaspoons snipped rosemary. Bring to boiling; reduce heat. Simmer, uncovered, for 3 minutes.

3. Spoon bean mixture onto 4 dinner plates; arrange 2 chops on each serving. If desired, garnish with rosemary sprigs and additional snipped rosemary. Makes 4 servings.

NUTRITION FACTS PER SERVING:

- 272 calories
- 9 g total fat
- 3 g saturated fat
- 67 mg cholesterol
- 466 mg sodium
- 24 g carbohydrate
- 6 g fiber
- 30 g protein

the ultimate sloppy joe

Chilly days bring requests for comfort foods such as sloppy joes. Dress up this favorite loose-meat sandwich with feta cheese, bulgur, and crispy romaine.

INGREDIENTS

- 1 pound lean ground lamb or ground beef
- 1 medium onion, chopped (½ cup)
- 1 15-ounce can tomato sauce
- ⅓ cup bulgur
- 1 teaspoon dried oregano, crushed
- 2 cups chopped romaine
- 6 kaiser rolls, split and toasted
- 2 ounces feta cheese with tomato and basil or plain feta cheese

Start to finish: 20 minutes

DIRECTIONS

1. In a 10-inch skillet cook ground lamb or beef and onion until meat is no longer pink. Drain off fat. Stir in tomato sauce, bulgur, and oregano. Bring to boiling; reduce heat. Simmer, uncovered, about 10 minutes or until desired consistency, stirring occasionally.

2. Arrange romaine on bottom halves of rolls. Spoon meat mixture on top. Crumble feta cheese over the meat. Cover with top halves of rolls. Makes 6 servings.

NUTRITION FACTS PER SERVING:

396 calories
15 g total fat
6 g saturated fat
59 mg cholesterol
889 mg sodium
43 g carbohydrate
3 g fiber
22 g protein

Fashion a colorful relish

platter from your pantry and refrigerator using ingredients such as cut-up vegetables, pickles, olives, and cubed cheese.

For another simple side dish, warm chunky applesauce with a dash of ground nutmeg, cinnamon, or apple pie spice.

greek-style pasta skillet

Lamb, cinnamon, and feta cheese add a Greek twist to this one-dish macaroni meal.

INGREDIENTS

- ¾ pound ground lamb or ground beef
- 1 medium onion, chopped (½ cup)
- 1 14½-ounce can diced tomatoes
- 1 5½-ounce can tomato juice
- ½ cup water
- ½ teaspoon instant beef bouillon granules
- ½ teaspoon ground cinnamon
- ⅛ teaspoon garlic powder
- 1 cup packaged dried medium shell macaroni or elbow macaroni
- 1 cup frozen loose-pack cut green beans
- ½ cup crumbled feta cheese (2 ounces)

Feta cheese has a wonderful sharp, salty flavor. This soft, white, crumbly cheese can be made from cow's, sheep's, or goat's milk. It's available in chunks or already crumbled.

Prep time: 15 minutes
Cooking time: 15 minutes

DIRECTIONS

1. In a large skillet cook ground lamb or beef and onion until meat is no longer pink. Drain off fat. Stir in undrained tomatoes, tomato juice, water, bouillon granules, cinnamon, and garlic powder. Bring to boiling.

2. Stir uncooked macaroni and green beans into meat mixture. Return to boiling; reduce heat. Cover and simmer about 15 minutes or until macaroni and green beans are tender. Sprinkle with feta cheese. Makes 4 servings.

NUTRITION FACTS PER SERVING:

362 calories
16 g total fat
7 g saturated fat
70 mg cholesterol
647 mg sodium
33 g carbohydrate
2 g fiber
22 g protein

52

INGREDIENTS

- ½ pound ground lamb, ground beef, or ground pork
- 1 14-ounce jar tomato and herb pasta sauce or spaghetti sauce
- 1¾ cups water
- ¼ cup dry red wine or water
- 1 9-ounce package refrigerated cheese-filled tortellini
- ½ cup shredded mozzarella cheese (2 ounces)

tortellini with meat sauce

For a spicier sauce, replace the ground lamb, beef, or pork with Italian sausage (remove casings, if present).

Prep time: 15 minutes
Cooking time: 15 minutes

DIRECTIONS

1. In a large saucepan cook ground lamb, beef, or pork over medium heat until no longer pink. Drain off fat.

2. Add pasta or spaghetti sauce, the 1¾ cups water, and ¼ cup wine or water to the meat. Bring to boiling; reduce heat. Stir in tortellini. Return to boiling. Simmer, uncovered, for 15 to 18 minutes or until tortellini are tender and sauce is of desired consistency. Spoon onto serving plates. Sprinkle with mozzarella cheese. Let stand for 2 to 3 minutes or until cheese is slightly melted. Makes 4 servings.

If refrigerated tortellini aren't available at your grocery store, use half of a 16-ounce package frozen cheese-filled tortellini instead.

NUTRITION FACTS PER SERVING:

466 calories
19 g total fat
7 g saturated fat
94 mg cholesterol
895 mg sodium
47 g carbohydrate
2 g fiber
25 g protein

broiling meat

When time is at a premium, broiling is an ideal way to cook a meal in a hurry. Place meat on the unheated rack of a broiler pan. For cuts less than 1½ inches thick, broil 3 to 4 inches from the heat. For cuts 1½ inches thick or thicker, broil 4 to 5 inches from the heat. Broil for the time given or until done, turning meat over after half of the broiling time.

Cut	Thickness	Doneness	Time
BEEF			
Flank steak	¾ inch	Medium	12 to 14 minutes
Steak (chuck, top round)	1 inch	Medium-rare	14 to 16 minutes
		Medium	16 to 20 minutes
	1½ inches	Medium-rare	18 to 20 minutes
		Medium	20 to 25 minutes
Steak (porterhouse, rib, rib eye, T-bone, sirloin, tenderloin, top loin)	1 inch	Medium-rare	10 to 12 minutes
		Medium	12 to 15 minutes
	1½ inches	Medium-rare	16 to 20 minutes
		Medium	20 to 25 minutes
VEAL			
Loin/rib chop	¾ to 1 inch	Medium	14 to 16 minutes
LAMB			
Loin/rib chop	1 inch	Medium	7 to 11 minutes
Sirloin chop	¾ to 1 inch	Medium	12 to 15 minutes
PORK			
Boneless loin chop	¾ to 1 inch	Medium (160°)	6 to 8 minutes
	1¼ to 1½ inches	Medium (160°)	11 to 15 minutes
Loin or rib chop (bone in)	¾ inch	Medium (160°)	8 to 10 minutes
	1¼ to 1½ inches	Medium (160°)	18 to 22 minutes
Ham slice	1 inch	Heated	14 to 16 minutes
SAUSAGES			
Fresh bratwurst		Well-done	10 to 12 minutes
Frankfurters and fully cooked sausages		Heated	3 to 5 minutes
GROUND MEAT PATTIES			
Ground beef patties	½ inch	Medium to well-done	10 to 12 minutes
	¾ inch	Medium to well-done	12 to 14 minutes
Ground lamb patties	½ inch	Medium to well-done	10 to 12 minutes
	¾ inch	Medium to well-done	12 to 14 minutes
Ground pork patties	½ inch	Medium to well-done	10 to 12 minutes
	¾ inch	Medium to well-done	12 to 14 minutes

panbroiling and panfrying meat

Shortcut meal preparation by relying on panbroiling and panfrying to cook meats quickly. To panbroil these meats, preheat a heavy skillet over high heat until extremely hot. Do not add water or fat. (For beef steaks and veal, brush skillet lightly with cooking oil before preheating.) Add meat. Do not cover. Reduce heat to medium and cook for the time given or until done, turning meat frequently. If meat browns too quickly, reduce heat to medium-low. Spoon off fat and juices as they accumulate during cooking.

To panfry these meats, in a heavy skillet melt 1 to 2 tablespoons margarine, butter, or cooking oil over medium heat. Add meat. Do not cover. Cook for time given or until done, turning meat over after half of the cooking time.

Cut	Thickness	Doneness	Panbroiling Time	Panfrying Time
BEEF				
Cubed steak	½ inch	Well-done	5 to 8 minutes	6 to 8 minutes
Steak (rib eye, sirloin, tenderloin, top loin, top round)	1 inch	Medium rare	6 to 8 minutes	8 to 11 minutes
		Medium	9 to 12 minutes	12 to 14 minutes
VEAL				
Cutlet	⅛ inch	Medium	2 to 3 minutes	3 to 4 minutes
	¼ inch	Medium	3 to 5 minutes	4 to 6 minutes
LAMB				
Chop	1 inch	Medium	7 to 9 minutes	8 to 10 minutes
PORK*				
Chop	¾ inch	Medium	7 to 9 minutes	8 to 10 minutes
		Well-done	9 to 11 minutes	11 to 13 minutes

To panbroil these meats, place meat in a cool skillet. (If using an electric range, preheat the burner for 2 to 4 minutes.) Turn heat to medium. Turn meat halfway through cooking time (for bacon, turn occasionally). If meat browns too quickly, reduce heat slightly.

Cut	Thickness	Doneness	Panbroiling Time
PORK*			
Bacon slices		Well-done	8 to 10 minutes
Canadian-style bacon	¼ inch	Heated	3 to 5 minutes
Ham slice	1 inch	Heated	14 to 16 minutes
GROUND MEAT			
Ground meat patties (beef, lamb, pork*)	¾ inch (4 to a pound)	Medium to Well-done	10 to 12 minutes

*Pork should be cooked until the juices run clear.

Jamaican Chicken Salad
See recipe, page 88

poultry

pesto chicken breasts with summer squash

This study in green is all about great taste and true simplicity. Crisp-tender pieces of zucchini accompany juicy, pan-seared chicken breasts flavored with basil-specked pesto sauce and smoky Asiago cheese (count 'em, four ingredients!).

INGREDIENTS

- 4 small skinless, boneless chicken breast halves (about ¾ pound total)
- 2 tablespoons pesto
- 2 cups chopped zucchini and/or yellow summer squash
- 2 tablespoons shredded Asiago or Parmesan cheese

To rinse the chicken pieces, run each piece under cold running water, then pat dry with paper towels.

Start to finish: 15 minutes

DIRECTIONS

1. Rinse chicken; pat dry. Skim 1 tablespoon oil off pesto (or substitute 1 tablespoon olive oil). In a large nonstick skillet cook chicken in hot oil over medium heat for 4 minutes.

2. Turn chicken; add squash. Cook for 4 to 6 minutes more or until the chicken is tender and no longer pink and squash is crisp-tender, stirring squash gently once or twice. Transfer chicken and squash to 4 dinner plates. Spread pesto over chicken; sprinkle with cheese. Makes 4 servings.

NUTRITION FACTS PER SERVING:

169 calories
8 g total fat
1 g saturated fat
48 mg cholesterol
158 mg sodium
4 g carbohydrate
1 g fiber
19 g protein

INGREDIENTS

- 4 medium skinless, boneless chicken breast halves (about 1 pound total)
- 2 or 3 cloves garlic, peeled and thinly sliced
- 1 tablespoon butter or margarine
- 1 teaspoon finely shredded lime peel
- 2 tablespoons lime juice
- ¼ teaspoon ground ginger
- ⅛ teaspoon crushed red pepper
- 1 orange
  Finely shredded orange peel (optional)

keys-style citrus chicken

The tropical-island-inspired cooking of the Florida Keys draws on the best of both of its worlds. Here it combines fresh Florida citrus with the Caribbean penchant for fiery peppers. Soak up the delicious juice with hot cooked rice.

Start to finish: 20 minutes

DIRECTIONS

1. Rinse chicken; pat dry. In a large skillet cook chicken and garlic in hot butter or margarine over medium heat for 8 to 10 minutes or until chicken is tender and no longer pink, turning chicken once and stirring garlic occasionally.

2. Meanwhile, in a small bowl combine lime peel, lime juice, ginger, and red pepper; set aside. Peel and slice orange, reserving juice. Cut orange slices into quarters. Add any reserved orange juice and the lime juice mixture to skillet. Place orange slices on top of chicken. Cook, covered, for 1 to 2 minutes or until heated through. Spoon drippings over chicken to serve. If desired, garnish with shredded orange peel. Makes 4 servings.

NUTRITION FACTS PER SERVING:

 167 calories
6 g total fat
3 g saturated fat
67 mg cholesterol
84 mg sodium
5 g carbohydrate
1 g fiber
22 g protein

Garlic tastes great roasted, braised, baked, or, as in this recipe, sautéed. Cooking of any kind caramelizes the sugar in garlic, mellowing its pungent smell and taming its assertive flavor.

Because it is sautéed with the chicken in this recipe, the garlic cooks long enough to turn light brown. This adds a toasty flavor that pairs well with the tangy lime juice.

margarita chicken

The classic margarita flavors of lime and tequila are a delicious complement to chicken.

INGREDIENTS

- ½ teaspoon finely shredded lime peel
- ¼ cup lime juice
- 2 tablespoons tequila
- 2 tablespoons honey
- 1 tablespoon cooking oil
- 2 teaspoons cornstarch
- ¼ teaspoon garlic salt
- ¼ teaspoon coarsely ground black pepper
- 4 medium skinless, boneless chicken breast halves (about 1 pound total)
- 4 flour tortillas, warmed
- 1 medium tomato, cut into 8 wedges
- 1 medium avocado, seeded, peeled, and cut up
- Lime slices, cut in half (optional)

For soft, warm tortillas, wrap them in foil and heat in a 350° oven about 10 minutes. Or, micro-cook each unwrapped tortilla for 10 to 20 seconds on 100% power (high).

Prep time: 15 minutes
Broiling time: 12 minutes

DIRECTIONS

1. For glaze, in a small saucepan stir together lime peel, lime juice, tequila, honey, cooking oil, cornstarch, garlic salt, and pepper. Cook and stir over medium heat until thickened and bubbly. Cook and stir for 2 minutes more.

2. Rinse chicken; pat dry. Place on the unheated rack of a broiler pan. Broil 4 to 5 inches from the heat for 12 to 15 minutes or until chicken is tender and no longer pink, turning once after half of the broiling time and brushing with some of the glaze during the last 5 minutes.

3. Arrange chicken, warmed tortillas, tomato, and avocado on 4 dinner plates. Drizzle chicken with the remaining glaze. If desired, garnish with lime slices. Makes 4 servings.

NUTRITION FACTS PER SERVING:

415 calories
16 g total fat
3 g saturated fat
59 mg cholesterol
356 mg sodium
39 g carbohydrate
3 g fiber
26 g protein

chicken with honey-cranberry sauce

A can of red cranberry sauce sweetened with honey and spiced with ginger makes a flavorful addition to quick-cooked chicken breasts.

INGREDIENTS

4 medium skinless, boneless chicken breast halves (about 1 pound total)
1 tablespoon margarine or butter
½ of a 16-ounce can (1 cup) whole cranberry sauce
2 tablespoons honey
½ teaspoon ground ginger

Prep time: 10 minutes
Cooking time: 10 minutes

DIRECTIONS

1. Rinse chicken; pat dry. In a large skillet cook chicken in hot margarine or butter over medium heat about 10 minutes or until chicken is tender and no longer pink, turning once. Remove chicken from skillet, reserving drippings in skillet. Keep warm.

2. Stir cranberry sauce, honey, and ginger into the reserved drippings in the skillet. Cook and stir until heated through. Spoon over chicken. Makes 4 servings.

To keep chicken warm while you prepare the honey-cranberry sauce, place the pieces on a serving platter and cover the platter with foil.

NUTRITION FACTS PER SERVING:

284 calories
6 g total fat
1 g saturated fat
59 mg cholesterol
108 mg sodium
36 g carbohydrate
1 g fiber
22 g protein

lemon chicken

This delectable chicken dish boasts the flavor of the Oriental restaurant favorite of the same name—without the mess of deep frying.

INGREDIENTS

- 4 medium skinless, boneless chicken breast halves (about 1 pound total)
- ⅓ cup all-purpose flour
- ¼ teaspoon pepper
- 2 tablespoons margarine or butter
- 1 cup chicken broth
- ¼ cup lemon juice
- 1 tablespoon cornstarch
- 2 green onions, sliced (¼ cup)
  Lemon slices, cut in half (optional)
  Hot cooked couscous (optional)
  Cooked artichoke halves (optional)

Quick-cooking COUSCOUS is the perfect main dish accompaniment for time-pressured cooks. Simply pour boiling water over the couscous; let it stand for 5 minutes. Fluff it with a fork, and it's ready to eat.

Start to finish: 25 minutes

DIRECTIONS

1. Rinse chicken; pat dry. Place each chicken breast half, boned side up, between 2 sheets of plastic wrap. Working from the center to the edges, pound lightly with the flat side of a meat mallet to ¼-inch thickness. Remove plastic wrap. In a shallow dish stir together flour and pepper. Lightly coat each piece of chicken with the flour mixture.

2. In a large skillet cook chicken in hot margarine or butter over medium heat for 4 to 6 minutes or until chicken is tender and no longer pink, turning once. Remove chicken from skillet. Keep warm.

3. For sauce, in a small mixing bowl stir together chicken broth, lemon juice, and cornstarch. Add to skillet. Cook and stir over medium heat until thickened and bubbly. Cook and stir for 2 minutes more. Stir in green onions. If desired, top chicken with lemon slices.

Serve chicken with sauce and, if desired, hot cooked couscous. If desired, garnish with artichoke halves. Makes 4 servings.

NUTRITION FACTS PER SERVING:

226 calories
9 g total fat
2 g saturated fat
60 mg cholesterol
315 mg sodium
10 g carbohydrate
0 g fiber
24 g protein

INGREDIENTS

- **2** tablespoons frozen orange juice concentrate, thawed
- **2** tablespoons molasses
- **¼** teaspoon onion powder
- **4** medium skinless, boneless chicken breast halves (about 1 pound total) or 8 small skinless, boneless chicken thighs
- **Salt**
- **Pepper**
- **Hot cooked spinach fettuccine or plain fettuccine (optional)**
- **Orange peel strips (optional)**

molasses-orange glazed chicken

This easy glaze gives the chicken a golden color and a sweet citrus flavor.

Prep time: 5 minutes
Broiling time: 12 minutes

DIRECTIONS

1. For glaze, in a small mixing bowl stir together orange juice concentrate, molasses, and onion powder.

2. Rinse chicken; pat dry. Season with salt and pepper. Place on the unheated rack of a broiler pan. Broil 4 to 5 inches from the heat for 6 minutes. Brush with some of the glaze. Turn chicken; brush with remaining glaze. Broil for 6 to 9 minutes more or until chicken is tender and no longer pink. If desired, serve with fettuccine and garnish with orange peel strips. Makes 4 servings.

For the orange peel strips, use a
vegetable peeler to cut thin strips of peel from the surface of an orange. Make sure to remove only the orange part of the peel.

NUTRITION FACTS PER SERVING:

- 160 calories
- 3 g total fat
- 1 g saturated fat
- 59 mg cholesterol
- 56 mg sodium
- 10 g carbohydrate
- 0 g fiber
- 22 g protein

sesame chicken

The appealing nutty flavor of these quick-to-fix chicken breasts comes from both sesame seed and toasted sesame oil.

INGREDIENTS

- 6 medium skinless, boneless chicken breast halves (about 1½ pounds total)
- ½ cup all-purpose flour
- 1½ teaspoons lemon-pepper seasoning
- ¾ teaspoon salt
- ⅓ cup sesame seeds
- 2 cups sliced fresh shiitake or button mushrooms
- ¼ cup finely chopped onion
- 2 teaspoons olive oil
- 1½ cups milk
- 1 tablespoon Dijon-style mustard
- 1 tablespoon snipped fresh parsley
- ⅓ cup milk
- 1 tablespoon olive oil
- 1 teaspoon toasted sesame oil

Start to finish: 30 minutes

DIRECTIONS

1. Rinse chicken; pat dry. Set aside. In a shallow bowl stir together the flour, lemon-pepper seasoning, and salt. Reserve 2 tablespoons flour mixture. Stir sesame seeds into remaining flour mixture. Set aside.

2. For sauce, in a medium saucepan cook mushrooms and onion in the 2 teaspoons olive oil until tender. Stir the reserved 2 tablespoons flour mixture into mushroom mixture until combined. Add the 1½ cups milk all at once. Cook and stir until thickened and bubbly. Cook and stir 1 minute more. Stir in the mustard and parsley. Keep sauce warm.

3. Meanwhile, dip chicken in the ⅓ cup milk; roll in sesame-seed-and-flour mixture. In a 12-inch skillet heat 1 tablespoon olive oil and the sesame oil over medium-high heat. Cook chicken in hot oil about 6 minutes or until chicken is tender and no longer pink, turning once. Serve sauce with chicken. Makes 6 servings.

NUTRITION FACTS PER SERVING:

362 calories
14 g total fat
3 g saturated fat
65 mg cholesterol
702 mg sodium
30 g carbohydrate
2 g fiber
30 g protein

INGREDIENTS

- 1 6-ounce package long grain and wild rice pilaf mix
- 2 green onions, thinly sliced (¼ cup)
- ½ cup water
- 1 cup broccoli flowerets
- 4 Italian-style or butter-garlic marinated boneless chicken breast halves
- 2 teaspoons olive oil
- 1 medium tomato, halved and thinly sliced
- 2 slices part-skim mozzarella cheese, halved (3 ounces)

marinated chicken breasts with mozzarella

Marinated yet quick-to-fix—it's possible when you start with purchased marinated chicken breasts.

Start to finish: 25 minutes

DIRECTIONS

1. Prepare rice according to package directions, adding green onions for the last 5 minutes of cooking. In a saucepan bring the water to boiling; add broccoli. Cover and cook for 3 minutes or until crisp-tender; drain and set aside.

2. In a large cast-iron skillet cook chicken breasts in hot oil over medium heat 8 to 10 minutes or until chicken is tender and no longer pink, turning once. Overlap halved tomato slices on top of chicken breasts. Spoon cooked broccoli over tomato slices; cover each with a half-slice of cheese. Broil chicken 3 to 4 inches from heat for 1 minute or until cheese is melted and bubbly. Serve over hot rice. Makes 4 servings.

Cut preparation time even more by using precut broccoli flowerets from your supermarket's salad bar or produce section.

NUTRITION FACTS PER SERVING:

377 calories
12 g total fat
4 g saturated fat
22 mg cholesterol
1,532 mg sodium
38 g carbohydrate
2 g fiber
31 g protein

french farmhouse garlic chicken

The classic version of this recipe requires stuffing and roasting a whole chicken. To speed dinner to the table, we've substituted chicken breasts cooked on the range top.

INGREDIENTS

- 4 small skinless, boneless chicken breast halves (about ¾ pound total)
- ¼ teaspoon salt
- ¼ teaspoon pepper
- 40 small cloves unpeeled garlic
- 1 tablespoon cooking oil
- ½ cup dry white wine or chicken broth
- ½ cup chicken broth
- 1 tablespoon lemon juice
- 1 teaspoon dried basil, crushed
- ½ teaspoon dried oregano, crushed
- 4 teaspoons all-purpose flour
- 2 tablespoons dry white wine or chicken broth
- Hot mashed potatoes or cooked rice

That's right— 40 cloves of garlic. As

the garlic cooks, the flavor mellows. Halve any large garlic cloves. If time allows, peel the garlic before cooking; otherwise, at the dinner table, use the tip of your knife to simply slip off the skins.

Prep time: 15 minutes
Cooking time: 10 minutes

DIRECTIONS

1. Rinse chicken; pat dry. Season with the salt and pepper. In a 10-inch skillet cook chicken and garlic in hot oil over medium-high heat for 4 to 6 minutes or just until browned, turning once. Slowly add ½ cup white wine or broth, ½ cup broth, lemon juice, basil, and oregano. Bring to boiling; reduce heat. Cover and simmer for 6 to 8 minutes or until chicken is tender and no longer pink. Use a slotted spoon to transfer the chicken and garlic to a warm serving platter. Keep warm.

2. In a small bowl stir together the flour and the 2 tablespoons dry white wine or broth. Stir into pan juices. Bring to boiling. Cook and stir for 1 minute more. Spoon sauce over chicken. Serve with potatoes or rice. Makes 4 servings.

NUTRITION FACTS PER SERVING:

327 calories
7 g total fat
2 g saturated fat
48 mg cholesterol
755 mg sodium
40 g carbohydrate
2 g fiber
22 g protein

chicken breasts with raspberry sauce

Convenient raspberry jam is the key ingredient in this mouthwatering sauce. Don't have seedless jam? Then stir regular raspberry jam to soften, and press through a strainer to remove seeds.

INGREDIENTS

- 4 medium skinless, boneless chicken breast halves (about 1 pound total)
- ½ teaspoon dried thyme, crushed
- ½ teaspoon dried sage, crushed
- ¼ teaspoon salt
- ¼ teaspoon pepper
  Nonstick cooking spray
- ¼ cup seedless raspberry jam
- 2 tablespoons orange juice
- 2 tablespoons wine vinegar
  Fresh raspberries (optional)

Prep time: 15 minutes
Cooking time: 8 minutes

DIRECTIONS

1. Rinse chicken; pat dry. Combine thyme, sage, salt, and pepper; rub over chicken breast halves, coating evenly.

2. Coat a 10-inch skillet with cooking spray. Add chicken to skillet. Cook over medium heat for 8 to 10 minutes or until tender and no longer pink, turning once. Remove from skillet. Keep warm.

3. Stir together jam, orange juice, and vinegar; add to skillet. Bring to boiling. Boil gently, uncovered, about 2 minutes or until sauce is reduced to desired consistency. Serve sauce over chicken. If desired, garnish with raspberries. Makes 4 servings.

NUTRITION FACTS PER SERVING:

 185 calories
4 g total fat
1 g saturated fat
59 mg cholesterol
189 mg sodium
15 g carbohydrate
0 g fiber
22 g protein

For a super quick yet elegant meal, make these two easy side dishes:

Prepare a package of quick-cooking long grain and wild rice mix according to package directions.

In the microwave oven cook peeled baby carrots (about 2 cups) with 2 tablespoons water, covered, on 100% power (high) about 5 minutes or until crisp-tender.

thyme chicken marsala

For a party meal, accompany this elegant chicken entrée with a loaf of crusty French bread and your favorite dessert.

INGREDIENTS

- 2 medium skinless, boneless chicken breast halves (about ½ pound total)
- 1 tablespoon all-purpose flour
- 2 tablespoons olive oil
- 1 medium carrot, cut into thin bite-size strips
- 1 small red or yellow sweet pepper, cut into thin bite-size strips
- 1 teaspoon bottled minced garlic or 2 cloves garlic, minced
- ¼ teaspoon salt
- ¼ teaspoon ground black pepper
- ⅓ cup dry marsala
- 1 tablespoon snipped fresh thyme or ¼ teaspoon dried thyme, crushed
  Hot cooked linguine or other pasta (optional)

Marsala is a rich
Sicilian wine that is available in both sweet and dry varieties. Sweet marsala makes a delicious after-dinner wine and dry marsala often is served as an aperitif or used in dishes such as this chicken entrée.

Prep time: 15 minutes
Cooking time: 13 minutes

DIRECTIONS

1. Rinse the chicken; pat dry. Place each breast half, boned side up, between 2 sheets of plastic wrap. Working from the center to the edges, pound lightly with the flat side of a meat mallet to ¼-inch thickness. Remove plastic wrap. Coat breasts lightly with the flour; shake off excess. Set aside.

2. In a large skillet heat 1 tablespoon of the oil. Add the carrot strips and cook for 3 minutes. Add the pepper strips, garlic, salt, and black pepper to the skillet. Cook and stir about 5 minutes or until crisp-tender. Arrange on 2 dinner plates. Cover and keep warm.

3. In the same skillet heat the remaining oil over medium heat. Add the chicken and cook for 4 to 6 minutes or until chicken is tender and no longer pink, turning once. Place chicken on top of vegetables.

4. Add the marsala and thyme to the skillet. Cook and stir for 1 minute, scraping up any browned bits from skillet. Pour mixture over chicken. If desired, serve with linguine or other pasta. Makes 2 servings.

NUTRITION FACTS PER SERVING:

311 calories
17 g total fat
3 g saturated fat
59 mg cholesterol
350 mg sodium
10 g carbohydrate
2 g fiber
23 g protein

INGREDIENTS

8 ounces packaged dried pappardelle, mafalda, fettuccine, or wide egg noodles

1 10-ounce package frozen baby lima beans

1 14½-ounce can Italian-style stewed tomatoes

6 ounces skinless, boneless chicken breasts

1 small onion, cut into wedges

¼ teaspoon coarsely ground black pepper

1 tablespoon olive oil

¼ cup chicken broth

¼ cup whipping cream

Shredded Parmesan cheese (optional)

Snipped fresh chives (optional)

wide noodles with chicken and lima beans

Any width pasta will do here, but the wider the noodle, the more luscious, creamy sauce you get per mouthful.

Start to finish: 30 minutes

DIRECTIONS

1. Cook pasta according to package directions, adding lima beans to water with the pasta. Drain pasta and beans; return to saucepan.

2. Meanwhile, place undrained tomatoes in a food processor bowl or blender container. Cover and process or blend until pureed. Set tomatoes aside.

3. Rinse chicken; pat dry. Cut chicken into bite-size pieces. For sauce, in a large skillet cook chicken, onion, and pepper in hot oil over medium-high heat for 2 to 3 minutes or until chicken is no longer pink. Reduce heat; stir in blended tomatoes and chicken broth. Simmer about 5 minutes or until liquid is reduced by half. Stir in cream; simmer for 2 to 3 minutes more or until sauce is desired consistency.

4. Pour sauce over pasta mixture; toss gently to coat. Transfer pasta mixture to a warm serving dish. If desired, sprinkle with Parmesan cheese and chives. Makes 4 servings.

If you prefer,

substitute lasagna noodles for the pappardelle. Cook them according to package directions. Drain and cut crosswise into 1-inch-wide pieces. (Cook the lima beans separately.)

NUTRITION FACTS PER SERVING:

503 calories
12 g total fat
4 g saturated fat
43 mg cholesterol
438 mg sodium
75 g carbohydrate
7 g fiber
25 g protein

north american chicken couscous

Quick-cooking couscous adds the finishing touch to this spiced-up stir-fry specialty.

INGREDIENTS

- 1 pound skinless, boneless chicken breasts
- 2 medium onions, cut into thin wedges
- 1 teaspoon bottled minced garlic or 2 cloves garlic, minced
- 1 tablespoon olive oil
- 16 packaged, peeled baby carrots (about ¾ cup)
- 2½ cups chicken broth
- 2 medium zucchini, quartered and cut into 2-inch-wide pieces
- ½ cup raisins
- 2 to 3 teaspoons curry powder
- 1 teaspoon ground cinnamon
- ½ teaspoon salt
- 1⅓ cups quick-cooking couscous
- ¼ cup slivered almonds, toasted (optional)

Cutting the chicken into even bite-size pieces is easier if the chicken is partially frozen.

Start to finish: 20 minutes

DIRECTIONS

1. Rinse chicken; pat dry. Cut chicken into bite-size pieces. In a large saucepan cook onions and garlic in hot oil about 3 minutes or until crisp-tender. Add chicken picces and carrots. Cook, uncovered, over medium heat for 5 minutes, stirring frequently. Stir in ½ cup of the chicken broth, zucchini, raisins, curry powder, ½ teaspoon of the cinnamon, and salt. Cover and cook over medium heat 3 to 4 minutes or until chicken is no longer pink and vegetables are crisp-tender.

2. Meanwhile, in a medium saucepan combine the remaining chicken broth and the remaining cinnamon; bring to boiling. Stir in couscous; cover. Remove from heat; let stand for 5 minutes. Fluff couscous lightly with fork. Serve couscous with chicken and vegetable mixture. If desired, garnish with toasted almonds. Makes 4 servings.

NUTRITION FACTS PER SERVING:

500 calories
8 g total fat
2 g saturated fat
60 mg cholesterol
833 mg sodium
72 g carbohydrate
13 g fiber
34 g protein

70

INGREDIENTS

- 1½ cups quick-cooking rice
- ¾ pound skinless, boneless chicken breasts
- 2 tablespoons cooking oil
- 1 medium onion, chopped (½ cup)
- 1 to 2 teaspoons curry powder
- 3 tablespoons all-purpose flour
- 1 cup chicken broth
- 1 5½-ounce can tomato juice
- 1 11-ounce can mandarin orange sections, drained, or one 8-ounce can pineapple tidbits, drained
- ½ cup raisins, chopped cashews, chopped peanuts, coconut, and/or chopped banana
- Fresh chives with flowers (optional)

chicken curry

Cooking the curry powder with the onion mellows the flavor yet retains the spiciness of this dish.

Start to finish: 20 minutes

DIRECTIONS

1. Cook rice according to package directions. Meanwhile, rinse chicken; pat dry. Cut chicken into ¾-inch pieces.

2. In a large skillet heat 1 tablespoon of the oil over medium heat. Add chicken to hot oil; cook and stir for 2 to 3 minutes or until no longer pink. Remove chicken from the skillet, reserving drippings. Set aside.

3. Add the remaining oil to the reserved drippings in skillet. Cook the onion and curry powder in the oil-drippings mixture until onion is tender. Stir in flour.

Stir in chicken broth and tomato juice. Cook and stir over medium heat until thickened and bubbly. Cook and stir for 1 minute more.

4. Return chicken to skillet. Gently stir in orange sections or pineapple. Cook until heated through. Serve over the hot cooked rice. Serve with raisins, cashews, peanuts, coconut, and/or banana. If desired, garnish with fresh chives. Makes 4 servings.

NUTRITION FACTS PER SERVING:

423 calories
10 g total fat
2 g saturated fat
45 mg cholesterol
385 mg sodium
62 g carbohydrate
2 g fiber
22 g protein

chicken and sausage couscous

Pick up a package of crisp breadsticks to go alongside this meal. For dessert try something light such as lemon or orange sherbet served with slices of cold, crisp melon—perfect palate refreshers.

INGREDIENTS

¼ pound skinless, boneless chicken breasts

6 ounces fully cooked smoked sausage (such as Polish sausage or Kielbasa), halved lengthwise and sliced into ½-inch pieces

2 stalks celery, sliced (1 cup)

2 medium carrots, thinly sliced (1 cup)

1⅓ cups chicken broth

1 cup couscous

1 medium green sweet pepper, cut into strips

1 cup chicken broth

1 tablespoon cornstarch

Get a jump start on dinner by cutting up the vegetables, sausage, and chicken the night before. Refrigerate them in separate covered containers until needed.

Start to finish: 30 minutes

DIRECTIONS

1. Rinse chicken; pat dry. Cut into bite-size strips; set aside. In a 10-inch skillet cook and stir sausage, celery, and carrots over medium-high heat about 5 minutes or until sausage is browned. Reduce heat; cover and cook for 3 to 5 minutes more or until carrots are nearly tender. Drain off fat.

2. Meanwhile, in a medium saucepan bring the 1⅓ cups broth to boiling. Stir in couscous; cover and remove from heat. Let stand while preparing meat and vegetable mixture.

3. Add chicken and green pepper to skillet; cook and stir over medium-high heat for 3 to 5 minutes or until chicken is no longer pink. Combine the 1 cup broth and cornstarch; stir into skillet. Cook and stir over medium heat until thickened and bubbly; cook and stir for 2 minutes more. Fluff couscous with a fork. Serve chicken mixture over couscous. Makes 4 servings.

NUTRITION FACTS PER SERVING:

400 calories
15 g total fat
5 g saturated fat
44 mg cholesterol
900 mg sodium
44 g carbohydrate
9 g fiber
21 g protein

chicken chop suey

Crisp chow mein noodles complement the savory chicken and vegetable mixture in this tasty one-dish meal.

INGREDIENTS

- 1 pound skinless, boneless chicken breasts
- 1¼ cups chicken broth or beef broth
- 2 tablespoons cornstarch
- 2 tablespoons soy sauce
- 1 tablespoon molasses
- ½ teaspoon ground ginger
- 1 tablespoon cooking oil
- 2 cups sliced celery
- 1 medium onion, chopped (½ cup)
- 2 cups fresh bean sprouts or one 16-ounce can bean sprouts, drained
- Chow mein noodles or hot cooked rice
- Tomato wedges (optional)

Start to finish: 25 minutes

DIRECTIONS

1. Rinse chicken; pat dry. Cut into ½-inch pieces. For sauce, stir together the broth, cornstarch, soy sauce, molasses, and ginger. Set aside.

2. Pour cooking oil in a wok or large skillet. (Add more oil as necessary during cooking.) Preheat over medium-high heat. Stir-fry the celery and onion in hot oil for 2 minutes. Add fresh bean sprouts, if using, and stir-fry for 1 to 2 minutes more or until celery and onion are crisp-tender. Remove vegetables from wok or skillet.

3. Add half of the chicken to the hot wok. Stir-fry for 3 to 4 minutes or until no longer pink. Remove chicken from the wok. Repeat with remaining chicken.

4. Return all chicken and cooked vegetables to the wok; push from the center of the wok. Stir sauce; add to the center of the wok. Cook and stir until thickened and bubbly. Add canned bean sprouts, if using. Stir to coat with sauce. Cook and stir about 1 minute more or until heated through. Serve immediately over chow mein noodles or hot cooked rice. If desired, garnish with tomato wedges. Makes 4 servings.

If you crave dessert, serve quarters of fresh pineapples, and drizzle them with chocolate syrup, if you like. Don't forget a pot of hot herbal tea to complete the meal.

NUTRITION FACTS PER SERVING:

343 calories
14 g total fat
3 g saturated fat
60 mg cholesterol
943 mg sodium
27 g carbohydrate
3 g fiber
28 g protein

sweet and sour chicken

Pineapple and brown sugar contribute the sweet and vinegar adds the sour to this first-rate version of an Oriental classic.

INGREDIENTS

- ¾ pound skinless, boneless chicken breasts
- 6 ounces rice noodles or 2 cups hot cooked rice
- 1 8-ounce can pineapple chunks (juice pack)
- ¾ cup chicken broth
- ¼ cup vinegar
- 3 tablespoons brown sugar
- 2 tablespoons cornstarch
- 2 tablespoons soy sauce
- 1 tablespoon cooking oil
- ½ teaspoon bottled minced garlic or 1 clove garlic, minced
- 1 cup sliced celery
- 1 medium onion, cut into thin wedges
- 1 small red or green sweet pepper, cut into thin bite-size strips

Rice noodles are a terrific timesaver because they need no cooking. Simply let them stand in warm water about 15 minutes to rehydrate. Rice noodles are sold in the Oriental section of large supermarkets and in Oriental markets.

Start to finish: 25 minutes

DIRECTIONS

1. Rinse chicken; pat dry. Cut into bite-size strips; set aside. Break rice noodles into a large bowl, if using; cover with warm water. Let stand for 15 minutes while preparing chicken mixture.

2. Drain pineapple, reserving juice (you should have about ⅓ cup). For sauce, in a small bowl stir together reserved pineapple juice, chicken broth, vinegar, brown sugar, cornstarch, and soy sauce. Set aside.

3. Pour cooking oil into a wok or large skillet. (Add more oil if necessary during cooking.) Preheat over medium-high heat. Stir-fry garlic in hot oil for 15 seconds. Add celery and onion; stir-fry for 2 minutes. Add the sweet pepper; stir-fry for 2 minutes more. Remove vegetables from wok.

4. Add the chicken to the hot wok. Stir-fry for 2 to 3 minutes or until no longer pink. Stir sauce; add to wok.

Cook and stir until thickened and bubbly. Add cooked vegetables and pineapple. Cook and stir for 2 minutes more or until heated through. Drain rice noodles, if using; arrange noodles or rice on 4 dinner plates. Top with chicken mixture. Makes 4 servings.

NUTRITION FACTS PER SERVING:

- 388 calories
- 6 g total fat
- 1 g saturated fat
- 45 mg cholesterol
- 706 mg sodium
- 64 g carbohydrate
- 2 g fiber
- 19 g protein

74

INGREDIENTS

- 2 tablespoons oyster-flavored sauce
- 1 tablespoon fish sauce or soy sauce
- 1 tablespoon brown sugar
- 2 teaspoons cornstarch
- ⅓ cup water
- ¾ pound skinless, boneless chicken breasts
- 2 tablespoons cooking oil
- 1 medium onion, sliced
- 2 to 4 fresh red chili peppers, seeded and cut into thin strips
- ½ teaspoon bottled minced garlic or 1 clove garlic, minced
- ½ cup unsalted or lightly salted roasted cashews
- Hot cooked rice

spicy stir-fried chicken with cashews

Pick up some fortune cookies to accompany this dynamite dish. Maybe you'll get a great fortune to go along with the guaranteed great meal.

Start to finish: 25 minutes

ZDIRECTIONS

1. For sauce, in a small bowl stir together the oyster-flavored sauce, fish sauce or soy sauce, brown sugar, and cornstarch. Stir in water. Rinse chicken; pat dry. Cut into bite-size strips. Set aside.

2. Pour cooking oil into a wok or large skillet. Preheat over medium-high heat. Add onion and stir-fry 1 minute. Add chili peppers and garlic and stir-fry 1 to 2 minutes more or until onion is crisp-tender. Remove with slotted spoon and set aside.

3. Add chicken to wok. Stir-fry 3 to 4 minutes or until no longer pink. Push chicken from center of wok.

Stir sauce; add to skillet. Cook and stir until thickened and bubbly. Return onion, chili peppers, and garlic to skillet. Cook and stir 1 minute more. Stir in cashews. Serve over rice. Makes 4 servings.

NUTRITION FACTS PER SERVING:

444 calories
18 g total fat
3 g saturated fat
47 mg cholesterol
549 mg sodium
48 g carbohydrate
2 g fiber
23 g protein

Because chili peppers contain very pungent oils, be sure to protect your hands when preparing them. Put plastic gloves or sandwich bags over your hands so your skin doesn't come in contact with the peppers. Always wash your hands and nails thoroughly in hot, soapy water after handling chili peppers.

75

stir-fried chicken with feta

Brighten each serving by accompanying the main dish with micro-cooked zucchini and yellow summer squash slices drizzled with olive oil and lemon juice.

INGREDIENTS

- ¾ pound skinless, boneless chicken breasts
- 1 cup orzo (rosamarina) pasta (about 6 ounces) or 1 cup couscous
- ⅓ cup chicken broth
- 2 tablespoons wine vinegar
- 1 tablespoon cornstarch
  Nonstick cooking spray
- 2 medium onions, chopped (1 cup)
- 1 teaspoon bottled minced garlic or 2 cloves garlic, minced
- 1 tablespoon olive oil
- 1 14½-ounce can Italian-style stewed tomatoes
- 1 teaspoon sugar
- ½ cup crumbled feta cheese (2 ounces)
  Snipped fresh basil or chopped ripe olives (optional)

To micro-cook zucchini and yellow summer squash slices, place 2½ cups sliced vegetables in a microwave-safe casserole with 2 tablespoons water. Microwave, covered, on 100% power (high) for 4 to 5 minutes or until crisp-tender, stirring twice.

Start to finish: 25 minutes

DIRECTIONS

1. Rinse chicken; pat dry. Cut chicken into thin bite-size strips. Set aside.

2. Prepare orzo or couscous according to package directions. Combine broth, vinegar, and cornstarch. Set aside.

3. Meanwhile, coat a 10-inch skillet with cooking spray. Add onions and garlic; stir-fry over medium-high heat for 2 minutes. Remove from skillet. Add oil; stir-fry chicken in hot oil for 3 to 4 minutes or until no longer pink. Stir in undrained tomatoes, sugar, onion mixture, and broth mixture. Cook and stir until thickened and bubbly. Cook and stir for 2 minutes more.

4. Drain orzo or fluff couscous with a fork. Serve chicken mixture over hot orzo or couscous. Top each serving with feta cheese and, if desired, basil or olives. Makes 4 servings.

NUTRITION FACTS PER SERVING:

382 calories
10 g total fat
3 g saturated fat
57 mg cholesterol
624 mg sodium
47 g carbohydrate
2 g fiber
26 g protein

stir-fried chicken pizza

Start with refrigerated pizza dough and it's easy to serve homemade pizza even on busy nights.

INGREDIENTS

- 1 10-ounce package refrigerated pizza dough
- 3 small skinless, boneless chicken breast halves (about 9 ounces total)
- 1 tablespoon cooking oil or olive oil
- 1 large onion, sliced and separated into rings
- 1 medium green or red sweet pepper, chopped
- 1 cup sliced fresh mushrooms
- 1 teaspoon bottled minced garlic or 2 cloves garlic, minced
- 1½ cups shredded mozzarella cheese (6 ounces)
- 1 tablespoon snipped fresh basil or ½ teaspoon dried basil, crushed
- 1 teaspoon sesame seeds (optional)

Prep time: 20 minutes
Baking time: 5 minutes

DIRECTIONS

1. Unroll pizza dough; pat into a greased 12-inch pizza pan. Bake in a 425° oven for 8 minutes. Meanwhile, rinse chicken and pat dry; cut chicken into thin bite-size strips and set aside.

2. Pour cooking oil into a large skillet. (Add more oil if necessary during cooking.) Preheat over high heat. Add the onion, pepper, mushrooms, and garlic and stir-fry for 2 to 3 minutes or until crisp-tender. Remove from skillet.

3. Add chicken to skillet and stir-fry for 2 to 3 minutes or until no longer pink. Return vegetables to skillet; toss to mix and heat through.

4. Sprinkle half of the cheese over pizza crust. Spoon chicken mixture evenly over cheese layer. Top with remaining cheese. Sprinkle with basil and, if desired, sesame seeds. Return to 425° oven for 5 to 7 minutes more or until cheese melts. Makes 4 servings.

Your kids will love to hear that pizza and pop are for supper. And you can feel good about serving this homemade version of soda pop: Stir together a 6-ounce can of their favorite frozen juice concentrate (orange, apple, or grape) with 3 juice cans (18 ounces total) filled with carbonated water. Serve over ice.

NUTRITION FACTS PER SERVING:

385 calories
15 g total fat
6 g saturated fat
57 mg cholesterol
457 mg sodium
34 g carbohydrate
2 g fiber
28 g protein

chicken with orzo

On your way home, stop at your supermarket's hot-food counter and pick up a rotisserie-cooked chicken for this Greek-style dinner that goes together in a matter of minutes.

INGREDIENTS

Nonstick cooking spray

1½ cups orzo (rosamarina) pasta
(8 ounces)

2 cups shredded fresh spinach

1½ cup crumbled feta cheese
(2 ounces)

1 teaspoon finely shredded lemon
peel

1 2- to 2½-pound hot deli-cooked
rotisserie chicken, cut into
serving-size pieces

1 medium tomato, cut in wedges

Those juicy cooked birds you

see whirling and twirling on rotisserie cookers in many grocery stores cut your time in the kitchen. Serve them whole with a side dish or two; shred them for soups, salads, and sandwiches; or cut them into serving-size pieces to put into a casserole, such as this simple recipe.

Prep time: 20 minutes
Baking time: 10 minutes

DIRECTIONS

1. Coat a 2-quart rectangular baking dish with cooking spray. Set aside.

2. Prepare orzo according to package directions. Drain well. Return orzo to saucepan. Add spinach, half of the feta cheese, and lemon peel; toss to mix.

3. Spread orzo mixture in the prepared baking dish. Arrange chicken pieces and tomato wedges on top. Sprinkle with the remaining feta cheese. Bake, uncovered, in a 450° oven about 10 minutes or until heated through. Serves 4 to 6.

NUTRITION FACTS PER SERVING:

459 calories
14 g total fat
6 g saturated fat
96 mg cholesterol
446 mg sodium
48 g carbohydrate
2 g fiber
35 g protein

INGREDIENTS

⅓ cup bottled hoisin sauce

1 to 1½ teaspoons five-spice
powder

Orange juice

1 1½- to 2-pound hot deli-cooked
rotisserie chicken

2 3-ounce packages ramen noodles

Fresh red chili peppers, sliced
(optional)

Steamed pea pods (optional)

Orange slices (optional)

five-spice chicken

The skin of this chicken should have a dark, lacquered look and give off a rich, spicy aroma.

Prep time: 15 minutes
Baking time: 15 minutes

DIRECTIONS

1. In a small bowl stir together the hoisin sauce, five-spice powder, and enough orange juice (1 to 2 tablespoons) to thin mixture for brushing. Brush about half of the mixture over entire chicken. Place chicken on a rack in a shallow roasting pan.

2. Bake, uncovered, in a 400° oven for 15 to 18 minutes or until heated through and glazed. Stir 1 to 2 tablespoons additional orange juice into remaining hoisin mixture until easy to drizzle. Place in a small saucepan; heat through.

3. Discard seasoning packets from ramen noodles. Cook and drain noodles according to package directions.

4. To serve, carve the chicken. Arrange chicken slices and ramen noodles on 4 dinner plates. Spoon half of the sauce over the chicken; pass the remaining sauce. If desired, garnish with fresh chili peppers. If desired, serve with pea pods and orange slices. Makes 4 servings.

NUTRITION FACTS PER SERVING:

317 calories
16 g total fat
4 g saturated fat
125 mg cholesterol
926 mg sodium
20 g carbohydrate
1 g fiber
24 g protein

You can find five-spice powder in

Asian specialty stores or most supermarkets. Or, to prepare your own, in a spice grinder or blender combine 3 tablespoons ground cinnamon, 6 star anise or 2 teaspoons aniseed, 1½ teaspoons fennel seed, 1½ teaspoons whole Szechwan peppers or whole black peppercorns, and ¾ teaspoon ground cloves. Cover and grind spices to a fine powder. Store in a tightly covered container for up to 2 months. Makes about ¼ cup.

turkey parmigiana

Turkey goes Italian in this six-ingredient entrée.

INGREDIENTS

- 8 ounces packaged dried spaghetti
- 4 turkey breast tenderloin steaks (about 1 pound total)
- 1 tablespoon margarine or butter
- 2 tablespoons grated Parmesan cheese
- 1 14-ounce jar tomato and herb pasta sauce
- ¾ cup shredded mozzarella cheese (3 ounces)

Turkey breast tenderloin steaks are ½-inch-thick lengthwise cuts from the turkey tenderloin. If you can't find these steaks, just buy two whole turkey tenderloins and cut each in half horizontally to make four steaks.

Start to finish: 20 minutes

DIRECTIONS

1. Cook spaghetti according to package directions. Drain.

2. Meanwhile, rinse turkey; pat dry. In a large skillet cook turkey in hot margarine or butter over medium heat for 10 to 12 minutes or until tender and no longer pink, turning once. Sprinkle turkey with Parmesan cheese. Spoon pasta sauce over turkey. Cover and cook for 1 to 2 minutes or until heated through.

3. Sprinkle turkey with mozzarella cheese. Cover and let stand for 1 to 2 minutes or until cheese is melted. Serve with hot cooked spaghetti. Makes 4 servings.

NUTRITION FACTS PER SERVING:

518 calories
12 g total fat
4 g saturated fat
64 mg cholesterol
561 mg sodium
62 g carbohydrate
0 g fiber
37 g protein

herbed turkey and broccoli

Soft-style cream cheese makes an ultrarich sauce for this one-pan pasta dish.

INGREDIENTS

- 2 quarts water
- 8 ounces packaged dried linguine or spaghetti, broken in half
- 3 cups small broccoli flowerets
- 1 8-ounce container soft-style cream cheese with garlic and herbs
- ⅔ cup milk
- ¼ teaspoon coarsely ground black pepper
- 6 ounces sliced smoked turkey breast, cut into bite-size strips

Start to finish: 30 minutes

DIRECTIONS

1. In a large pot or Dutch oven bring water to boiling. Add linguine or spaghetti a little at a time. Return to boiling. Reduce heat. Cook for 6 minutes. Add broccoli. Return to boiling. Cook for 2 to 3 minutes more or until pasta is tender and broccoli is crisp-tender. Drain.

2. In the same pot or Dutch oven combine cream cheese, milk, and pepper. Cook and stir over low heat until cream cheese is melted. Add pasta-broccoli mixture and turkey. Toss until coated with the cheese mixture. If necessary, stir in additional milk to make desired consistency. Makes 4 servings.

NUTRITION FACTS PER SERVING:

516 calories
21 g total fat
11 g saturated fat
81 mg cholesterol
675 mg sodium
57 g carbohydrate
4 g fiber
25 g protein

81

thai turkey

If your family enjoys spicy food, use the top of the range given for the crushed red pepper.

INGREDIENTS

⅔ cup water
2 tablespoons soy sauce
1 tablespoon honey
2 teaspoons toasted sesame oil
2 teaspoons curry powder
1 teaspoon cornstarch
⅛ to ¼ teaspoon crushed red pepper
Nonstick cooking spray
1 small onion, cut into thin wedges
1 red sweet pepper, cut into thin strips
¾ pound cooked turkey, cut into bite-size strips (about 3 cups)

½ teaspoon bottled minced garlic or 1 clove garlic, minced
Hot cooked rice
Sliced fresh serrano peppers (optional)

Choose either long grain or quick-cooking rice to accompany this saucy dish. If using long grain rice, put it on to cook before preparing the recipe. For quick-cooking rice, prepare it just before you cook the onion and sweet pepper.

Start to finish: 25 minutes

DIRECTIONS

1. For sauce, in a small mixing bowl stir together the water, soy sauce, honey, sesame oil, curry powder, cornstarch, and crushed red pepper. Set aside.

2. Coat a large skillet or wok with cooking spray. Add the onion wedges and sweet pepper strips; cook and stir over medium heat until tender. Stir in the turkey strips and garlic. Stir in sauce. Cook and stir until thickened and bubbly. Cook and stir for 1 minute more. Serve over hot cooked rice. If desired, garnish with serrano peppers. Makes 4 servings.

NUTRITION FACTS PER SERVING:

335 calories
11 g total fat
3 g saturated fat
81 mg cholesterol
576 mg sodium
31 g carbohydrate
1 g fiber
27 g protein

chicken, pear, and blue cheese salad

The pairing of mellow pears and tangy blue cheese is naturally fresh and simple. Combine this classic twosome with packaged assorted greens and chicken, and you have a dinner that's naturally elegant as well.

INGREDIENTS

- 6 cups packaged torn mixed salad greens or mesclun (about 8 ounces)
- 10 to 12 ounces roasted or grilled chicken breast, sliced
- ¾ cup bottled reduced-calorie or regular blue cheese salad dressing
- 2 pears, cored and sliced
  Freshly ground black pepper (optional)

Start to finish: 15 minutes

DIRECTIONS

1. In a large mixing bowl combine the salad greens, chicken, and salad dressing; toss gently to coat. Divide among 4 individual salad bowls or dinner plates.

2. Arrange pear slices on tops of salads. If desired, sprinkle with freshly ground pepper. Makes 4 servings.

NUTRITION FACTS PER SERVING:

208 calories
6 g total fat
2 g saturated fat
72 mg cholesterol
591 mg sodium
18 g carbohydrate
3 g fiber
23 g protein

When shopping for pears, look for ones
without bruises or cuts. The color of the pears won't tell you much because the color of some pear varieties does not change as the fruit ripens. The pears for this salad should yield to gentle pressure at the stem end. If the pears in the store aren't ripe, place them in a paper bag or loosely covered bowl and let them stand at room temperature for a few days.

83

chutney-chicken salad

Curry powder and sweet-hot mango chutney add exotic touches to this classic chicken salad with red grapes. Serve it over full-flavored salad greens with a side of fresh cherries, or try it as a sandwich filling for croissants or wraps.

INGREDIENTS

¼ cup sliced or slivered almonds

¼ cup mango chutney, snipped

2 tablespoons light mayonnaise dressing or plain low-fat yogurt

1 teaspoon curry powder

2 cups chopped or shredded deli-cooked rotisserie chicken or deli-roasted turkey breast (about 10 ounces)

1 cup seedless red grapes, halved
   Lettuce leaves
   Fresh cherries with stems (optional)

Remember this salad at
Thanksgiving time or whenever you serve roast turkey. It's a great way to use up leftovers.

Start to finish: 20 minutes

DIRECTIONS

1. In a shallow baking pan spread almonds in a single layer. Bake in a 350° oven for 5 to 10 minutes or until nuts are a light golden brown, stirring once or twice to prevent overbrowning. Cool almonds slightly.

2. Meanwhile, in a large mixing bowl combine chutney, mayonnaise dressing, and curry powder. Add chicken, grapes, and toasted nuts; toss gently to coat. Serve on lettuce leaves. If desired, garnish with cherries. Makes 4 servings.

NUTRITION FACTS PER SERVING:

311 calories
16 g total fat
4 g saturated fat
76 mg cholesterol
118 mg sodium
20 g carbohydrate
2 g fiber
21 g protein

citrusy chicken salad

INGREDIENTS

⅓ cup frozen orange juice concentrate, thawed

¼ cup olive oil

2 to 3 tablespoons white wine vinegar or white vinegar

1 teaspoon ground cumin

⅛ teaspoon ground red pepper

4 cups torn mixed salad greens

10 ounces cooked chicken, cut into bite-size pieces (2 cups)

2 medium oranges, peeled and sectioned

1 cup jicama cut into thin bite-size strips

1 medium red sweet pepper, cut into rings

A wide variety of packaged salad greens is available in supermarket produce sections. For this main-dish salad, choose the combination that suits your fancy.

Start to finish: 25 minutes

DIRECTIONS

1. For dressing, in a small bowl stir together orange juice concentrate, olive oil, vinegar, cumin, and ground red pepper. Set aside.

2. In a large bowl toss together salad greens, chicken, oranges, jicama, and sweet pepper. Pour dressing over salad; toss lightly to coat. Makes 4 servings.

NUTRITION FACTS PER SERVING:

348 calories
20 g total fat
3 g saturated fat
68 mg cholesterol
73 mg sodium
20 g carbohydrate
2 g fiber
24 g protein

Brown-skinned jicama tastes like a cross between an apple and a water chestnut. Long used in Mexican cooking, it traverses the globe to add snap to this bright-colored, cumin-flavored salad with Mediterranean flavors.

southwestern chicken and black bean salad

Caesar salad dressing and romaine are tossed with a list of Mexican ingredients, including black beans, tortilla chips, chili powder, and cilantro to create a flavorful new entrée.

INGREDIENTS

- 10 cups torn romaine
- 1 15-ounce can black beans, rinsed and drained
- 1½ cups chopped cooked chicken or turkey (about 8 ounces)
- 1½ cups red and/or yellow cherry tomatoes, halved
- ½ cup bottled reduced-calorie Caesar salad dressing
- 2 teaspoons chili powder
- ½ teaspoon ground cumin
- 2 tablespoons snipped fresh cilantro or parsley
- ½ cup broken tortilla chips

Make quick work of snipping fresh herbs such as cilantro or parsley by placing the leaves in a 1-cup glass measure and snipping them finely with kitchen shears.

Start to finish: 25 minutes

DIRECTIONS

1. In a large bowl combine romaine, black beans, chicken, and tomatoes.

2. For dressing, in a small bowl whisk together salad dressing, chili powder, and cumin. Pour dressing over salad. Toss lightly to coat. Sprinkle with cilantro or parsley and tortilla chips. Makes 4 servings.

NUTRITION FACTS PER SERVING:

295 calories
10 g total fat
1 g saturated fat
55 mg cholesterol
913 mg sodium
26 g carbohydrate
9 g fiber
27 g protein

teriyaki chicken noodle salad

INGREDIENTS

- 1 3-ounce package chicken- or Oriental-flavor ramen noodles
- ¼ cup rice vinegar or white wine vinegar
- 2 tablespoons orange juice
- 2 tablespoons salad oil
  Few dashes bottled hot pepper sauce
- 6 cups torn mixed salad greens
- 2 cups fresh vegetables (such as bean sprouts, halved pea pods, or sliced carrots, yellow summer squash, zucchini, cucumber, and/or onions)

- 2 oranges, peeled, halved, and thinly sliced
- ¾ pound skinless, boneless chicken breasts
- 2 tablespoons cooking oil
  Coarsely ground black pepper

This fresh chicken salad is "fast food" in the best possible sense. The crunchy noodles and mixture of Asian spices that enliven the dressing come ready-to-use in a package of ramen-style soup.

Start to finish: 30 minutes

DIRECTIONS

1. For dressing, in a screw-top jar combine the flavor packet from the ramen noodles, the vinegar, orange juice, salad oil, and hot pepper sauce. Cover and shake well. Set aside.

2. In a large salad bowl combine salad greens, desired vegetables, and orange slices; toss gently to mix. Break ramen noodles into pieces; add to salad. Cover and refrigerate.

3. Rinse chicken; pat dry. Cut chicken into thin bite-size strips. Pour cooking oil into a wok or large skillet. Preheat over medium-high heat. Add chicken; stir-fry for 2 to 3 minutes or until no longer pink.

4. While chicken is cooking, pour the dressing over the salad mixture; toss gently to coat. Let stand about 5 minutes to soften noodles, tossing occasionally.

5. Add chicken and pan juices to salad; toss gently. Sprinkle with pepper. Serve immediately. Makes 4 servings.

NUTRITION FACTS PER SERVING:

351 calories
17 g total fat
3 g saturated fat
45 mg cholesterol
521 mg sodium
30 g carbohydrate
4 g fiber
21 g protein

87

jamaican chicken salad

Look in the spice section of your supermarket for Jamaican jerk seasoning or make the homemade version of this spice blend.

INGREDIENTS

½ cup bottled fat-free honey-mustard salad dressing

1 teaspoon finely shredded lime peel

4 medium skinless, boneless chicken breast halves (about 1 pound total)

2 to 3 teaspoons purchased Jamaican jerk seasoning or Homemade Jerk Seasoning (see recipe, below)

2 teaspoons cooking oil

12 cups (16 ounces) packaged torn mixed salad greens (such as the European blend)

16 chilled bottled mango slices in light syrup, drained
Lime peel strips (optional)

Prep time: 15 minutes
Cooking time: 12 minutes

DIRECTIONS

1. For dressing, mix honey-mustard dressing and shredded lime peel. If necessary, add water to make of drizzling consistency. Cover and chill dressing until ready to serve.

2. Rinse chicken; pat dry. Sprinkle chicken with the jerk seasoning. In a 10-inch skillet cook the seasoned chicken in hot oil over medium-high heat about 12 minutes or until tender and no longer pink, turning once. Thinly bias slice each chicken breast.

3. Divide greens among 4 dinner plates. Arrange warm chicken and mango over greens; drizzle with dressing. If desired, top with strips of lime peel. Makes 4 servings.

Homemade Jerk Seasoning: Combine 2 teaspoons onion powder, 1 teaspoon sugar, 1 teaspoon crushed red pepper, 1 teaspoon crushed dried thyme, ½ teaspoon salt, ½ teaspoon ground cloves, and ½ teaspoon ground cinnamon. Store in a tightly covered container.

NUTRITION FACTS PER SERVING:

318 calories
6 g total fat
1 g saturated fat
45 mg cholesterol
572 mg sodium
35 g carbohydrate
8 g fiber
22 g protein

curried chicken salad

INGREDIENTS

- 2 medium oranges or one 11-ounce can mandarin orange sections, drained
- 3 cups cubed cooked chicken (about 1 pound)
- 2 cups seedless red grapes, halved
- 1 8-ounce can sliced water chestnuts, drained
- 1 cup thinly sliced celery
- ⅓ cup light mayonnaise dressing or salad dressing
- ⅓ cup lemon-flavored low-fat yogurt
- 2 teaspoons soy sauce
- 1 teaspoon curry powder

Ladies' luncheons have changed and so has chicken salad. Today's version is a riot of color—red grapes, green celery, orange sections—and looks to the East for its flavorings of soy sauce and curry.

Start to finish: 30 minutes

DIRECTIONS

1. If using fresh oranges, peel and slice; halve or quarter each slice. In a large mixing bowl combine oranges, chicken, grapes, water chestnuts, and celery.

2. For dressing, in a small bowl stir together light mayonnaise dressing, yogurt, soy sauce, and curry powder. Pour dressing over chicken mixture; toss lightly to coat. Makes 6 servings.

NUTRITION FACTS PER SERVING:

♥ 275 calories
11 g total fat
3 g saturated fat
68 mg cholesterol
299 mg sodium
22 g carbohydrate
2 g fiber
24 g protein

Starting with chilled ingredients is

essential to preparing a main-dish salad in just 30 minutes. Put the mandarin orange sections, grapes, and water chestnuts in the refrigerator the night before you want to serve this tasty salad.

If you want to prepare the salad ahead, you can store it in the refrigerator for up to 24 hours.

strawberry-peppercorn vinaigrette with turkey

An enduring combination is the mix of hot and sweet. See what the fuss is about with a dressing that combines sweet strawberries and pungent cracked pepper. It gives turkey salad a wake-up call.

INGREDIENTS

- 8 cups mesclun, or 6 cups torn romaine and 2 cups torn curly endive, chicory, or escarole
- 2½ cups cooked turkey or chicken cut into bite-size strips (about ¾ pound)
- 2 cups sliced, peeled kiwifruit and/or sliced carambola (star fruit)
- 1½ cups enoki mushrooms (3 ounces)
- 1 cup red cherry tomatoes and/or yellow baby pear tomatoes, halved
- 1 cup cut-up fresh or thawed frozen strawberries
- 2 tablespoons red wine vinegar
- ⅛ teaspoon cracked black pepper

Kiwifruit taste like a mixture of strawberries, melons, and peaches. These fuzzy, brown-skinned fruits should yield to gentle pressure when ripe. Look for ones with no bruises or soft spots.

Carambola or star fruit, on the other hand, taste like a medley of lemon, pineapple, and apple. This small oval fruit should be waxy-looking with deep lengthwise grooves and a bright yellow skin. Look for firm, shiny-skinned fruit. If the carambola are more green than gold, they will be very tart.

Start to finish: 25 minutes

DIRECTIONS

1. Divide mesclun among 4 plates. Top each with turkey, kiwifruit, mushrooms, and tomatoes.

2. For dressing, in a food processor bowl or blender container combine strawberries, vinegar, and black pepper. Cover and process or blend until smooth.

3. Drizzle dressing over salads. Toss lightly to coat. Makes 4 servings.

NUTRITION FACTS PER SERVING:

251 calories
8 g total fat
2 g saturated fat
84 mg cholesterol
102 mg sodium
15 g carbohydrate
5 g fiber
31 g protein

INGREDIENTS

- 6 ounces packaged dried rotini or radiatore
- 1 medium apple, chopped
- 1 tablespoon lime juice or lemon juice
- ½ pound smoked turkey breast, cut into bite-size pieces
- 1 cup raspberries or cut-up strawberries
- ½ cup sliced celery
- ¼ cup plain fat-free yogurt
- 2 tablespoons fat-free mayonnaise dressing or salad dressing
- 2 tablespoons skim milk
- 4 teaspoons Dijon-style mustard
- 1 tablespoon snipped fresh marjoram
- ¼ teaspoon celery seed

turkey and pasta salad

It's Waldorf salad with a twist! This delicious version builds on the classic, but goes modern with smoked turkey, raspberries, curly rotini pasta, and a low-fat dressing.

Start to finish: 25 minutes

DIRECTIONS

1. Cook pasta according to package directions; drain. Rinse with cold water and drain well.

2. Toss chopped apple with lime juice or lemon juice. In a large mixing bowl combine the cooked pasta, chopped apple, turkey, raspberries or strawberries, and celery.

3. For dressing, in a small mixing bowl combine yogurt, mayonnaise dressing, milk, mustard, marjoram, and celery seed. Drizzle dressing over pasta mixture; toss gently to coat. Makes 4 servings.

To save last-minute prep

time, cook the pasta ahead and chill it until you're ready to assemble the salad.

NUTRITION FACTS PER SERVING:

278 calories
2 g total fat
0 g saturated fat
25 mg cholesterol
820 mg sodium
45 g carbohydrate
3 g fiber
19 g protein

91

quick chicken fajitas

Splurge by offering sour cream, guacamole, and chopped fresh jalapeño peppers—in addition to salsa—as toppers for the fajitas.

INGREDIENTS

8 7-inch flour tortillas

1 tablespoon lime juice or lemon juice

½ teaspoon ground cumin

½ teaspoon ground coriander

¼ teaspoon dried oregano, crushed

¾ pound skinless, boneless chicken breasts or turkey tenderloin steaks, thinly sliced into bite-size pieces

¼ cup clear Italian salad dressing (not reduced-oil dressing)

1 small red and/or green sweet pepper, cut into strips

1 small onion, halved and sliced

¼ cup frozen guacamole dip, thawed (optional)

Salsa

After a Tex-Mex meal, serve Almost-Fried Ice Cream: Scoop your favorite ice cream into a shallow pan and place the balls, covered, in the freezer until firm. Stir together 1½ cups almond cluster multigrain cereal, coarsely crushed, and 2 teaspoons melted margarine. Roll ice cream scoops in cereal mixture; return to freezer until ready to serve. To serve, drizzle honey over ice cream and sprinkle with cinnamon.

Start to finish: 20 minutes

DIRECTIONS

1. Wrap tortillas in foil; heat in a 350° oven for 10 to 15 minutes or until heated through. [Or, wrap in paper towels or waxed paper and heat in a microwave oven on 100% power (high) for 15 to 20 seconds.]

2. Meanwhile, in a medium bowl combine lime juice, cumin, coriander, and oregano. Stir in chicken.

3. Pour salad dressing into a large skillet. Preheat over medium-high heat. Add chicken mixture. Stir-fry for 2 minutes. With a slotted spoon, remove chicken from skillet. Add sweet pepper and onion to skillet; stir-fry for 2 to 3 minutes or until crisp-tender. Return chicken to skillet; heat through.

4. Spoon mixture onto warm tortillas; roll up. If desired, top with guacamole dip. Top with salsa. Makes 4 servings.

NUTRITION FACTS PER SERVING:

425 calories
17 g total fat
4 g saturated fat
51 mg cholesterol
600 mg sodium
45 g carbohydrate
1 g fiber
23 g protein

INGREDIENTS

- ½ cup plain yogurt
- ¼ cup finely chopped cucumber
- ½ teaspoon dried dillweed
- ¼ teaspoon dried mint, crushed
- 4 large pita bread rounds
- 4 lettuce leaves
- 6 ounces thinly sliced cooked chicken breast
- 1 small tomato, thinly sliced
- ⅓ cup crumbled feta cheese

cucumber-chicken pita sandwiches

When it's too hot to cook, try this refreshing sandwich.

Start to finish: 15 minutes

DIRECTIONS

1. For dressing, in a small mixing bowl stir together yogurt, cucumber, dillweed, and mint. Set aside.

2. For each sandwich, place a pita bread round on a plate. Top with lettuce, chicken, and tomato. Spoon dressing on top. Sprinkle with feta cheese. Roll up the pita bread. Secure with toothpicks. Serve immediately. Makes 4 servings.

Round out this warm-weather

entrée with your favorite fresh fruit and, if you like, chips or celery and carrot sticks. Ice cream makes a perfect cooling finale.

NUTRITION FACTS PER SERVING:

377 calories
14 g total fat
5 g saturated fat
55 mg cholesterol
793 mg sodium
43 g carbohydrate
1 g fiber
18 g protein

93

fabulous focaccia sandwiches

Perfect picnic food in a flash, these hearty sandwiches of juicy rotisserie chicken, herbed mayonnaise, and vegetables on chewy focaccia require only fresh fruit and a bottle of chilled white wine to make an idyllic alfresco meal.

INGREDIENTS

- 1 8- to 10-inch tomato or onion Italian flatbread (focaccia) or 1 loaf sourdough bread
- 3 to 4 tablespoons light mayonnaise dressing
- 1 to 2 tablespoons shredded fresh basil
- 1½ cups fresh spinach leaves
- 1½ cups sliced or shredded deli-cooked rotisserie chicken
- ½ of a 7-ounce jar roasted red sweet peppers, drained and cut into strips (about ½ cup)
- Snipped fresh chives (optional)

That's foh-KAH-chee-ah!
Focaccia is a flatbread—akin to deep-dish pizza crust—that originated in the Italian region of Liguria. Olive oil is often incorporated into the dough, as well as being generously brushed on top before the focaccia is finished with the desired toppings, such as minced garlic, onions, fresh herbs, tomatoes, olives, or a dusting of cheese. Generally, focaccia can be found at bakeries or large supermarkets.

Start to finish: 15 minutes

DIRECTIONS

1. Using a long serrated knife, cut bread in half horizontally. In a small bowl stir together mayonnaise dressing and basil.

2. Spread cut sides of bread halves with mayonnaise mixture. Layer spinach, chicken, and roasted sweet peppers between bread halves. If desired, sprinkle with chives. Cut into quarters. Makes 4 servings.

NUTRITION FACTS PER SERVING:

370 calories
11 g total fat
4 g saturated fat
51 mg cholesterol
148 mg sodium
43 g carbohydrate
4 g fiber
25 g protein

thai chicken wraps

Join the wrap rage with this all-in-one meal of Pacific Rim flavors: seasoned chicken, a confetti of gingered vegetables, and a sweet and savory peanut sauce.

INGREDIENTS

- 6 8- to 10-inch plain, red, and/or green flour tortillas
- ¾ pound skinless, boneless chicken breasts
- ½ teaspoon garlic salt
- ¼ to ½ teaspoon pepper
- 1 tablespoon cooking oil
- 4 cups packaged shredded broccoli (broccoli slaw mix)
- 1 medium red onion, cut into thin wedges
- 1 teaspoon grated fresh ginger
- 1 recipe Peanut Sauce (see recipe, below)

Start to finish: 25 minutes

DIRECTIONS

1. Wrap tortillas in paper towels. Microwave on 100% power (high) for 30 seconds to soften.

2. Meanwhile, rinse chicken; pat dry. Cut into bite-size strips. In a small bowl combine garlic salt and pepper. Add chicken; toss to coat evenly. In a large skillet cook and stir seasoned chicken in hot oil over medium-high heat for 2 to 3 minutes or until no longer pink. Remove from skillet; keep warm. Add broccoli, onion, and ginger to skillet. Cook and stir for 2 to 3 minutes or until vegetables are crisp-tender.

3. To assemble, spread each tortilla with about 1 tablespoon Peanut Sauce. Top with chicken strips and vegetable mixture. Roll each tortilla, securing with a toothpick. Serve immediately with remaining sauce. Makes 6 servings.

Peanut Sauce: In a small saucepan combine ¼ cup sugar, ¼ cup creamy peanut butter, 3 tablespoons soy sauce, 3 tablespoons water, 2 tablespoons cooking oil, and 1 teaspoon bottled minced garlic. Heat until sugar is dissolved, stirring frequently.

To heat the tortillas in the oven, wrap the tortillas in foil. Heat in a 350° oven for 10 minutes.

NUTRITION FACTS PER SERVING:

330 calories
16 g total fat
3 g saturated fat
30 mg cholesterol
911 mg sodium
30 g carbohydrate
3 g fiber
17 g protein

barbecued turkey tenderloins

Southern barbecue goes gourmet! These substantial sandwiches feature spicy grilled turkey tucked into crusty French rolls with grilled tomatillos and fresh spinach. Try them with sweet potato chips, a tasty alternative to regular chips.

INGREDIENTS

- ½ cup bottled onion-hickory barbecue sauce
- 1 small fresh jalapeño pepper, seeded and finely chopped
- 1 tablespoon tahini (sesame butter)
- 4 tomatillos, husked and halved lengthwise, or ½ cup salsa verde
- 2 turkey breast tenderloins (about 1 pound total)
- 4 French-style rolls, split
  Fresh spinach leaves

Tahini is a thick paste that is made by crushing sesame seeds. It is most often used in Middle Eastern dishes and can be found in the ethnic foods section of most supermarkets.

Prep time: 10 minutes
Grilling time: 20 minutes

DIRECTIONS

1. For sauce, in a small bowl combine barbecue sauce, jalapeño pepper, and tahini. Transfer half of the sauce to another bowl for basting. Reserve remaining sauce until ready to serve. On two 8- to 10-inch skewers thread tomatillos, if using. Set aside.

2. Rinse turkey; pat dry. Brush both sides of turkey with basting sauce. Grill turkey on the greased rack of an uncovered grill directly over medium heat about 20 minutes or until the turkey is tender and no longer pink, turning and brushing once with basting sauce. Place tomatillos on the grill rack next to the turkey for the last 8 minutes of grilling or until tender, turning once. Thinly slice turkey and chop tomatillos.

3. Toast the rolls on the grill. To serve, fill the rolls with a few spinach leaves, the grilled turkey, and tomatillos or salsa verde. Spoon on the reserved sauce. Makes 4 servings.

NUTRITION FACTS PER SERVING:

378 calories
8 g total fat
2 g saturated fat
50 mg cholesterol
776 mg sodium
45 g carbohydrate
1 g fiber
30 g protein

INGREDIENTS

- ½ cup fine dry bread crumbs
- 3 green onions, finely chopped (⅓ cup)
- 1 tablespoon soy sauce
- ¼ teaspoon ground ginger
- ¼ teaspoon garlic powder
- ¼ teaspoon bottled hot pepper sauce
- 1 pound ground raw turkey or ground raw chicken
- 1 tablespoon cooking oil
- 1 medium carrot, shredded
- 1 cup fresh bean sprouts
- 1 tablespoon margarine or butter
- Soy sauce (optional)
- Honey mustard (optional)
- 4 hamburger buns, split and toasted

veggie-topped turkey burgers

Bean sprouts add a delightful crunch and fresh flavor to these out-of-the-ordinary burgers.

Prep time: 15 minutes
Cooking time: 12 minutes

DIRECTIONS

1. In a bowl combine bread crumbs, green onions, the 1 tablespoon soy sauce, ginger, garlic powder, and hot pepper sauce. Add ground turkey or chicken; mix well. Shape into 4 patties, each about ¾ inch thick.

2. In a 10- or 12-inch skillet cook patties in hot oil over medium heat for 10 to 12 minutes or until no longer pink in centers, turning once. Remove from skillet. Keep warm.

3. Add shredded carrot, bean sprouts, and margarine or butter to skillet. Cook and stir for 2 to 3 minutes or until carrot is crisp-tender. If desired, season vegetables with a few drops soy sauce. If desired, spread honey mustard on cut sides of bun tops. Place burgers on cut sides of bun bottoms. Top with cooked vegetables. Makes 4 servings.

NUTRITION FACTS PER SERVING:

385 calories
17 g total fat
4 g saturated fat
42 mg cholesterol
682 mg sodium
35 g carbohydrate
1 g fiber
21 g protein

All this burger needs on the

side is a fresh spinach salad with a bit of Far East flair. Look in the supermarket produce section for bags of spinach already cleaned and ready for tossing into a bowl. Top with chilled canned mandarin orange sections and a package of broken ramen noodles (omit the seasoning packet). Serve with poppy seed dressing or your favorite bottled dressing for flavor and to soften the uncooked noodles.

smoked turkey salad sandwiches

On a hot summer day, this quick sandwich is light and refreshing. And, using fat-free mayonnaise dressing and fat-free yogurt keeps it low in fat.

INGREDIENTS

¼ cup fat-free mayonnaise dressing or regular mayonnaise or salad dressing

¼ cup plain fat-free yogurt

½ cup corn relish

2 cups chopped smoked turkey

1 stalk celery, thinly sliced

4 kaiser rolls, split

1 medium tomato, sliced

Simply pass a serve-yourself

relish tray filled with assorted pickles (try some pickled watermelon for a change), crisp cucumber slices, olives, and fresh berries to go with the turkey sandwiches.

Start to finish: 15 minutes

DIRECTIONS

1. For dressing, in a small mixing bowl stir together mayonnaise dressing and yogurt. Stir in corn relish.

2. In a large mixing bowl combine turkey and celery. Add dressing; toss gently to coat. Serve on rolls with tomato slices. Makes 4 servings.

NUTRITION FACTS PER SERVING:

292 calories
10 g total fat
1 g saturated fat
0 mg cholesterol
527 mg sodium
3 g carbohydrate
2 g fiber
18 g protein

italian turkey sandwiches

A minty tomato spread elevates these submarine sandwiches from ordinary to super.

INGREDIENTS

- ⅓ cup chopped onion
- 2 oil-packed dried tomato halves, drained and thinly sliced (about 3 tablespoons)
- 1 teaspoon bottled minced garlic or 2 cloves garlic, minced
- 1 teaspoon dried Italian seasoning, crushed
- 1 tablespoon olive oil
- ¼ cup snipped fresh parsley
- ¼ cup snipped fresh mint
- 2 tablespoons lime juice
- 1 tablespoon Worcestershire sauce
  Dash pepper
- 4 6- to 7-inch French-style rolls, split horizontally
- 1 6-ounce package thinly sliced turkey ham, smoked turkey breast, or ham
- 2 medium tomatoes, thinly sliced
- ½ cup shredded mozzarella cheese (2 ounces)

Prep time: 20 minutes
Baking time: 7 minutes

DIRECTIONS

1. In a small saucepan cook and stir onion, dried tomatoes, garlic, and Italian seasoning in hot oil for 3 minutes. Add parsley, mint, lime juice, Worcestershire sauce, and pepper. Cook and stir for 1 minute more.

2. To assemble, spread parsley mixture onto bottom halves of rolls. Top with turkey or ham, tomato slices, and cheese; add top halves of rolls. Arrange sandwiches in a shallow baking pan. Bake, uncovered, in a 350° oven for 7 to 10 minutes or until heated through and cheese is melted. Makes 4 servings.

Fresh mint not available? You can substitute 1 teaspoon dried mint, crushed, and add an extra ¼ cup snipped fresh parsley.

NUTRITION FACTS PER SERVING:

- 385 calories
- 11 g total fat
- 3 g saturated fat
- 30 mg cholesterol
- 1,114 mg sodium
- 52 g carbohydrate
- 1 g fiber
- 21 g protein

broiling poultry

When you need a meal in a hurry, turn to poultry. It's quick to broil and so delicious. If desired, remove the skin from the poultry. Rinse and pat dry with paper towels. If desired, sprinkle with salt and pepper.

Remove the broiler pan from the oven and preheat the broiler for 5 to 10 minutes. Arrange the poultry on the unheated rack of the broiler pan with the bone side up. If desired, brush poultry with cooking oil.

Place the pan under the broiler so the surface of the poultry is 4 to 5 inches from the heat; place chicken and Cornish game hen halves 5 to 6 inches from the heat. Turn the pieces over when browned on one side, usually after half of the broiling time. Chicken halves and meaty pieces should be turned after 20 minutes. Brush again with oil. The poultry is done when the meat is no longer pink and the juices run clear. If desired, brush with a sauce the last 5 minutes of cooking.

Type of Bird	Weight	Broiling Time
Chicken, broiler-fryer, half	1¼ to 1½ pounds	28 to 32 minutes
Chicken breast halves, skinned and boned	4 to 5 ounces	12 to 15 minutes
Chicken breast halves, thighs, and drumsticks	2 to 2½ pounds total	25 to 35 minutes
Chicken kabobs (boneless breast, cut into 2½-inch strips and threaded loosely onto skewers)	1 pound	8 to 10 minutes
Cornish game hen, half	10 to 12 ounces	30 to 40 minutes
Turkey breast steak or slice	2 ounces	6 to 8 minutes
Turkey breast tenderloin steak	4 to 6 ounces	8 to 10 minutes
Turkey patties (ground raw turkey)	¾ inch thick	10 to 12 minutes

microwaving poultry

Cooking poultry in your microwave oven is a surefire way to save precious minutes at mealtime. To microwave a whole bird, rinse thoroughly and pat the bird dry. Tie the legs to the tail and twist the wing tips under the back. Place the bird, breast side down, on a rack in a microwave-safe baking dish. Brush with melted margarine or butter. Cover with waxed paper. Microwave on the power specified below and for the time given or until done. After half of the cooking time, turn the breast side up and brush again with melted margarine or butter. (If desired, insert a temperature probe into the thigh, but don't let it touch the bone.)

The bird is done when the drumsticks move easily in their sockets, the temperature is 185° in several spots, no pink remains, and the juices run clear. If the wing and leg tips or other areas are done before the rest, shield these areas with small pieces of foil (check your owner's manual to see if foil is allowed in your oven). Let cooked birds weighing more than 2 pounds stand, covered with foil, for 15 minutes.

To microwave poultry parts, rinse thoroughly and pat dry. Arrange pieces in a microwave-safe baking dish with meaty portions toward edges of dish, tucking under thin boneless portions. If pieces are crowded in the dish, omit the neck, back, and wings. Cover with waxed paper. (Or, for skinless poultry, cover with a lid or vented plastic wrap.) Microwave on the power level specified below and for the time given or until done, rearranging, stirring, and turning pieces over after half of the cooking time.

Type of Bird	Amount	Power Level	Cooking Time
Chicken, broiler-fryer, cut up	One 2½- to 3-pound bird	100% (high)	9 to 17 minutes
Chicken, broiler-fryer, whole	One 2½- to 3-pound bird	50% (medium)	30 to 37 minutes
Chicken breasts, halved	Two 12-ounce breasts	100% (high)	8 to 10 minutes
	Two 16-ounce breasts	100% (high)	8 to 11 minutes
Chicken breast, whole	One 12-ounce breast	100% (high)	5 to 7 minutes
	Two 12-ounce breasts	100% (high)	13 to 15 minutes
Chicken drumsticks	2 drumsticks	100% (high)	2½ to 5 minutes
	6 drumsticks	100% (high)	6 to 10 minutes
Chicken pieces	1 pound	100% (high)	2½ to 5 minutes
Cornish game hen, whole	One 1¼- to 1½-pound bird	100% (high)	7 to 10 minutes
	Two 1¼- to 1½-pound birds	100% (high)	13 to 18 minutes
Turkey, ground, raw	1 pound	100% (high)	4 to 7 minutes
Turkey breast, half	One 3- to 4-pound half	50% (medium)	40 to 55 minutes
Turkey breast tenderloin steaks	Four 4-ounce steaks	100% (high)	5 to 8 minutes
Turkey drumstick	One 1-pound drumstick	100% (high)	7 to 9 minutes

Snapper Veracruz
See recipe, page 116

fish & seafood

broiled fish steaks with tarragon cheese sauce

This elegant three-ingredient sauce is equally delicious on salmon, swordfish, or tuna steaks.

INGREDIENTS

1¼ pounds fresh or frozen salmon, swordfish, or tuna steaks (about ¾ inch thick)

½ cup plain yogurt or light dairy sour cream

½ cup shredded mozzarella or Monterey Jack cheese (2 ounces)

2 teaspoons snipped fresh tarragon or ½ teaspoon dried tarragon, crushed

Salt

Ground black pepper

Hot cooked pasta (optional)

Fresh tarragon sprigs (optional)

Red sweet pepper strips (optional)

Serve the broiled fish on a bed

of pasta such as large bow tie, linguine, or fettuccine. Add a handful of red sweet pepper strips to the pasta during the last 5 minutes of cooking. Drain the pasta and sweet peppers, then toss with olive oil. If desired, top with cracked black pepper.

Prep time: 10 minutes
Broiling time: 6½ minutes

DIRECTIONS

1. Thaw fish, if frozen. Rinse fish; pat dry. Cut fish steaks into 4 equal portions, if necessary.

2. Stir together the yogurt or sour cream, cheese, and snipped or dried tarragon. Set aside.

3. Place fish on unheated rack of broiler pan. Sprinkle fish with salt and ground black pepper. Broil 4 inches from the heat for 6 to 9 minutes or until fish flakes easily when tested with a fork. Spoon yogurt mixture over fish steaks. Broil 30 to 60 seconds more or until heated through and cheese starts to melt. If desired, serve over hot cooked pasta and garnish with fresh tarragon sprigs and red pepper strips. Makes 4 servings.

NUTRITION FACTS PER SERVING:

188 calories
8 g total fat
3 g saturated fat
36 mg cholesterol
236 mg sodium
3 g carbohydrate
0 g fiber
25 g protein

citrus sole

INGREDIENTS

- 4 fresh or frozen sole or whitefish fillets (about ¾ pound total)
- 2 oranges or 1 grapefruit
- ½ cup light dairy sour cream
- 2 tablespoons frozen orange juice concentrate, thawed
- ¼ teaspoon dried herbes de Provence, crushed
- 2 teaspoons margarine or butter, melted
- ¼ teaspoon salt
- ¼ teaspoon paprika
- ⅛ teaspoon pepper

If the herb blend herbes de Provence isn't available at your supermarket, substitute an equal measure of crushed dried thyme.

Prep time: 10 minutes
Broiling time: 4 minutes

DIRECTIONS

1. Thaw fish, if frozen. Rinse fish; pat dry. If desired, peel oranges or grapefruit; cut into ¼-inch slices. Set aside.

2. In small bowl combine sour cream, orange juice concentrate, and herbes de Provence.

3. Place fish on a greased, unheated rack of a broiler pan. Tuck under any thin edges so fish cooks evenly. Combine melted margarine or butter, salt, paprika, and pepper; brush the tops of fish. Arrange orange or grapefruit slices around fish on broiler pan. Broil about 4 inches from the heat for 4 to 6 minutes or until fish flakes easily when tested with a fork and fruit is heated through. Serve fish and fruit slices with the sauce. Makes 4 servings.

NUTRITION FACTS PER SERVING:

- 162 calories
- 5 g total fat
- 2 g saturated fat
- 44 mg cholesterol
- 253 mg sodium
- 13 g carbohydrate
- 1 g fiber
- 17 g protein

Before cooking the Citrus Sole, prepare 1 cup seven grain and sesame breakfast pilaf or 1 cup long grain rice according to package directions, except stir in 1 cup chopped fresh broccoli for the last 5 minutes of cooking. Season to taste.

herb-buttered fish steaks

If you can't find small fish steaks, buy two large ones and cut them in half before serving. As long as the steaks are 1 inch thick, the cooking time will be the same.

INGREDIENTS

4 small fresh or frozen halibut, salmon, shark, or swordfish steaks, cut 1 inch thick (about 1 pound total)

2 tablespoons butter or margarine, softened

1 teaspoon finely shredded lime peel or lemon peel

1 teaspoon lime juice or lemon juice

1 teaspoon snipped fresh tarragon or rosemary or ¼ teaspoon dried tarragon or rosemary, crushed

1 teaspoon butter or margarine, melted

To thaw fish,

place the unopened package in a container in the refrigerator, allowing a 1-pound package to thaw overnight. To thaw fish in the microwave oven, place 1 pound frozen steaks or fillets in a microwave-safe baking dish; cover with vented plastic wrap. Micro-cook on 30% power (medium-low) for 4 to 6 minutes, turning and separating fish after 3 minutes. Let steaks stand 15 minutes; fillets 10 minutes. Fish should be pliable and cold on the outside and slightly icy in the center of thick areas.

Prep time: 10 minutes
Broiling time: 8 minutes

DIRECTIONS

1. Thaw fish, if frozen. Rinse fish; pat dry. For the herb butter, in a small mixing bowl stir together the 2 tablespoons butter or margarine, the lime or lemon peel, lime or lemon juice, and tarragon or rosemary. Set aside.

2. Place the fish steaks on the lightly greased rack of a broiler pan. Brush with the 1 teaspoon melted butter or margarine. Broil 4 to 5 inches from the heat for 8 to 12 minutes or until fish flakes easily, turning once after half of the broiling time. To serve, top with herb butter. Makes 4 servings.

NUTRITION FACTS PER SERVING:

184 calories
9 g total fat
2 g saturated fat
36 mg cholesterol
140 mg sodium
0 g carbohydrate
0 g fiber
24 g protein

vegetable-topped fish

Salsa and summer squash make an easy sauce for baked fish fillets.

INGREDIENTS

- 1 **pound fresh or frozen fish fillets**
- 2 **teaspoons margarine or butter, melted**
- ⅛ **teaspoon salt**
- ⅛ **teaspoon pepper**
- 1 **8-ounce jar (about 1 cup) salsa**
- 1 **small yellow summer squash or zucchini, halved lengthwise and cut into ¼-inch slices**

Start to finish: 15 minutes

DIRECTIONS

1. Thaw fish, if frozen. Rinse fish; pat dry. Measure thickness of fish. Place the fish in a greased shallow baking pan, tucking under any thin edges so fish cooks evenly. Brush fish with melted margarine or butter. Sprinkle with the salt and pepper. Bake, uncovered, in a 450° oven until fish flakes easily when tested with a fork. (Allow 4 to 6 minutes per ½-inch thickness of fish.)

2. Meanwhile, in a small saucepan stir together salsa and summer squash or zucchini. Bring to boiling; reduce heat. Cover and simmer for 5 to 6 minutes or until squash is crisp-tender. Serve squash mixture over baked fish fillets. Makes 4 servings.

Delicately flavored, skinless, and firm-textured fish fillets work best in this recipe. Orange roughy, cod, flounder, sea bass, and sole are excellent choices.

NUTRITION FACTS PER SERVING:

 202 calories
10 g total fat
2 g saturated fat
44 mg cholesterol
638 mg sodium
13 g carbohydrate
1 g fiber
19 g protein

pizza fish fillets

Green spinach fettuccine makes a colorful bed for the fish fillets, but regular fettuccine is equally tasty.

INGREDIENTS

1½ pounds fresh or frozen haddock, cod, or orange roughy fillets, ½ to ¾ inch thick

   Nonstick cooking spray

½ teaspoon lemon-pepper seasoning

12 ounces packaged dried spinach fettuccine

2 cups sliced fresh mushrooms

1 medium green sweet pepper, chopped

1 medium onion, chopped (½ cup)

¼ cup water

1 8-ounce can pizza sauce

½ cup shredded mozzarella cheese (2 ounces)

Frozen fruit makes a refreshing dessert when served partially thawed. While the sauce for the fish is heating, set out two 10-ounce packages of frozen mixed fruit in light syrup (in the quick-thaw pouch). At dessert time, spoon the fruit into sherbet dishes; add a splash of lemon juice and 2 tablespoons ginger ale to each dish.

Start to finish: 25 minutes

DIRECTIONS

1. Thaw fish, if frozen. Cut the fish into 6 serving-size pieces. Rinse fish; pat dry. Coat a 2-quart rectangular baking dish with nonstick spray. Place fish in the prepared baking dish, tucking under any thin edges so fish cooks evenly. Measure the thickness of the fish. Sprinkle the fish with the lemon-pepper seasoning.

2. Bake fish, uncovered, in a 450° oven until fish flakes easily when tested with a fork. (Allow 6 to 9 minutes per ½-inch thickness.) Drain off any liquid.

3. Meanwhile, cook fettuccine according to the package directions. In a medium saucepan combine mushrooms, green pepper, onion, and water; cover and cook about 5 minutes or just until tender. Drain; add pizza sauce. Heat through.

4. Serve fish on fettuccine; spoon sauce over fish. Sprinkle with cheese. Makes 6 servings.

NUTRITION FACTS PER SERVING:

342 calories
4 g total fat
1 g saturated fat
50 mg cholesterol
604 mg sodium
46 g carbohydrate
2 g fiber
29 g protein

INGREDIENTS

- 1 to 1¼ pounds fresh or frozen halibut steaks, cut ¾ inch thick
- ½ cup chunky salsa
- 2 tablespoons honey
- 2 tablespoons Dijon-style mustard

sweet mustard halibut

While the fish bakes, put 4 brown-and-serve rolls in the oven and bake about 5 minutes or until light brown. For an easy side dish, put your microwave oven to work—cook frozen green beans or broccoli while the fish and bread bake.

Start to finish: 15 minutes

DIRECTIONS

1. Thaw fish, if frozen. Rinse fish; pat dry. Arrange fish in a shallow 2-quart rectangular baking dish. Bake, uncovered, in a 450° oven 6 to 9 minutes or until fish flakes easily when tested with a fork. Drain off any liquid.

2. Meanwhile, in a small bowl stir together the salsa and honey. Spread mustard over drained fish; spoon salsa mixture over mustard. Bake for 2 to 3 minutes more or until mustard and salsa mixture are hot. Makes 4 servings.

NUTRITION FACTS PER SERVING:

176 calories
4 g total fat
0 g saturated fat
36 mg cholesterol
362 mg sodium
11 g carbohydrate
0 g fiber
24 g protein

No one likes to cope with busy grocery store aisles. Here are some hints to help you avoid the hassle:

- Shop just once a week and make a list. One well-organized trip saves time as well as money.
- Organize your grocery list. Eliminate backtracking by grouping items according to the grocery store's floor plan.
- Use the same in-store routine every time you shop. It reduces your shopping time.
- Shop when others don't—early morning or late evening. You'll miss crowded aisles and long waits at the checkout lines.

crispy oven-fried fish

A high oven temperature assures that the crumb coating gets crisp—and cooks the fish in under 10 minutes.

INGREDIENTS

- 1 **pound fresh or frozen haddock, orange roughy, or cod fillets, ½ to ¾ inch thick**
  Nonstick cooking spray
- 2 **tablespoons plain yogurt or dairy sour cream**
- 2 **tablespoons Dijon-style mustard**
- 1 **tablespoon snipped fresh chives**
  Dash ground red pepper
  Dash chili powder
- ⅔ **cup fine dry bread crumbs**
- 2 **tablespoons margarine or butter, melted**
  Lemon slices, halved (optional)
  Fresh chives (optional)

For a home-style dinner, fix a saucepan of instant mashed potatoes to serve with the crunchy fish fillets. Perk up the mashed potatoes by stirring in onion or garlic powder, snipped fresh chives or parsley, diced green chili peppers, crumbled bacon, or snipped dried tomatoes. Cooked fresh broccoli completes your meal.

Prep time: 15 minutes
Baking time: 6 minutes

DIRECTIONS

1. Thaw fish, if frozen. Rinse fish; pat dry. Cut fish into 4 serving-size pieces. Coat a baking sheet with nonstick spray.

2. In a small bowl combine yogurt or sour cream, mustard, snipped chives, red pepper, and chili powder. Coat fish on all sides with yogurt mixture; roll in bread crumbs to coat evenly.

3. Place fish on prepared baking sheet, tucking under any thin edges so fish cooks evenly. Drizzle fish with melted margarine or butter. Bake in a 450° oven for 6 to 10 minutes or until fish flakes easily when tested with a fork. Serve immediately. If desired, garnish with lemon slices and fresh chives. Makes 4 servings.

NUTRITION FACTS PER SERVING:

275 calories
12 g total fat
3 g saturated fat
44 mg cholesterol
540 mg sodium
19 g carbohydrate
1 g fiber
21 g protein

catfish olé

INGREDIENTS

- 1 to 1¼ pounds fresh or frozen catfish fillets, ½ to ¾ inch thick
- ½ cup finely crushed tortilla chips
- ½ teaspoon dried oregano, crushed
- ¼ teaspoon garlic powder
- 2 tablespoons milk
- 1 cup shredded cheddar or Monterey Jack cheese (4 ounces)
- Shredded lettuce (optional)
- ⅔ cup chunky salsa

Try this tasty tortilla fix-up to go with the crispy fish: Warm flour tortillas in the microwave oven or wrap them in foil and heat them along with the fish until softened. Stir a spoonful of honey and a little shredded orange peel into softened margarine or butter and serve with the tortillas.

Prep time: 10 minutes
Baking time: 9 minutes

DIRECTIONS

1. Thaw catfish, if frozen. Rinse fish; pat dry. Combine the crushed tortilla chips, oregano, and garlic powder.

Dip fish portions in milk; coat all sides with tortilla-chip mixture. Place coated fish in a shallow baking dish, tucking under any thin edges so fish cooks evenly. Sprinkle with any remaining tortilla-chip mixture. Bake in a 450° oven for 6 minutes.

2. Top fish portions with cheese. Return to oven and bake about 3 minutes more or until cheese melts and fish flakes easily when tested with a fork.

3. If desired, serve fish on shredded lettuce. Top with salsa. Makes 4 servings.

For the crushed tortilla chips,

use the leftover crumbs in the bottom of an almost-empty bag of chips. Or, place a handful in a plastic bag and close. Roll with a rolling pin until finely crushed.

NUTRITION FACTS PER SERVING:

232 calories
10 g total fat
6 g saturated fat
74 mg cholesterol
594 mg sodium
7 g carbohydrate
0 g fiber
26 g protein

111

sole-slaw sandwiches

Keep prep time to a minimum by using deli coleslaw to top these hearty sandwiches. But if you happen to have a few minutes to spare, stir together your favorite coleslaw recipe, use some of it as a sandwich topper, and refrigerate the rest for tomorrow night's supper.

INGREDIENTS

1 to 1¼ pounds fresh or frozen
    sole or flounder fillets
    Nonstick cooking spray
⅓ cup seasoned fine dry bread
    crumbs
⅓ cup grated Parmesan cheese
¼ teaspoon pepper
3 tablespoons all-purpose flour
¼ cup milk
1 cup deli coleslaw
4 multigrain hamburger buns, split
    and toasted

For a picnic-style supper,

heat a can of pork and beans zipped up with a dab or two of mustard. Serve the hot beans and crunchy chips or canned peach slices with the fish sandwiches.

Prep time: 15 minutes
Baking time: 8 minutes

DIRECTIONS

1. Thaw fish, if frozen. Rinse fish; pat dry. Cut into 4 serving-size pieces. Coat a baking sheet with nonstick spray. Set aside.

2. In a shallow bowl or pie plate combine bread crumbs, Parmesan cheese, and pepper. Place flour and milk in 2 separate shallow bowls or pie plates.

3. Fold under ends of fish portions so each portion is slightly larger than bun. Coat fish with the flour; dip into milk. Coat completely with crumb mixture. Arrange fish portions on prepared baking sheet so they don't touch each other.

4. Bake fish in a 400° oven for 8 to 10 minutes or until fish flakes easily when tested with a fork. Meanwhile, drain excess liquid from coleslaw. Place fish fillets on toasted buns; top with coleslaw. Makes 4 servings.

NUTRITION FACTS PER SERVING:

308 calories
6 g total fat
3 g saturated fat
70 mg cholesterol
700 mg sodium
32 g carbohydrate
3 g fiber
31 g protein

poached orange roughy with lemon sauce

Despite its speed, poaching is an inherently gentle way to cook. It's also one of the lightest and most healthful. Here, poaching in lemon-and-pepper-infused broth preserves the delicate flavor and texture of one of the most popular kinds of white fish.

INGREDIENTS

- 1 pound fresh or frozen orange roughy or red snapper, ½ inch thick
- 1 pound fresh asparagus spears
- 1 14½-ounce can reduced-sodium chicken broth
- 2 teaspoons finely shredded lemon peel
- ⅛ teaspoon ground black pepper
- 1 medium yellow sweet pepper, cut into bite-size strips
- 4 teaspoons cornstarch
- 2 cups hot cooked couscous or rice
- 2 tablespoons snipped fresh chives

Start to finish: 20 minutes

DIRECTIONS

1. Thaw fish, if frozen. Rinse fish; pat dry. Cut fish into 4 serving-size pieces; set aside. Snap off and discard woody bases from asparagus. Set aside.

2. In a 10-inch skillet combine 1 cup of the broth, the lemon peel, and black pepper. Bring to boiling; reduce heat. Carefully add the fish and asparagus. Cover and cook over medium-low heat for 4 minutes. Add sweet pepper strips. Cover and cook 2 minutes more or until fish flakes easily when tested with a fork. Using a slotted spatula, transfer fish and vegetables to a serving platter, reserving liquid in skillet. Keep fish and vegetables warm.

3. For sauce, stir together remaining broth and cornstarch. Stir into liquid in skillet. Cook and stir until thickened and bubbly. Cook and stir for 2 minutes more. Arrange fish and vegetables on couscous or rice; top with sauce. Sprinkle with chives. Makes 4 servings.

NUTRITION FACTS PER SERVING:

249 calories
2 g total fat
0 g saturated fat
60 mg cholesterol
390 mg sodium
29 g carbohydrate
6 g fiber
28 g protein

fettuccine and salmon

Remember this sensational salmon dish when you're looking for a sophisticated yet simple entrée for a dinner party.

INGREDIENTS

- 1 pound fresh or frozen skinless salmon fillet
  Nonstick cooking spray
- ⅓ cup finely chopped onion
- 1½ cups skim milk
- 1½ teaspoons cornstarch
- 6 ounces reduced-fat cream cheese (Neufchâtel), cubed and softened
- ½ cup finely shredded smoked Gouda cheese (2 ounces)
- 1 tablespoon snipped fresh chives
- ¼ to ½ teaspoon coarsely ground black pepper
- ½ of a 9-ounce package refrigerated linguine and ½ of a 9-ounce package refrigerated spinach fettuccine
  Fresh chives with blossoms (optional)

The combination of green spinach fettuccine and white linguine makes for a beautiful presentation, but if you prefer, you can use a 9-ounce package of either.

Start to finish: 20 minutes

DIRECTIONS

1. Thaw fish, if frozen. Rinse fish; pat dry. Cut fish into 4 serving-size pieces. In a large skillet bring 2 cups water to boiling. Measure thickness of fish. Add fish to skillet. Return to boiling; reduce heat. Cover and simmer until fish flakes easily when tested with a fork. (Allow 4 to 6 minutes per ½-inch thickness.) Drain; keep warm.

2. Meanwhile, coat a medium saucepan with nonstick spray. Add onion and cook until tender. Stir together the milk and cornstarch. Add to saucepan. Cook and stir until slightly thickened and bubbly. Cook and stir 2 minutes more. Add cream cheese and Gouda cheese. Cook and stir until melted. Stir in snipped chives and coarsely ground pepper.

3. Meanwhile, cook pasta according to package

directions; drain. Divide hot pasta among 4 dinner plates; place salmon over pasta. Spoon sauce over salmon. If desired, garnish with chives with blossoms. Makes 4 servings.

NUTRITION FACTS PER SERVING:

566 calories
26 g total fat
13 g saturated fat
131 mg cholesterol
579 mg sodium
43 g carbohydrate
0 g fiber
40 g protein

spicy fillets with toasted pecans

The crispy coating and toasted pecans earmark this pan-fried fish as a sample of southern-style cooking.

INGREDIENTS

- 1 pound fresh or frozen firm-textured fish fillets, ½ to 1 inch thick
- ¼ cup all-purpose flour
- 2 tablespoons yellow cornmeal
- 1 teaspoon chili powder
- ½ teaspoon garlic salt
- 3 tablespoons margarine or butter
- ¼ cup broken pecans
- 1 tablespoon lemon juice
- ⅛ teaspoon ground red pepper

Start to finish: 15 minutes

DIRECTIONS

1. Thaw fish, if frozen. Rinse fish; pat dry. Cut fish into 4 serving-size pieces. In a shallow dish stir together flour, cornmeal, chili powder, and garlic salt. Dip fish into flour mixture.

2. In a 12-inch skillet cook fish in 2 tablespoons of the margarine or butter over medium heat until fish flakes easily when tested with a fork and coating is golden, turning once. (Allow 4 to 6 minutes per ½-inch thickness.) Remove fish from skillet; keep warm.

3. Melt the remaining margarine or butter in the skillet. Add pecans; cook and stir over medium heat for 3 to 5 minutes or until lightly toasted. Stir in lemon juice and red pepper. Spoon pecan mixture over fish fillets. Makes 4 servings.

Choose from a

number of firm-textured fish options for this dish, including catfish, pike, lake trout, or orange roughy.

NUTRITION FACTS PER SERVING:

267 calories
14 g total fat
2 g saturated fat
45 mg cholesterol
407 mg sodium
11 g carbohydrate
1 g fiber
24 g protein

snapper veracruz

With its location on the Gulf of Mexico, it's no wonder Veracruz is famous for seafood. It was once the only East Coast port allowed to operate in New Spain. Snapper Veracruz, one of Mexico's best-known fish recipes, is a melding of flavors—Spanish green olives and capers with jalapeño peppers from nearby Jalapa, the capital of the state of Veracruz. To douse the fire caused by the peppers, this meal typically includes boiled potatoes.

INGREDIENTS

1½ pounds fresh or frozen skinless red snapper or other fish fillets

⅛ teaspoon salt

⅛ teaspoon ground black pepper

1 large onion, sliced and separated into rings

1 teaspoon bottled minced garlic or 2 cloves garlic, minced

1 tablespoon cooking oil

2 large tomatoes, chopped (2 cups)

¼ cup sliced pimiento-stuffed olives

¼ cup dry white wine

2 tablespoons capers, drained

1 to 2 fresh jalapeño or serrano peppers, seeded and chopped, or 1 to 2 canned jalapeño peppers, rinsed, drained, seeded, and chopped

½ teaspoon sugar

1 bay leaf

Snipped fresh parsley

To prepare boiled potatoes,

peel and quarter 1½ pounds potatoes. In covered medium saucepan cook potatoes in a small amount of boiling salted water for 20 to 25 minutes or until tender. Drain.

Start to finish: 30 minutes

DIRECTIONS

1. Thaw fish, if frozen. Rinse fish; pat dry. Cut fish into 6 serving-size pieces. Sprinkle fish fillets with the salt and black pepper.

2. For sauce, in a large skillet cook onion and garlic in hot oil until onion is tender. Stir in tomatoes, olives, wine, capers, jalapeño or serrano peppers, sugar, and bay leaf. Bring to boiling. Add fillets to skillet. Return to boiling; reduce heat. Cover and simmer for 6 to 10 minutes or until fish flakes easily when tested with a fork.

3. Use a slotted spatula to carefully transfer fish from skillet to a serving platter. Cover and keep warm.

4. Boil sauce in skillet for 5 to 6 minutes or until reduced to about 2 cups, stirring occasionally. Discard bay leaf. Spoon sauce over fish. Sprinkle with some parsley. Makes 6 servings.

NUTRITION FACTS PER SERVING:

174 calories
5 g total fat
1 g saturated fat
42 mg cholesterol
260 mg sodium
7 g carbohydrate
6 g fiber
24 g protein

INGREDIENTS

1   pound fresh or frozen cod fillets,
      about ½ inch thick
1   4.3- to 4.7-ounce envelope
      quick-cooking rice and pasta
      mix with vegetables
1   8-ounce can tomatoes, cut up
¼   teaspoon ground black pepper
⅛   teaspoon ground red pepper
      (optional)
½   medium green sweet pepper, cut
      into strips or rings

creole cod and rice

When your family asks, "What can I do to help?" suggest they fix a tossed salad to cool the spicy entrée. If the greens weren't rinsed ahead, a salad spinner is a time-saver for busy, health-conscious families. Rinse, spin, and dry crisp greens in 5 minutes.

Start to finish: 25 minutes

DIRECTIONS

1. Thaw fish, if frozen. Rinse fish; pat dry. In 10-inch skillet prepare rice mix as directed on the envelope, except substitute undrained tomatoes for ½ cup of the liquid and add the black pepper and, if desired, red pepper to mixture. Cover and cook rice for half of the time directed on rice mix package.

2. Place fish fillets and green pepper on top of the rice mixture. Cover and cook over low heat about 10 minutes more or until fish flakes easily when tested with a fork. Makes 4 servings.

NUTRITION FACTS PER SERVING:

263 calories
5 g total fat
1 g saturated fat
49 mg cholesterol
649 mg sodium
28 g carbohydrate
1 g fiber
25 g protein

For the mix in this recipe, you'll find a variety of quick-cooking rice and pasta mixes with different vegetables (and some with cheese) at the grocery store. Any type in the range of 4.3 to 4.7 ounces will work. Just use what appeals to you.

117

tangy thyme fish

Bottled salad dressing is the base for the creamy sauce that complements these fish fillets.

INGREDIENTS

- 1 pound fresh or frozen salmon, sole, flounder, cod, or orange roughy fillets, ½ to ¾ inch thick
- 1 cup chicken broth
- ¼ cup chopped onion
- ⅛ teaspoon pepper
- ⅛ teaspoon dried thyme or marjoram, crushed
- 2 tablespoons cold water
- 1 teaspoon cornstarch
- ¼ cup bottled original-style buttermilk ranch salad dressing
- 2 tablespoons snipped fresh parsley

Look in the frozen vegetable section of your supermarket for a 16-ounce package of colorful vegetables, such as broccoli, peppers, and mushrooms. While you prepare the fish, cook the vegetables in your microwave oven following the package directions.

Start to finish: 25 minutes

DIRECTIONS

1. Thaw fish, if frozen. Rinse fish; pat dry. Measure the thickness of the fish.

2. In a 10-inch skillet combine the broth, onion, pepper, and thyme or marjoram. Bring to boiling. Place fish in skillet, tucking under any thin edges so fish cooks evenly. Return to simmering. Cover and simmer until fish flakes easily when tested with a fork. (Allow 4 to 6 minutes per ½-inch thickness.) Remove fish to a hot platter. Keep warm.

3. Bring liquid in skillet to boiling; boil, uncovered, over medium-high heat for 3 to 5 minutes or until reduced to about ½ cup. Combine water and cornstarch; stir into liquid in skillet. Cook and stir until thickened and bubbly. Cook and stir 2 minutes more. Stir in salad dressing and parsley. Serve sauce with fish. Makes 4 servings.

NUTRITION FACTS PER SERVING:

236 calories
13 g total fat
2 g saturated fat
50 mg cholesterol
417 mg sodium
3 g carbohydrate
0 g fiber
24 g protein

INGREDIENTS

- 4 frozen battered or breaded fish fillets
- 3 tablespoons mayonnaise or salad dressing
- 1 teaspoon finely shredded lime peel
- 2 teaspoons lime juice
- 1 cup packaged shredded cabbage with carrots (coleslaw mix)
- 2 tablespoons capers, drained (optional)
- 4 individual French-style or club rolls (3½ to 4 inches long)
- ½ cup salsa
- ½ cup sliced pitted kalamata or ripe olives

fish fillet muffuletta

To keep fish captivatingly crisp, assemble these hearty meal-size sandwiches just before serving.

Start to finish: 25 minutes

DIRECTIONS

1. Cook fish according to package directions. Meanwhile, in a medium bowl stir together mayonnaise or salad dressing, lime peel, and lime juice. Add cabbage and, if desired, capers. Stir until well combined. Set aside.

2. Split rolls horizontally. Hollow out the insides of top halves of rolls, leaving a ½-inch-thick shell. Spoon cabbage mixture on the bottom halves of rolls. Top with fish and salsa. Sprinkle with olives. Add tops of rolls. Makes 4 servings.

Capers are often used to add flavor to dishes. These flower buds of the caper bush have a pungent, slightly bitter flavor and are usually pickled in vinegar or packed in salt. Look for them with the pickles at the grocery store.

NUTRITION FACTS PER SERVING:

447 calories
25 g total fat
4 g saturated fat
26 mg cholesterol
937 mg sodium
45 g carbohydrate
1 g fiber
14 g protein

119

grilled fish sandwiches

Pick your choice of tongue-tingling seasoning to rub onto the fish—each yields a distinctly different flavor. It's like getting three recipes in one.

INGREDIENTS

- 4 fresh or frozen fish fillets (about 4 ounces each)
- 1 tablespoon lemon juice or lime juice
- 1 teaspoon lemon-pepper seasoning, Jamaican jerk seasoning, or Cajun seasoning (see recipes, pages 88 and 121)
- ½ cup mayonnaise or salad dressing
- 4 teaspoons Dijon-style mustard
- 1 to 3 teaspoons honey

- 4 individual focaccia, or 4 hamburger buns or kaiser rolls, split and toasted
- Watercress or lettuce leaves (optional)
- Roasted red sweet pepper strips or tomato slices (optional)

Look for focaccia at Italian

bakeries and larger supermarkets. It is sold plain as well as seasoned. Onion- or herb-flavored focaccia is especially tasty for sandwiches such as this one.

Start to finish: 15 minutes

DIRECTIONS

1. Thaw fish, if frozen. Rinse fish; pat dry. Brush fish fillets with lemon or lime juice. Rub desired seasoning evenly onto all sides of fish. Place the seasoned fish fillets in a well-greased wire grill basket. Grill on an uncovered grill directly over medium coals until fish flakes easily when tested with a fork. (Allow 4 to 6 minutes for each ½-inch thickness.)

2. Meanwhile, for spread, in a small mixing bowl stir together mayonnaise or salad dressing and mustard. Stir in honey to taste.

3. To serve, spread sides of focaccia, buns, or rolls with spread. If desired, cover bottom halves of focaccia, buns, or rolls with watercress or lettuce. Top with fish, additional spread, red pepper strips or tomato slices (if desired), and top halves of focaccia, buns, or rolls. Makes 4 servings.

NUTRITION FACTS PER SERVING:

311 calories
14 g total fat
2 g saturated fat
51 mg cholesterol
676 mg sodium
24 g carbohydrate
1 g fiber
22 g protein

blackened fishwich

Most large supermarkets carry the spicy seasoning blend called Cajun seasoning. If your grocery doesn't have it, look for it at your fish market or make the homemade version given in the recipe below.

INGREDIENTS

- 1 pound fresh or frozen cod or orange roughy fillets, ¾ to 1 inch thick
- 2 teaspoons Cajun seasoning or Homemade Cajun Seasoning (see recipe, below)
- 2 tablespoons cooking oil
  Leaf lettuce
- 4 kaiser rolls, split and toasted
- 1 small tomato, sliced
- ¼ cup frozen guacamole dip, thawed

Start to finish: 15 minutes

DIRECTIONS

1. Thaw fish, if frozen. Rinse fish; pat dry. Cut into 4 serving-size pieces. Rub seasoning onto both sides of fish.

2. In a large skillet heat oil until very hot (a drop of water sizzles in skillet). Carefully cook fish fillets in hot oil over medium heat about 6 minutes or until fish flakes easily when tested with a fork, turning once. Place leaf lettuce and fish on bottom half of each toasted roll. Place tomato slices and guacamole dip on roll tops. Makes 4 servings.

Homemade Cajun Seasoning: Stir together ½ teaspoon onion powder, ½ teaspoon garlic powder, ¼ teaspoon salt, ¼ teaspoon ground thyme, ¼ teaspoon ground black pepper, and ⅛ to ¼ teaspoon ground red pepper.

NUTRITION FACTS PER SERVING:

  352 calories
12 g total fat
2 g saturated fat
45 mg cholesterol
711 mg sodium
35 g carbohydrate
1 g fiber
26 g protein

The blackened style of cooking fish

originated in New Orleans, so a Southern favorite like black-eyed peas makes a great accompaniment to this spicy dish. For a quick side salad with below-the-Mason-Dixon-line flavor, toss together a can of drained black-eyed peas, sliced celery, sliced green onion, and shredded carrot; finish by adding some bottled Italian salad dressing. Quick-chill the salad in the freezer about 10 minutes.

121

salmon caesar salad

Smoked salmon turns a classic side-dish salad into a hearty entrée for three.

INGREDIENTS

- 1   10-ounce package Caesar salad mix (includes greens, dressing, croutons, and Parmesan cheese)
- 1   small yellow, red, and/or green sweet pepper, cut into thin strips
- ¼   cup sliced pitted ripe olives
- 6   ounces smoked salmon, skinned, boned, and broken into chunks; or 3 to 4 ounces thinly sliced smoked salmon (lox-style), cut into bite-size strips

If you can't find packaged Caesar salad, substitute 5 cups torn mixed salad greens, ⅓ cup croutons, 3 tablespoons bottled Caesar or ranch salad dressing, and 2 tablespoons grated Parmesan cheese.

Start to finish: 10 minutes

DIRECTIONS

1. In a large salad bowl combine the lettuce and dressing from the salad mix, the sweet pepper strips, and olives. Toss mixture gently to coat. Add the croutons and cheese from the mix and the salmon. Toss gently. Makes 3 servings.

NUTRITION FACTS PER SERVING:

254 calories
18 g total fat
2 g saturated fat
19 mg cholesterol
971 mg sodium
10 g carbohydrate
1 g fiber
14 g protein

INGREDIENTS

1	16-ounce Italian bread shell (Boboli)
2	medium tomatoes, very thinly sliced
4	ounces sliced provolone cheese
3	ounces thinly sliced smoked salmon (lox-style)
½	cup crumbled semisoft goat cheese or garlic-and-herb feta cheese
	Fresh marjoram sprigs (optional)

smoked salmon pizza

A purchased Italian bread shell is the deliciously chewy crust for this sophisticated pizza.

Prep time: 10 minutes
Baking time: 11 minutes

DIRECTIONS

1. Place bread shell on a baking sheet. Arrange tomatoes, provolone cheese, and salmon on top. Sprinkle with goat or feta cheese. Bake in a 400° oven for 11 to 13 minutes or until heated through. If desired, garnish with fresh marjoram sprigs. Cut into wedges. Makes 6 to 8 servings.

NUTRITION FACTS PER SERVING:

358 calories
16 g total fat
6 g saturated fat
38 mg cholesterol
812 mg sodium
35 g carbohydrate
2 g fiber
20 g protein

For a flavor variation, top this pizza with a little roasted garlic. To roast a head of garlic, peel away the dry outer leaves, leaving the skin of the cloves intact. Cut off the pointed top portion of the head, exposing the individual cloves. Place, cut side up, in a small baking dish. Drizzle with a little olive oil. Bake in a 400° oven for 25 to 35 minutes or until the cloves feel soft when pressed. To season the pizza, squeeze the roasted garlic from as many cloves as you like into a bowl. Then dab the garlic over the pizza.

123

hot tuna hoagies

This may be a sandwich, but you'll need a knife and fork to eat it.

INGREDIENTS

- 1½ cups packaged shredded cabbage with carrot (coleslaw mix)
- 1 9¼-ounce can tuna (water pack), drained and broken into chunks
- 2 tablespoons mayonnaise or salad dressing
- 2 tablespoons buttermilk ranch, creamy cucumber, or creamy Parmesan salad dressing
- 2 hoagie buns, split and toasted
- 2 ounces cheddar cheese or Swiss cheese, thinly sliced

Prep time: 10 minutes
Broiling time: 2½ minutes

DIRECTIONS

1. In a medium mixing bowl toss together shredded cabbage with carrot and tuna. In a small mixing bowl stir together mayonnaise or salad dressing and ranch, cucumber, or Parmesan salad dressing. Toss salad dressing mixture with tuna mixture.

2. Spread tuna mixture evenly on the 4 bun halves. Place on the unheated rack of a broiler pan. Broil 4 to 5 inches from the heat for 2 to 3 minutes or until heated through. Top with cheese. Broil 30 to 60 seconds more or until cheese is melted. Makes 4 servings.

NUTRITION FACTS PER SERVING:

417 calories
16 g total fat
5 g saturated fat
40 mg cholesterol
788 mg sodium
41 g carbohydrate
3 g fiber
27 g protein

INGREDIENTS

- 1 5-ounce jar cream cheese spread with olives or pimiento, or American cheese spread
- 1 6½-ounce can tuna, drained and broken into chunks
- 3 English muffins, split and toasted
- 6 slices tomato, halved
  Pimiento-stuffed olives, quartered or sliced (optional)

tuna muffin melt

Keep the ingredients for the filling ready and waiting on your pantry shelf so you can make this tasty sandwich anytime. Accompany the sandwich with pickles.

Prep time: 15 minutes
Broiling time: 4 minutes

DIRECTIONS

1. In a mixing bowl combine ⅓ cup of the cheese spread and the tuna. Spread tuna mixture onto muffin halves. Place halves on the unheated rack of a broiler pan. Broil 4 inches from the heat about 3 minutes or until sandwiches are heated through.

2. Top each tuna-topped muffin half with 2 tomato-slice halves and a spoonful of the remaining cheese spread.

Broil about 1 minute more or until heated through. If desired, top each sandwich with olives. Makes 3 servings.

NUTRITION FACTS PER SERVING:

367 calories
12 g total fat
7 g saturated fat
61 mg cholesterol
1,235 mg sodium
33 g carbohydrate
2 g fiber
32 g protein

How do you choose between

convenience foods and the extra cost? These hints may help:

- Compare the cost per serving. If a convenience food costs three times more than the from-scratch ingredients, the cost is probably not worth the time saved.
- Check the cost per pound of meats. Boneless cuts will have less waste.
- Add up the cost of food items, then divide the cost by the number of meals you plan to serve. Is it less than eating out?

shrimp and plum tomatoes with pasta

Plum tomatoes and tarragon impart a garden-fresh flavor to this delightful combination.

INGREDIENTS

- 1   12-ounce package frozen, peeled, and deveined shrimp
- 1   9-ounce package refrigerated spinach or plain fettuccine
- 1   medium onion, chopped (½ cup)
- 1   teaspoon bottled minced garlic or 2 cloves garlic, minced
- 1   tablespoon olive oil or cooking oil
- 4   medium plum tomatoes, chopped (about 1⅔ cups)
- 2   teaspoons snipped fresh tarragon or ½ teaspoon dried tarragon, crushed
- ¼   teaspoon coarsely ground black pepper

Got a spare minute?
Use it to chop an extra onion or green pepper by hand or with a food processor. Then store it by spreading the chopped onion or green pepper in a single layer in a shallow baking pan and freezing. Next break up the frozen vegetables into pieces and put them into freezer bags or containers. Seal, label, and store them in the freezer for up to 1 month. To use, just add the amount you need to what you're cooking—no need to thaw!

Start to finish: 15 minutes

DIRECTIONS

1. In a large saucepan cook the shrimp with the fettuccine according to the package directions for the fettuccine. Drain. Return to the hot saucepan.

2. Meanwhile, in a medium saucepan cook onion and garlic in hot oil until onion is tender. Stir in tomatoes, tarragon, and pepper. Cook over low heat, stirring occasionally, for 2 to 3 minutes or until heated through.

3. Add tomato mixture to fettuccine mixture in saucepan. Toss to mix. Makes 4 servings.

NUTRITION FACTS PER SERVING:

277 calories
5 g total fat
1 g saturated fat
131 mg cholesterol
173 mg sodium
37 g carbohydrate
1 g fiber
20 g protein

INGREDIENTS

1½ cups water
¼ teaspoon salt
1½ cups quick-cooking rice
½ cup chicken broth
1½ teaspoons cornstarch
1 medium red sweet pepper, cut into thin strips
1 medium green sweet pepper, cut into thin strips
1 small onion, cut into thin wedges
2 teaspoons bottled minced garlic or 4 cloves garlic, minced
1 tablespoon margarine or butter
1 12-ounce package frozen, peeled, deveined shrimp, thawed
1 tablespoon margarine or butter
2 tablespoons snipped fresh parsley

shrimp in garlic sauce

Stir-fry the shrimp just until they turn pink. Overcooking toughens them.

Start to finish: 20 minutes

DIRECTIONS

1. In a medium saucepan bring the water and salt to boiling. Stir in rice. Cover; remove from heat. Let stand until serving time. For sauce, stir together chicken broth and cornstarch. Set aside.

2. In a wok or large skillet cook red pepper, green pepper, onion, and garlic in 1 tablespoon hot margarine or butter over medium-high heat about 3 minutes or until pepper and onion are crisp-tender. Remove vegetables from the wok or skillet. Add shrimp and 1 tablespoon margarine or butter. Stir-fry over medium-high heat for 3 to 4 minutes or until shrimp turn pink.

3. Push shrimp from the center of the wok or skillet. Stir sauce; add to the center of the wok. Cook and stir until thickened and bubbly. Return vegetables to the wok or skillet. Stir to coat with sauce. Cook and stir about 1 minute more or until heated through.

4. Stir parsley into rice. Immediately serve shrimp mixture over hot rice. Makes 4 servings.

NUTRITION FACTS PER SERVING:

♥ 285 calories
7 g total fat
1 g saturated fat
131 mg cholesterol
453 mg sodium
37 g carbohydrate
1 g fiber
18 g protein

sizzling shrimp with tangy coconut sauce

Another time, serve this intriguing dish as an appetizer. (Plan 3 shrimp per appetizer serving.)

INGREDIENTS

- 15 to 18 fresh or frozen jumbo shrimp in shells (1 pound)
- ⅓ cup purchased unsweetened coconut milk
- 1 teaspoon cornstarch
- 2 to 4 teaspoons wasabi paste
- 2 teaspoons grated fresh ginger
- 2 tablespoons lime juice
- 2 teaspoons cooking oil
- 1 tablespoon soy sauce
- 1 tablespoon bottled minced garlic or 6 cloves garlic, minced
- ¼ to 1 teaspoon crushed red pepper (optional)

The zip in the coconut sauce comes from wasabi (WAH-suh-bee)—also called Japanese horseradish. It's a large, pale-green relative of the common horseradish and is purchased in raw, paste, or powder form. Look for tubes of wasabi paste in Asian markets.

Start to finish: 25 minutes

DIRECTIONS

1. Thaw shrimp, if frozen. Rinse shrimp; pat dry and set aside. For dipping sauce, in a small saucepan stir together the coconut milk and cornstarch. Cook and stir over low heat for 3 to 5 minutes.

2. Meanwhile, in a small mixing bowl combine the wasabi paste, ginger, and ½ to 1 teaspoon of the lime juice. Stir in thickened coconut milk mixture. Cover and cool mixture in the refrigerator while preparing the shrimp.

3. Peel and devein shrimp, leaving tails on, if desired. In a large skillet or wok heat oil over medium-high heat for 30 seconds. Cook shrimp in hot oil for 2 minutes, turning once. Carefully add soy sauce, garlic, and, if desired, crushed red pepper. Cook for 30 seconds to 1 minute more or until shrimp turn pink.

4. Remove skillet or wok from heat. Sprinkle remaining lime juice over shrimp mixture. Serve with dipping sauce. Makes 3 servings.

NUTRITION FACTS PER SERVING:

- 177 calories
- 9 g total fat
- 5 g saturated fat
- 174 mg cholesterol
- 576 mg sodium
- 4 g carbohydrate
- 0 g fiber
- 20 g protein

128

southern seafood and rice

This spicy one-dish meal is reminiscent of jambalaya, a Cajun classic.

INGREDIENTS

- ¾ **pound fresh or frozen peeled and deveined shrimp or scallops**
- 2⅓ **cups chicken broth**
- 4 **green onions, sliced (½ cup)**
- 1 **teaspoon Worcestershire sauce**
- ½ **teaspoon dried thyme, crushed**
- ½ **teaspoon bottled minced garlic or 1 clove garlic, minced**
- ⅛ **to ¼ teaspoon ground red pepper or bottled hot pepper sauce**
- 1 **14½-ounce can stewed tomatoes or Cajun-style stewed tomatoes**
- 1 **cup long grain rice**
- 1 **10-ounce package frozen cut okra, partially thawed**
  Snipped fresh parsley

Prep time: 10 minutes
Cooking time: 18 minutes

DIRECTIONS

1. Thaw shrimp or scallops, if frozen. Rinse shrimp or scallops; pat dry and set aside. In a 3-quart saucepan combine the broth, green onions, Worcestershire sauce, thyme, garlic, and ground red pepper or hot pepper sauce. Bring to boiling. Stir in stewed tomatoes, rice, and okra. Return to boiling; reduce heat. Cover and simmer for 15 to 20 minutes or until rice is just tender, stirring once or twice.

2. Stir in shrimp or scallops. Cover and simmer for 3 to 5 minutes more or until shrimp turn pink or scallops turn opaque and rice is tender. Stir to fluff rice. Sprinkle with parsley. Makes 4 servings.

NUTRITION FACTS PER SERVING:

329 calories
2 g total fat
1 g saturated fat
131 mg cholesterol
1,062 mg sodium
52 g carbohydrate
2 g fiber
23 g protein

For a Louisiana-seasoned meal, serve corn-bread sticks with seafood and rice. Try this quick recipe: Stir together one 8½-ounce package corn muffin mix, 1 beaten egg, and one 8-ounce carton sour cream, stirring just until moistened. Grease corn-bread stick pans or muffin cups; fill ⅔ full. Bake in 400° oven for 15 to 20 minutes or until light brown. Makes 10.

129

caesar shrimp and asparagus salad

Tender asparagus, succulent shrimp, homemade croutons, and bottled Caesar salad dressing all do their parts to make this garden-fresh medley a candidate for the salad hall of fame.

INGREDIENTS

- 1 cup Herb Croutons (see recipe, below)
- 12 ounces fresh asparagus spears
- 4 green onions, sliced (½ cup)
- ½ cup bottled Caesar salad dressing
- ½ teaspoon finely shredded lemon peel
- ¼ teaspoon pepper
- 6 cups torn mixed salad greens
- 1 pound cooked, peeled, and deveined large or jumbo shrimp (with tails left on)

Finely shredded Parmesan cheese (optional)
Lemon peel strips (optional)

Start to finish: 30 minutes

DIRECTIONS

1. Prepare Herb Croutons. While croutons are baking, rinse asparagus. Snap woody bases from spears and discard. In a covered saucepan cook asparagus spears in a small amount of boiling water for 4 to 6 minutes or until crisp-tender; drain. Set aside; keep warm.

2. Meanwhile, in a covered small skillet cook green onions in 2 tablespoons water for 2 to 3 minutes or until tender. Stir in the salad dressing, shredded lemon peel, and pepper; heat through.

3. Divide greens among 4 dinner plates. Arrange asparagus spears, cooked shrimp, and Herb Croutons among greens. Spoon warm dressing mixture over salads. If desired, sprinkle with finely shredded Parmesan cheese and lemon peel strips. Serve salad immediately. Makes 4 servings.

Herb Croutons: In a large skillet melt ¼ cup margarine or butter. Remove from heat. Stir in ½ teaspoon dried thyme, crushed, and ⅛ teaspoon garlic powder. Add 2 cups French or sourdough bread cubes; stir until cubes are coated with margarine mixture. Spread in a single layer in a baking pan. Bake in a 300° oven about 15 minutes or until dry and crisp, stirring twice; cool. Tightly cover and store at room temperature for up to 1 week.

NUTRITION FACTS PER SERVING:

387 calories
27 g total fat
3 g saturated fat
174 mg cholesterol
407 mg sodium
12 g carbohydrate
2 g fiber
22 g protein

INGREDIENTS

- 12 slices party rye bread or 12 large crackers
- 3 tablespoons reduced-fat cream cheese (Neufchâtel)
- ⅓ cup shredded cucumber
- ⅓ cup thinly sliced red onion
  Fresh herb (optional)
- 6 cups torn mixed salad greens
- ¾ pound cooked, peeled, and deveined shrimp
- ¼ cup bottled fat-free white wine vinaigrette salad dressing
- 1 tablespoon snipped fresh dill
  Fresh dill (optional)

scandinavian shrimp salad

Create a Scandinavian smorgasbord with vinaigrette-coated shrimp flanked by rye bread topped with cream cheese and cucumbers. A critical ingredient is dillweed, which is sprinkled onto the bread and snipped into the vinaigrette.

Start to finish: 25 minutes

DIRECTIONS

1. Spread rye bread slices or crackers with cream cheese; top with cucumber and onion. If desired, garnish with fresh herb.

2. Divide salad greens among 4 salad plates or bowls; top with shrimp. Stir together salad dressing and the 1 tablespoon dill; drizzle over salads. If desired, garnish salad with fresh dill. Serve with rye bread slices or crackers. Makes 4 servings.

For a change-of-pace presentation, serve this colorful shrimp salad in oversize coffee cups or mugs.

NUTRITION FACTS PER SERVING:

218 calories
5 g total fat
2 g saturated fat
174 mg cholesterol
641 mg sodium
20 g carbohydrate
1 g fiber
23 g protein

131

pan-seared scallops

This is a flash in the pan! Sweet scallops are given a Cajun-flavored crust, then tossed with balsamic vinegar-dressed spinach and bacon. Serve with corn bread and cold beer and you have a meal that's both homey and elegant in no time flat.

INGREDIENTS

- 1 pound fresh or frozen sea scallops
- 2 tablespoons all-purpose flour
- 1 to 2 teaspoons blackened steak seasoning or Cajun seasoning or Homemade Cajun Seasoning (see recipe, page 121)
- 1 tablespoon cooking oil
- 1 10-ounce package prewashed spinach
- 1 tablespoon water
- 2 tablespoons balsamic vinegar
- ¼ cup cooked bacon pieces

Sea scallops

are the larger of the two most widely available varieties of this shellfish. Bay scallops, the smaller variety, have a sweet flavor similar to sea scallops. Scallops should be firm, sweet smelling, and free of excess cloudy liquid. Chill shucked scallops covered with their own liquid in a closed container for up to 2 days.

Start to finish: 20 minutes

DIRECTIONS

1. Thaw scallops, if frozen. Rinse scallops; pat dry. In a plastic bag combine flour and seasoning. Add scallops; toss to coat.

2. In a large skillet cook scallops in hot oil over medium heat about 6 minutes or until browned and opaque, turning once. Remove scallops from skillet.

3. Add spinach to skillet; sprinkle with water. Cover and cook over medium-high heat 2 minutes or until spinach is slightly wilted. Add vinegar; toss to coat evenly. Return scallops to skillet; heat through. Sprinkle with bacon. Makes 4 servings.

NUTRITION FACTS PER SERVING:

158 calories
6 g total fat
1 g saturated fat
37 mg cholesterol
323 mg sodium
9 g carbohydrate
2 g fiber
18 g protein

INGREDIENTS

- ¾ **pound fresh or frozen bay or sea scallops**
- 6 **cups water**
- 8 **ounces Chinese egg noodles or vermicelli, broken into 3- to 4-inch-long pieces**
- ¼ **cup soy sauce**
- 3 **tablespoons dry sherry or apple juice**
- ½ **teaspoon ground ginger**
- 1 **tablespoon cooking oil**
- 1½ **teaspoons bottled minced garlic or 3 cloves garlic, minced**
- 2 **cups frozen loose-pack stir-fry vegetables**

no-chop scallop stir-fry

Both bay and sea scallops are delicious in this easy stir-fry dish, but cut the larger sea scallops in half before cooking.

Start to finish: 15 minutes

DIRECTIONS

1. Thaw scallops, if frozen. Rinse scallops; pat dry and set aside. In a large saucepan bring water to boiling. Cook egg noodles or vermicelli in boiling water until al dente (tender, but still slightly firm when bitten). (Allow 3 to 4 minutes for egg noodles or 5 to 7 minutes for vermicelli.) Drain. Rinse and drain again; set aside.

2. Meanwhile, for sauce, stir together soy sauce, sherry or apple juice, and ginger; set aside. Cut any large scallops in half; set aside.

3. Pour cooking oil into a wok or large skillet. (Add more oil as necessary during cooking.) Preheat over medium-high heat. Stir-fry garlic in hot oil for 15 seconds. Add frozen vegetables. Stir-fry for 2 to 3 minutes or until crisp-tender. Remove the vegetables from the wok.

4. Add the scallops to the hot wok. Stir-fry for 2 to 3 minutes or until opaque. Push scallops from the center of the wok. Stir sauce. Add sauce to the center of the wok. Return vegetables to the wok. Add noodles to the wok. Toss to coat with sauce. Serve immediately. Makes 4 servings.

NUTRITION FACTS PER SERVING:

285 calories
6 g total fat
1 g saturated fat
62 mg cholesterol
1,178 mg sodium
37 g carbohydrate
0 g fiber
18 g protein

133

new crab cakes

This new take on a classic balances tender crab with the crunch of potato chips.

INGREDIENTS

- 1 recipe Herb Sauce (see recipe, below)
  Shredded lemon peel (optional)
- 1 beaten egg
- ½ cup finely crushed potato chips
- 2 tablespoons shredded coconut, toasted
- 1 green onion, finely chopped (2 tablespoons)
- 2 tablespoons mayonnaise or salad dressing
- 1 tablespoon snipped fresh parsley
- ½ teaspoon ground coriander
- 6 ounces cooked crabmeat, cut into bite-size pieces, or one 6-ounce can crabmeat, drained, flaked, and cartilage removed
- 2 tablespoons cooking oil

Toasting heightens the flavor of coconut and adds an appealing golden color. To toast, spread the coconut in a single layer in a shallow baking pan. Bake in a 350° oven for 5 to 10 minutes or until light golden brown, watching carefully and stirring once or twice so the coconut doesn't burn.

Start to finish: 25 minutes

DIRECTIONS

1. Prepare Herb Sauce. Cover and refrigerate at least 20 minutes to allow flavors to mellow. If desired, garnish with shredded lemon peel.

2. In a medium mixing bowl combine egg, ¼ cup of the crushed potato chips, the coconut, green onion, mayonnaise or salad dressing, parsley, and coriander. Stir in crabmeat; mix well. Shape crabmeat mixture into eight ½-inch-thick patties. Coat patties with remaining crushed potato chips.

3. In a large skillet heat oil. (Add additional oil if necessary during cooking.) Add crab cakes. Cook over medium heat 4 to 6 minutes or until golden and heated through, turning once. Serve immediately with Herb Sauce. Makes 4 servings.

Herb Sauce: In a small bowl combine ¼ cup mayonnaise or salad dressing, 1 tablespoon snipped fresh cilantro, and 1 teaspoon finely shredded lemon peel.

NUTRITION FACTS PER SERVING:

365 calories
32 g total fat
5 g saturated fat
108 mg cholesterol
351 mg sodium
10 g carbohydrate
1 g fiber
12 g protein

INGREDIENTS

½ cup mayonnaise or salad
    dressing

1 green onion, sliced
    (2 tablespoons)

1 tablespoon frozen orange juice
    concentrate, thawed

½ teaspoon ground ginger
    Dash ground red pepper

½ pound lump crabmeat or one
    8-ounce package flake-style
    imitation crabmeat

6 cups torn mixed salad greens

2 cups fresh strawberries, halved

1 11-ounce can mandarin orange
    sections, drained

¼ cup pecan pieces (optional)

crab and fruit salad

Store the can of mandarin orange sections in the refrigerator, and the oranges will be icy cold when you are ready to add them to the salad.

Start to finish: 20 minutes

DIRECTIONS

1. In a medium mixing bowl stir together mayonnaise or salad dressing, green onion, orange juice concentrate, ginger, and red pepper. Gently stir in crabmeat or crab-flavored fish. Cover and chill in the freezer about 10 minutes or until cold.

2. Meanwhile, toss together salad greens, strawberries, and mandarin oranges. Arrange on 4 salad plates. Divide the crab mixture among the salad plates. If desired, sprinkle with pecans. Makes 4 servings.

NUTRITION FACTS PER SERVING:

334 calories
24 g total fat
3 g saturated fat
73 mg cholesterol
358 mg sodium
19 g carbohydrate
3 g fiber
14 g protein

Cut down on last-minute

work by tearing the salad greens ahead of time. When storing the torn greens, refrigerate them in a sealed plastic bag or a covered plastic container. Place a white paper towel in the bottom of the bag or container to absorb any excess water from the greens. For maximum freshness, prepare the greens only a day or two ahead.

ravioli with red clam sauce

Loaded with slices of zucchini and bits of clam, this full-flavored sauce is delectable ladled over just about any type of pasta. Next time try it over spinach fettuccine.

INGREDIENTS

- 1 9-ounce package refrigerated cheese ravioli or cheese tortellini
- 1 14½-ounce can stewed tomatoes
- 1 6½-ounce can minced clams
- 1 medium zucchini, halved lengthwise and thinly sliced (1½ cups)
- 2 teaspoons dried Italian seasoning, crushed
- 1 8-ounce can tomato sauce
- 1 tablespoon cornstarch
  Grated Parmesan cheese

Go Italian tonight.
Serve a crisp tossed salad with this hearty clam-sauced ravioli. Personalize your salads by topping with fish-shaped pretzels or broken bagel chips. For an almost homemade salad dressing, stir a little Dijon-style mustard into bottled Italian salad dressing. To complete your Italiano feast, serve a bottle of Chianti.

Start to finish: 20 minutes

DIRECTIONS

1. Cook ravioli or tortellini according to package directions.

2. Meanwhile, in a medium saucepan combine stewed tomatoes, undrained clams, zucchini, and Italian seasoning. Bring to boiling; reduce heat. Simmer, uncovered, for 1 minute. Stir together the tomato sauce and cornstarch until well blended; stir into hot mixture. Cook and stir over medium heat until thickened and bubbly. Cook and stir for 2 minutes more. Serve clam sauce over hot pasta. Sprinkle Parmesan cheese over each serving. Makes 3 servings.

NUTRITION FACTS PER SERVING:

406 calories
16 g total fat
1 g saturated fat
113 mg cholesterol
1,380 mg sodium
46 g carbohydrate
3 g fiber
24 g protein

cooking fish

Minutes count when cooking fish. Use a ruler to measure the thickness of the fish in order to better estimate when to check for doneness. Properly cooked fish is opaque, begins to flake easily when tested with a fork, and comes away from the bones readily; the juices should be a milky white. Fish may be cooked while still frozen, but you will need to increase the cooking time (see directions, below).

Cooking Method	Preparation	Fresh or Thawed Fillets or Steaks	Frozen Fillets or Steaks	Dressed Whole
Bake	Place in a single layer in a greased shallow baking pan. For fillets, tuck under any thin edges. Brush with melted margarine or butter.	Bake, uncovered, in a 450° oven for 4 to 6 minutes per ½-inch thickness.	Bake, uncovered, in a 450° oven for 9 to 11 minutes per ½-inch thickness.	Bake, uncovered, in a 350° oven for 6 to 9 minutes per ½ pound.
Broil	Preheat broiler. Place fish on greased unheated rack of a broiler pan. For fillets, tuck under any thin edges. Brush with melted margarine or butter.	Broil 4 inches from the heat for 4 to 6 minutes per ½-inch thickness. If fish is 1 inch or more thick, turn it over halfway through broiling.	Broil 4 inches from the heat for 6 to 9 minutes per ½-inch thickness. If fish is 1 inch or more thick, turn it over halfway through broiling.	Not recommended.
Poach	Add 1½ cups water, broth, or wine to a large skillet. Bring to boiling. Add fish. Return to boiling; reduce heat.	Simmer, uncovered, for 4 to 6 minutes per ½-inch thickness.	Simmer, uncovered, for 6 to 9 minutes per ½-inch thickness.	Simmer, covered, for 6 to 9 minutes per ½ pound.
Microwave	Remove head and tail of dressed fish. Arrange fish in a single layer in a shallow baking dish. For fillets, tuck under any thin edges. Cover with vented clear plastic wrap.	Cook on 100% power (high). For ½ pound of ½-inch-thick fillets, allow 2 to 4 minutes; for 1 pound of ½-inch-thick fillets, allow 3 to 5 minutes. For 1 pound of ¾- to 1-inch-thick steaks, allow 5 to 7 minutes.	Not recommended.	Cook on 100% power (high). For two 8- to 10-ounce fish, allow 4½ to 7 minutes, giving dish a half-turn once. Let stand for 5 minutes.

Soup with Mixed Pastas
See recipe, page 151

soups

allspice meatball stew

The exotic flavor of this hearty stew comes from the allspice—a berry of the pimiento tree. Allspice, which can be purchased ground or whole, gets its name because it tastes like a combination of cinnamon, nutmeg, and cloves.

INGREDIENTS

1 16-ounce package frozen prepared Italian-style meatballs

3 cups fresh green beans cut into 1½-inch-long pieces, or frozen cut green beans

2 cups packaged peeled baby carrots

1 14½-ounce can beef broth

2 teaspoons Worcestershire sauce

½ to ¾ teaspoon ground allspice

½ teaspoon ground cinnamon

2 14½-ounce cans stewed tomatoes

Freeze some of this soup for later. Place 1-, 2-, or 4-serving portions in sealed freezer containers. To reheat, place the frozen soup in a large saucepan. Heat, covered, over medium heat about 30 minutes, stirring occasionally to break apart.

Start to finish: 30 minutes

DIRECTIONS

1. In a 4-quart kettle or Dutch oven combine the meatballs, green beans, carrots, beef broth, Worcestershire sauce, allspice, and cinnamon. Bring to boiling; reduce heat. Cover and simmer for 10 minutes.

2. Stir in undrained tomatoes. Return to boiling; reduce heat. Cover and simmer about 5 minutes more or until vegetables are crisp-tender. Makes 8 servings.

NUTRITION FACTS PER SERVING:

233 calories
13 g total fat
6 g saturated fat
37 mg cholesterol
938 mg sodium
18 g carbohydrate
4 g fiber
12 g protein

INGREDIENTS

- 1 **pound ground beef**
- 2 **14½-ounce cans beef broth**
- 3 **cups frozen pasta with broccoli, corn, and carrots in garlic-seasoned sauce**
- 1 **14½-ounce can diced tomatoes**
- 1 **5½-ounce can tomato juice or ⅔ cup no-salt-added tomato juice**
- 2 **teaspoons dried Italian seasoning, crushed**
- ¼ **cup grated Parmesan cheese**

italian beef soup

Keep the ingredients on hand for this easy soup, and you'll always be prepared to whip up a hearty supper.

Prep time: 15 minutes
Cooking time: 20 minutes

DIRECTIONS

1. In a large saucepan cook ground beef until no longer pink. Drain off fat.

2. Add beef broth, pasta with mixed vegetables, undrained tomatoes, tomato juice, and Italian seasoning to beef in saucepan. Bring to boiling; reduce heat. Simmer, uncovered, about 10 minutes or until vegetables and pasta are tender. Ladle into soup bowls. Sprinkle with Parmesan cheese. Makes 6 servings.

If diced tomatoes aren't

available at your grocery store, purchase a can of whole tomatoes and cut them up with kitchen shears. Just snip the tomatoes right in the can.

NUTRITION FACTS PER SERVING:

258 calories
14 g total fat
6 g saturated fat
54 mg cholesterol
929 mg sodium
13 g carbohydrate
1 g fiber
20 g protein

141

heartland steak and vegetable soup

Big bowls of this rib-sticking soup and a loaf of crusty French bread are all you need for supper on a chilly night.

INGREDIENTS

- 2 4-ounce beef cubed steaks
- ¼ teaspoon garlic salt
- ⅛ teaspoon pepper
- 1 tablespoon cooking oil
- ⅓ cup margarine or butter
- 1 medium onion, chopped (½ cup)
- ½ cup chopped carrot
- ½ cup chopped celery
- ½ cup frozen loose-pack baby lima beans
- ½ cup all-purpose flour
- 4 cups water
- 1 7½-ounce can tomatoes, cut up
- ½ cup frozen loose-pack whole kernel corn
- ½ cup frozen loose-pack peas
- 1 tablespoon snipped fresh basil or 1 teaspoon dried basil, crushed
- 2 teaspoons instant beef bouillon granules
- 2 teaspoons Worcestershire sauce

Chopping onions is no work at all if you first cut them in half. Then place one half cut side down on a cutting board. Slice the onion half in one direction. Next, holding the slices together, slice at a 90-degree angle to the first cuts. Repeat with the other onion half.

Start to finish: 30 minutes

DIRECTIONS

1. Sprinkle steaks with garlic salt and pepper. In a 4-quart kettle or Dutch oven cook steaks in hot oil about 3 minutes or until done, turning once. Remove steaks from pan and cut into cubes; set meat aside. Drain fat from pan.

2. In the same pan melt margarine or butter. Add onion, carrot, celery, and lima beans. Cook and stir until onion is tender. Stir in flour. Stir water into flour mixture all at once. Cook and stir until thickened and bubbly.

3. Stir in undrained tomatoes, corn, peas, basil, bouillon granules, Worcestershire sauce, and cubed meat. Return to boiling; reduce heat. Cover and simmer about 5 minutes or until heated through. Makes 4 servings.

NUTRITION FACTS PER SERVING:

410 calories
22 g total fat
4 g saturated fat
36 mg cholesterol
924 mg sodium
33 g carbohydrate
4 g fiber
21 g protein

easy hamburger vegetable soup

Sprinkle the crispy, cheesy cracker topping on any of your favorite soups, stews, or chilies.

INGREDIENTS

- 1 pound ground beef or ground pork
- 1 medium onion, chopped (½ cup)
- ½ cup chopped green sweet pepper
- 4 cups beef broth
- 1 cup frozen loose-pack whole kernel corn
- 1 7½-ounce can tomatoes, cut up
- ½ of a 9-ounce package frozen lima beans
- ½ cup chopped, peeled potato or ½ cup frozen loose-pack hash brown potatoes
- 1 medium carrot, cut into thin bite-size strips (½ cup)
- 1 tablespoon snipped fresh basil or 1 teaspoon dried basil, crushed
- 1 teaspoon Worcestershire sauce
- ⅛ teaspoon ground black pepper
- 1 bay leaf
- 1 cup Cracker Mix (optional) (see recipe, below)

Prep time: 15 minutes
Cooking time: 15 minutes

DIRECTIONS

1. In a large saucepan or Dutch oven cook ground beef or pork, onion, and green pepper until meat is no longer pink. Drain fat from pan.

2. Stir in beef broth, corn, undrained tomatoes, lima beans, potato, carrot, basil, Worcestershire sauce, black pepper, and bay leaf. Bring to boiling; reduce heat. Cover and simmer for 15 to 20 minutes or until vegetables are tender. Discard bay leaf. Ladle into soup bowls. If desired, top each serving with ¼ cup of the Cracker Mix. Makes 4 servings.

Cracker Mix: In a large bowl combine 1 cup bite-size fish-shape pretzel or cheese-flavored crackers, 1 cup oyster crackers, 1 cup bite-size shredded wheat biscuits, and 1 cup miniature rich round crackers. In a small bowl combine 2 tablespoons cooking oil, ½ teaspoon Worcestershire sauce, ⅛ teaspoon garlic powder, and dash bottled hot pepper sauce; pour over cracker mixture, tossing to coat. Sprinkle cracker mixture with 2 tablespoons grated Parmesan cheese; toss to coat. Spread mixture on a shallow baking sheet. Bake in a 300° oven for 10 to 15 minutes or until golden, stirring once. Cool completely. Store in an airtight container. Makes about 4 cups.

NUTRITION FACTS PER SERVING:

401 calories
15 g total fat
6 g saturated fat
71 mg cholesterol
956 mg sodium
34 g carbohydrate
4 g fiber
31 g protein

143

sausage-vegetable soup

For a Louisiana spin on this hearty soup, use Cajun-style stewed tomatoes and add a couple dashes of bottled hot pepper sauce.

INGREDIENTS

1   14½-ounce can beef broth
1   14½-ounce can diced tomatoes with Italian herbs or Italian-style stewed tomatoes, cut up
1½ cups water
2   cups frozen loose-pack diced hash brown potatoes
1   10-ounce package frozen mixed vegetables
½   pound smoked turkey sausage, halved lengthwise and cut into ½-inch-thick pieces
⅛   teaspoon pepper
2   tablespoons grated Parmesan cheese (optional)

Look for smoked turkey sausage in your supermarket's meat case. It has the same tempting flavor as regular sausage, with less fat.

Prep time: 15 minutes
Cooking time: 5 minutes

DIRECTIONS

1. In a large saucepan combine beef broth, undrained tomatoes, and water. Bring to boiling. Stir in hash brown potatoes, mixed vegetables, sausage, and pepper. Return to boiling; reduce heat. Cover and simmer for 5 to 10 minutes or until vegetables are tender.

2. Ladle into soup bowls. If desired, sprinkle with Parmesan cheese. Makes 4 servings.

NUTRITION FACTS PER SERVING:

257 calories
9 g total fat
3 g saturated fat
36 mg cholesterol
1,202 mg sodium
29 g carbohydrate
1 g fiber
16 g protein

INGREDIENTS

- 4 cups chicken broth
- 2 15-ounce cans white kidney beans (cannellini), great northern beans, or red kidney beans, rinsed and drained
- ½ pound cooked turkey kielbasa, halved lengthwise and cut into ½-inch-thick pieces
- 1 medium onion, chopped (½ cup)
- 1 teaspoon dried basil, crushed
- ¼ teaspoon coarsely ground black pepper
- ½ teaspoon bottled minced garlic or 1 clove garlic, minced, or ⅛ teaspoon garlic powder
- 3 cups packaged fresh spinach

turkey sausage and bean soup

This soup tastes like it simmered all day even though it can be ready in less than 25 minutes. The secret is in the smoky flavor of the turkey kielbasa.

Start to finish: 25 minutes

DIRECTIONS

1. In a large saucepan or Dutch oven combine chicken broth, beans, kielbasa, onion, basil, pepper, and garlic or garlic powder. Bring to boiling; reduce heat. Cover and simmer for 10 to 15 minutes or until onion is tender.

2. Meanwhile, remove stems from spinach. Stack the leaves one on top of the other and cut into 1-inch-wide strips. Just before serving, stir spinach into soup. Makes 4 servings.

Kielbasa, or Polish sausage, is a smoked sausage that is traditionally made with pork and sometimes beef. The turkey version is equally flavorful.

NUTRITION FACTS PER SERVING:

- 257 calories
- 6 g total fat
- 2 g saturated fat
- 39 mg cholesterol
- 1,620 mg sodium
- 35 g carbohydrate
- 11 g fiber
- 28 g protein

145

chicken noodle soup florentine

Look in the supermarket's spice section for fines herbes—an herb blend most commonly containing chervil, chives, parsley, and tarragon.

INGREDIENTS

- 1 49½-ounce can chicken broth
- 8 ounces fresh mushrooms, sliced (about 3 cups)
- 8 green onions, sliced (1 cup)
- 1½ teaspoons dried fines herbes, crushed
- ¼ teaspoon pepper
- 2½ cups packaged dried medium noodles (5 ounces)
- 1 9-ounce package frozen diced cooked chicken (about 2 cups)
- 3 cups chopped fresh spinach or half of a 10-ounce package frozen chopped spinach (see tip, page 42)

While the soup simmers, prepare and bake a brownie mix according to package directions. Immediately sprinkle the hot brownies with almond brickle pieces and semisweet chocolate pieces. Cool brownies completely.

Prep time: 15 minutes
Cooking time: 7 minutes

DIRECTIONS

1. In a 4½-quart kettle or Dutch oven combine chicken broth, mushrooms, green onions, fines herbes, and pepper. Bring to boiling; add noodles. Cook and stir until the mixture returns to boiling; reduce heat.

2. Cover and boil gently for 7 to 9 minutes or until noodles are tender (do not overcook). Add chicken and spinach to soup; heat through. Makes 6 servings.

Note: You can freeze half of the soup in a covered container for another meal. To reheat frozen soup, place in a medium saucepan over medium heat. Cover and heat through for 20 to 25 minutes, stirring occasionally.

146

NUTRITION FACTS PER SERVING:

222 calories
6 g total fat
1 g saturated fat
59 mg cholesterol
866 mg sodium
20 g carbohydrate
1 g fiber
22 g protein

INGREDIENTS

- 1½ cups small broccoli flowerets
- 1 cup sliced fresh mushrooms
- ½ cup shredded carrot
- ¼ cup chopped onion
- ¼ cup margarine or butter
- ¼ cup all-purpose flour
- 1½ teaspoons snipped fresh basil or ½ teaspoon dried basil, crushed
- ¼ teaspoon pepper
- 3 cups milk
- 1 cup half-and-half or light cream
- 1 tablespoon white wine Worcestershire sauce
- 1½ teaspoons instant chicken bouillon granules
- 1½ cups chopped cooked chicken or turkey

creamy broccoli-chicken soup

This incredibly creamy soup is packed with vegetables, poultry, and just the right amount of seasoning.

Start to finish: 20 minutes

DIRECTIONS

1. In a medium saucepan cook and stir broccoli, mushrooms, carrot, and onion in hot margarine or butter for 6 to 8 minutes or until vegetables are tender.

2. Stir in flour, basil, and pepper. Add milk and half-and-half or light cream all at once; add Worcestershire sauce and bouillon granules. Cook and stir until thickened and bubbly. Stir in chicken or turkey; heat through. Makes 4 servings.

NUTRITION FACTS PER SERVING:

435 calories
26 g total fat
10 g saturated fat
86 mg cholesterol
675 mg sodium
23 g carbohydrate
2 g fiber
27 g protein

This hearty soup is an ideal way to use up leftover chicken or turkey. But if you don't have any on hand, purchase roasted chicken from your supermarket's deli section. Or, look in the freezer case for frozen chopped cooked chicken. If you prefer to cook your own, simmer skinless, boneless chicken breasts in water for 12 to 14 minutes or until tender and no longer pink. Plan that ¾ pound boneless breasts will give you about 1½ cups cooked chicken.

147

mexican chicken posole

In parts of Mexico, one day a week is designated as "posole day." Shops and businesses close early and people retire to temporary posole "restaurants" to enjoy a steaming bowl of this hearty soup. Make this streamlined version of the Mexican favorite and see what all the fuss is about (without all the fuss).

INGREDIENTS

- ¾ pound skinless, boneless chicken thighs or breast halves
- 3 to 4 teaspoons Mexican seasoning or chili powder
- 2 teaspoons cooking oil or olive oil
- 1 red or yellow sweet pepper, cut into bite-size pieces
- 2 14½-ounce cans reduced-sodium or regular chicken broth
- 1 15-ounce can hominy or black-eyed peas, rinsed and drained

  Salsa, light dairy sour cream, and/or lime wedges (optional)

Mexican seasoning is a blend of traditional Mexican flavorings. Look for it in the spice aisle of your supermarket, or substitute chili powder.

Start to finish: 20 minutes

DIRECTIONS

1. Rinse chicken; pat dry. Cut into 1-inch pieces. Sprinkle chicken with Mexican seasoning or chili powder; toss to coat evenly.

2. In a large saucepan cook and stir seasoned chicken in hot oil over medium-high heat for 3 minutes. Add sweet pepper; cook and stir about 1 minute more or until chicken is no longer pink.

3. Carefully add broth and hominy or black-eyed peas.

Bring to boiling; reduce heat. Cover and simmer about 3 minutes or until heated through. If desired, serve with salsa, sour cream, and/or lime wedges. Makes 4 servings.

NUTRITION FACTS PER SERVING:

192 calories
8 g total fat
2 g saturated fat
41 mg cholesterol
905 mg sodium
14 g carbohydrate
1 g fiber
15 g protein

INGREDIENTS

1 6¼- or 6¾-ounce package
quick-cooking long grain and
wild rice mix

5 cups water

½ pound ground raw chicken or
ground raw turkey

1 12-ounce can evaporated milk,
chilled

2 tablespoons all-purpose flour
Cracked black pepper (optional)

chicken and rice soup

For a quick soup lunch or supper, cut up fresh vegetable sticks or purchase cleaned and ready-to-eat vegetables at your supermarket. Slice your favorite bread and dish up the soup!

Start to finish: 25 minutes

DIRECTIONS

1. In a 3-quart saucepan combine the rice mix with seasoning packet and the water. Bring to boiling.

2. Drop the ground chicken or turkey by small spoonfuls into the boiling mixture (about 36 pieces total). Reduce heat. Cover and simmer for 5 minutes.

3. Gradually stir chilled milk into flour until smooth; add to boiling mixture. Cook and stir until slightly thickened and bubbly. Cook and stir for 1 minute more. Ladle into soup bowls. If desired, sprinkle cracked black pepper over each serving. Makes 6 servings.

NUTRITION FACTS PER SERVING:

226 calories
6 g total fat
3 g saturated fat
35 mg cholesterol
728 mg sodium
30 g carbohydrate
0 g fiber
13 g protein

Ready-to-cook mixes, such as the rice mix used in this soup, offer a great deal of convenience. Keep several—including rice mixes, noodle mixes, and potato mixes—on hand for last-minute meals. Any of these will go well with a simple entrée such as broiled fish, poultry, or meat. If you're concerned about sodium, prepare the packaged mix using about half of the seasoning packet.

dilled spinach soup

The essence of summer in a bowl. There are few things so satisfying at the end of a warm summer day as sitting down to a refreshing cold soup seasoned with fragrant herbs. Pair the soup with purchased croissants and follow it with fresh peaches for dessert.

INGREDIENTS

- 9 cups fresh spinach (about 10 ounces)
- 2 cups milk
- 1 small onion, cut up
- 2 tablespoons snipped fresh dill
- 1 teaspoon lemon-pepper seasoning
- 2 8-ounce cartons plain fat-free yogurt
- 1 cup cubed cooked chicken or ham or cooked small shrimp

  Edible flowers (such as nasturtiums) (optional)

  Slivered almonds (optional)

To save time, buy

packaged precleaned spinach that just needs a quick rinsing. Or, clean regular spinach by rinsing it thoroughly to remove any sand. You may need to rinse it several times.

Start to finish: 20 minutes

DIRECTIONS

1. In a blender container or food processor bowl combine about one-third of the spinach, 1 cup of the milk, the onion, dill, and lemon-pepper seasoning.

Cover; blend or process until nearly smooth. Add another one-third of the spinach; cover and blend until smooth. Pour blended mixture into a serving bowl or large storage container.

2. In the blender container or food processor bowl combine remaining spinach, remaining milk, and the yogurt; cover and blend until nearly smooth. Stir into the mixture in serving bowl; stir in chicken. (If desired, cover and store in refrigerator for up to 24 hours.)

3. Ladle into 4 soup bowls. If desired, garnish each serving with edible flowers and slivered almonds. Makes 4 servings.

NUTRITION FACTS PER SERVING:

217 calories
6 g total fat
2 g saturated fat
45 mg cholesterol
508 mg sodium
18 g carbohydrate
2 g fiber
24 g protein

150

INGREDIENTS

- 4 cups reduced-sodium chicken broth
- 1 cup water
- 3 bay leaves
- 1 large onion, chopped (1 cup)
- 1 large carrot, chopped
- 2 teaspoons bottled minced garlic or 4 cloves garlic, minced
- ¼ pound skinless, boneless chicken breasts, coarsely chopped
- 1 teaspoon olive oil or cooking oil
- 2 ounces packaged dried small pastas in various shapes (such as shells, rotini, ditalini, alphabetini, and/or broken spaghetti)
- Several fresh sage leaves

soup with mixed pastas

With this recipe, you can make creative use of any extra pastas tucked away in your pantry. Break up longer pastas into small pieces.

Prep time: 10 minutes
Cooking time: 18 minutes

DIRECTIONS

1. In a large saucepan bring chicken broth and water to boiling. Add bay leaves, onion, carrot, and garlic. Reduce heat and simmer, uncovered, 10 minutes.

2. In a skillet cook and stir chicken in hot oil 3 minutes or until cooked through. Add chicken, pastas, and sage to soup. Simmer, uncovered, for 8 to 10 minutes or until larger pieces of pasta are tender but slightly firm. Remove the bay leaves. Makes 3 servings.

NUTRITION FACTS PER SERVING:

220 calories
6 g total fat
1 g saturated fat
20 mg cholesterol
896 mg sodium
28 g carbohydrate
2 g fiber
14 g protein

To speed up chopping ingredients,
keep your knives sharp. It's much easier and faster to chop vegetables with a sharp knife. Clean and chop vegetables in advance and all at once. You'll have just one mess to clean up and vegetables will be ready to use when needed. When a recipe calls for a whole vegetable, chopped, don't bother measuring it. A little more or a little less won't hurt the recipe.

asian chicken noodle soup

Chicken soup is known universally as a comforting cure-all for the body and soul. Soy sauce, fresh ginger, and pea pods add an Asian flair to this classic favorite.

INGREDIENTS

- 2 14½-ounce cans chicken broth
- 1 cup water
- ¾ cup packaged dried fine egg noodles
- 1 tablespoon soy sauce
- 1 teaspoon grated fresh ginger
- ⅛ teaspoon crushed red pepper
- 1 medium red sweet pepper, cut into ¾-inch pieces
- 1 medium carrot, chopped
- ⅓ cup thinly sliced green onions
- 1 cup chopped cooked chicken or turkey
- 1 cup fresh pea pods, halved crosswise, or ½ of a 6-ounce package frozen pea pods, thawed and halved crosswise

Fresh ginger is easy

to use. Choose a plump, firm root with light-colored skin and no soft spots or wrinkles. Wrap the fresh ginger in paper towels and store in the refrigerator for up to a month. Or, freeze whole or grated fresh ginger for up to 3 months. Leave the skin on until you're ready to use the fresh ginger. Then peel it, if desired. Grate the ginger using a fine grater and discard any stringy fibers left on the root. A 2×1-inch piece should yield about 2 tablespoons grated ginger. If you prefer, look for already grated ginger in your supermarket's produce section.

Start to finish: 20 minutes

DIRECTIONS

1. In a large saucepan combine chicken broth, water, noodles, soy sauce, fresh ginger, and crushed red pepper. Bring to boiling. Stir in the sweet pepper, carrot, and green onions. Return to boiling; reduce heat. Cover and simmer for 4 to 6 minutes or until vegetables are crisp-tender and noodles are tender.

2. Stir in chicken and pea pods. Simmer, uncovered, for 1 to 2 minutes more or until pea pods are crisp-tender. Makes 3 servings.

NUTRITION FACTS PER SERVING:

224 calories
6 g total fat
2 g saturated fat
58 mg cholesterol
1,280 mg sodium
17 g carbohydrate
2 g fiber
24 g protein

INGREDIENTS

1¾ cups water

1 14½-ounce can reduced-sodium chicken broth

½ pound skinless, boneless chicken, cut into bite-size pieces

1 to 2 teaspoons chili powder

1 11-ounce can whole kernel corn with sweet peppers, drained

1 cup chunky garden-style salsa

3 cups broken baked or fried corn tortilla chips

2 ounces Monterey Jack cheese with jalapeño peppers, shredded

chicken and salsa soup

Decide how zesty you want this soup to be, then choose from mild, medium, or hot salsa.

Prep time: 10 minutes
Cooking time: 13 minutes

DIRECTIONS

1. In a 3-quart saucepan combine water, chicken broth, chicken, and chili powder. Bring to boiling; reduce heat. Cover and simmer for 8 minutes. Add corn. Simmer, uncovered, for 5 minutes more. Stir in salsa; heat through.

2. Ladle soup into bowls. Top with chips and sprinkle with cheese. Makes 4 servings.

Before starting the salsa soup,

fix up a 15-ounce package of corn bread mix by stirring one 4-ounce can diced green chili peppers, drained, into the batter; spread the batter into the baking pan. Sprinkle with paprika; bake as directed. Serve with honey butter.

NUTRITION FACTS PER SERVING:

319 calories
9 g total fat
3 g saturated fat
42 mg cholesterol
989 mg sodium
32 g carbohydrate
3 g fiber
20 g protein

153

chicken and shrimp tortilla soup

Your family will be intrigued when you sprinkle shreds of crisp-baked corn tortillas over the top of this eye-catching Southwestern soup. Make the tortilla shreds ahead of time and store them in an airtight container.

INGREDIENTS

6 ounces peeled and deveined fresh or frozen medium shrimp with tails

1 recipe Crisp Tortilla Shreds (see recipe, below)

1 large onion, chopped (1 cup)

1 teaspoon cumin seed

1 tablespoon cooking oil

4½ cups reduced-sodium chicken broth

1 14½-ounce can Mexican-style stewed tomatoes

3 tablespoons snipped fresh cilantro

2 tablespoons lime juice

1⅔ cups shredded cooked chicken breast

Start to finish: 30 minutes

DIRECTIONS

1. Thaw shrimp, if frozen. Prepare Crisp Tortilla Shreds; set aside.

2. In a large saucepan cook the onion and cumin seed in hot oil about 5 minutes or until onion is tender. Carefully add chicken broth, undrained tomatoes, cilantro, and lime juice.

3. Bring to boiling; reduce heat. Cover and simmer for 8 minutes. Stir in shrimp and chicken. Cook about 3 minutes more or until shrimp turn pink, stirring occasionally. Ladle into soup bowls. Top each serving with tortilla shreds. Makes 6 servings.

Crisp Tortilla Shreds:
Brush four 5½-inch corn tortillas with 1 tablespoon cooking oil. In a small bowl combine ½ teaspoon salt and ⅛ teaspoon pepper; sprinkle mixture over tortillas. Cut tortillas into thin shreds. Arrange in a single layer on a baking sheet. Bake in a 350° oven about 8 minutes or until crisp.

NUTRITION FACTS PER SERVING:

160 calories
5 g total fat
1 g saturated fat
80 mg cholesterol
794 mg sodium
8 g carbohydrate
0 g fiber
21 g protein

INGREDIENTS

1	cup small broccoli flowerets
1	cup frozen loose-pack whole kernel corn
½	cup water
¼	cup chopped onion
1½	teaspoons snipped fresh thyme or ½ teaspoon dried thyme, crushed
2	cups milk
1½	cups chopped cooked chicken or turkey
1	10¾-ounce can condensed cream of potato soup
¾	cup shredded cheddar cheese (3 ounces)

Dash pepper
¼ cup shredded cheddar cheese (1 ounce)

easy cheesy vegetable-chicken chowder

This hearty chowder lives up to its name. It's easy—only takes about 20 minutes to cook—and with a cup of cheddar cheese, it's definitely cheesy!

Start to finish: 20 minutes

DIRECTIONS

1. In a large saucepan combine broccoli, corn, water, onion, and thyme. Bring to boiling; reduce heat. Cover and simmer for 8 to 10 minutes or until vegetables are tender. Do not drain.

2. Stir milk, chicken or turkey, potato soup, the ¾ cup cheddar cheese, and pepper into vegetable mixture. Cook and stir over medium heat until cheese melts and mixture is heated through. Sprinkle the ¼ cup cheddar cheese over soup. Makes 4 servings.

NUTRITION FACTS PER SERVING:

368 calories
18 g total fat
9 g saturated fat
94 mg cholesterol
901 mg sodium
23 g carbohydrate
1 g fiber
30 g protein

Get a head start on meal preparation by stocking your shelves with products that are already shredded, chopped, or crumbled. They may cost a little more, but when you're racing the clock, every minute counts. For this recipe, buy precut broccoli flowerets and shredded cheese.

curried chicken soup

This spiced chicken noodle soup can be ready in just 20 minutes. It's a good way to use leftover chicken. Or, if you don't have any, buy a roasted chicken from your supermarket's deli.

INGREDIENTS

- **5   cups water**
- **1   3-ounce package chicken-flavored ramen noodles**
- **2   to 3 teaspoons curry powder**
- **1   cup sliced fresh mushrooms**
- **2   cups cubed cooked chicken**
- **1   medium apple, cored and coarsely chopped**
- **½   cup sliced water chestnuts**

Use an apple wedger to quickly core and cut the apple into wedges. Then chop the wedges. There's no need to peel the apple.

Prep time: 15 minutes
Cooking time: 5 minutes

DIRECTIONS

1. In a large saucepan combine the water, the flavoring packet from noodles, and curry powder. Bring to boiling. Break up noodles and add to mixture in saucepan along with the mushrooms. Return to boiling; reduce heat. Simmer, uncovered, for 3 minutes.

2. Stir in chicken, apple, and water chestnuts. Heat through. Makes 5 servings.

NUTRITION FACTS PER SERVING:

217 calories
8 g total fat
1 g saturated fat
54 mg cholesterol
449 mg sodium
17 g carbohydrate
1 g fiber
20 g protein

156

INGREDIENTS

- 1 large onion, chopped (1 cup)
- 2 teaspoons bottled minced garlic or 4 cloves garlic, minced
- 2 to 4 fresh Anaheim or poblano peppers, seeded and chopped
- 1 tablespoon cumin seed
- 2 tablespoons cooking oil
- 1½ cups frozen loose-pack whole kernel corn or fresh-cut corn kernels (about 3 ears)
- 3 medium tomatoes, chopped
- 2 14½-ounce cans (3½ cups total) reduced-sodium chicken broth

- 1½ cups coarsely shredded cooked chicken
- ½ cup snipped fresh cilantro
- 2 cups coarsely crushed tortilla chips
- 1 cup shredded Monterey Jack cheese (4 ounces) (optional)
- Tortilla chips (optional)
- Lime wedges (optional)
- Fresh cilantro sprigs (optional)

tortilla soup

Anaheim and poblano peppers add a lively beat to corn and tomatoes in this aromatic broth.

Prep time: 15 minutes
Cooking time: 15 minutes

DIRECTIONS

1. In a large kettle or Dutch oven cook onion, garlic, Anaheim or poblano peppers, and cumin seed in hot oil about 5 minutes or until onion is tender, stirring constantly. Add corn, tomatoes, chicken broth, shredded cooked chicken, and the snipped cilantro. Bring mixture to boiling; reduce heat. Cover and simmer for 10 minutes.

2. To serve, divide crushed tortilla chips among 6 soup bowls. Ladle soup over chips. If desired, garnish each serving with cheese, extra tortilla chips, lime wedges, and fresh cilantro sprigs. Makes 6 servings.

Anaheim chili peppers are mild green peppers with a long, slender shape. Poblano peppers are a darker green than Anaheim peppers and can be mild or spicy. They are triangular in shape and are usually 4 to 5 inches long. You'll find both types in the produce section of your grocery store or at Mexican markets.

NUTRITION FACTS PER SERVING:

274 calories
13 g total fat
2 g saturated fat
29 mg cholesterol
504 mg sodium
26 g carbohydrate
4 g fiber
16 g protein

157

quick-to-fix turkey and rice soup

Turn your leftover Thanksgiving turkey into a meal your family will love.

INGREDIENTS

- 4 cups chicken broth
- 1 cup water
- 1 teaspoon snipped fresh rosemary or ¼ teaspoon dried rosemary, crushed
- ¼ teaspoon pepper
- 1 10-ounce package frozen mixed vegetables (2 cups)
- 1 cup quick-cooking rice
- 2 cups chopped cooked turkey or chicken
- 1 14½-ounce can tomatoes, cut up

Fresh herbs are highly perishable,

so purchase them only as you need them. For short-term storage, immerse the freshly cut stems in water about 2 inches deep. Cover the leaves loosely with a plastic bag or plastic wrap. Store the herbs in the refrigerator for up to several days.

Prep time: 10 minutes
Cooking time: 10 minutes

DIRECTIONS

1. In a large saucepan or Dutch oven combine chicken broth, water, rosemary, and pepper. Bring to boiling.

2. Stir in mixed vegetables and rice. Return to boiling; reduce heat. Cover and simmer for 10 to 15 minutes or until vegetables and rice are tender. Stir in turkey or chicken and undrained tomatoes; heat through. Makes 6 servings.

NUTRITION FACTS PER SERVING:

231 calories
6 g total fat
2 g saturated fat
49 mg cholesterol
681 mg sodium
23 g carbohydrate
1 g fiber
21 g protein

INGREDIENTS

- ¾ **pound fresh or frozen fish fillets**
- 1 **24-ounce can vegetable juice**
- 1 **11-ounce can whole kernel corn with sweet peppers**
- 4 **green onions, sliced (½ cup)**
- ¼ **cup chicken broth**
- 1½ **teaspoons snipped fresh thyme or ½ teaspoon dried thyme, crushed**
- 1 **teaspoon Worcestershire sauce Several dashes bottled hot pepper sauce**

manhattan fish chowder

Manhattan-style chowders are tomato-based and may contain other vegetables in place of the potatoes found in milk-based New England-style chowders.

Prep time: 15 minutes
Cooking time: 11 minutes

DIRECTIONS

1. Thaw fish, if frozen. Rinse fish; pat dry. Cut fish into ¾-inch pieces. In a large saucepan combine vegetable juice, corn, green onions, chicken broth, thyme, Worcestershire sauce, and hot pepper sauce. Bring to boiling; reduce heat. Cover and simmer for 8 minutes.

2. Add fish to saucepan. Return to boiling; reduce heat. Cover and simmer for 3 to 5 minutes more or until fish flakes easily when tested with a fork, stirring once. Makes 4 servings.

NUTRITION FACTS PER SERVING:

173 calories
2 g total fat
0 g saturated fat
45 mg cholesterol
1,021 mg sodium
22 g carbohydrate
4 g fiber
19 g protein

Complete this soup supper with crusty French bread and slices of fresh apple or pear.

159

shrimp and greens soup

Although great any time of year, this fresh-tasting seafood soup is light enough to serve during the summer. The savory combination of shrimp, shredded bok choy, and leek is embellished with an accent of lemon pepper.

INGREDIENTS

- ¾ pound peeled and deveined fresh or frozen shrimp
- 1 large leek, sliced
- 1 teaspoon bottled minced garlic or 2 cloves garlic, minced
- 1 tablespoon olive oil
- 3 14½-ounce cans reduced-sodium chicken broth or vegetable broth
- 1 tablespoon snipped fresh Italian flat-leaf parsley or parsley
- 1 tablespoon snipped fresh marjoram or thyme
- ¼ teaspoon lemon-pepper seasoning
- 2 cups shredded bok choy or fresh spinach leaves

Bok choy, a variety of Chinese cabbage,
has long, white celerylike stalks and large green leaves. It's crisp like celery with a sweet, mild cabbagelike flavor. Avoid heads that are wilted or have mushy leaves. Store bok choy in a plastic bag in the refrigerator and use it within a few days.

Start to finish: 30 minutes

DIRECTIONS

1. Thaw shrimp, if frozen. Rinse shrimp; pat dry. In a large saucepan cook leek and garlic in hot oil over medium-high heat about 2 minutes or until leek is tender. Carefully add chicken broth, parsley, marjoram, and lemon-pepper seasoning. Bring to boiling; add shrimp. Return to boiling; reduce heat.

2. Simmer, uncovered, for 2 minutes. Stir in the bok choy or spinach. Cook about 1 minute more or until the shrimp turn pink. Makes 4 servings.

NUTRITION FACTS PER SERVING:

147 calories
6 g total fat
1 g saturated fat
131 mg cholesterol
1,093 mg sodium
5 g carbohydrate
2 g fiber
18 g protein

160

INGREDIENTS

- 8 fresh or frozen cleaned baby clams and/or fresh or frozen mussels in shells
- ¼ pound fresh or frozen peeled and deveined shrimp with tails
- 12 ounces fresh or frozen firm white-fleshed fish (such as cod, haddock, or grouper)
- 2 medium onions, sliced and separated into rings
- 1 teaspoon bottled minced garlic or 2 cloves garlic, minced
- 2 tablespoons olive oil
- 2 cups chicken broth or clam juice

- 1 cup dry white wine or chicken broth
- 1 14½-ounce can stewed tomatoes, cut up
- 1 teaspoon finely shredded orange peel
- 1 teaspoon dried thyme, crushed
- 1 teaspoon fennel seed
- ½ teaspoon salt
- ½ teaspoon pepper
- ⅛ teaspoon ground saffron
- 1 7-ounce can sweet potatoes, drained and cut up
- 6 slices French bread, toasted (optional)

root cellar bouillabaisse

Traditional bouillabaisse used to take hours to assemble and simmer; this version is quick and easy to prepare, and the flavor is a match for any bistro's recipe.

Start to finish: 25 minutes

DIRECTIONS

1. Thaw seafood, if frozen. Rinse seafood; pat dry. Cut fish into 1½-inch pieces.

2. In a large saucepan cook the onions and garlic in hot oil 3 minutes or until just tender, stirring frequently. Add the 2 cups broth, wine, undrained tomatoes, orange peel, thyme, fennel seed, salt, pepper, and saffron. Bring to boiling; add seafood and fish. Return to boiling; reduce heat. Cover and simmer for 3 to 5 minutes. Add sweet potatoes; heat through, stirring gently.

3. To serve, remove and discard clams or mussels that have not opened. If desired, ladle soup into bowls over bread. Makes 6 servings.

NUTRITION FACTS PER SERVING:

334 calories
7 g total fat
1 g saturated fat
61 mg cholesterol
889 mg sodium
40 g carbohydrate
3 g fiber
22 g protein

Saffron, the filaments of a special
variety of purple crocus, is reddish orange in color and imparts a bright yellow color, bittersweet flavor, and exotic aroma to bouillabaisse. Because the delicate filaments must be picked by hand, saffron is the world's most expensive spice. It is sold in tiny threads or ground into a powder. When using saffron threads, release the wonderful flavor by rubbing the threads against the side of the pan with a spoon until they are crushed.

161

fish provençale

The sweet essence of fresh fennel blends nicely with fish, tomatoes, garlic, and onion. This orange-scented soup tastes as good as it smells.

INGREDIENTS

½ pound fresh or frozen skinless haddock, grouper, or halibut fillets

1 small fennel bulb

3 cups vegetable broth or chicken broth

1 large onion, finely chopped (1 cup)

1 cup yellow summer squash and/or zucchini cut into bite-size pieces

1 cup dry white wine

1 teaspoon finely shredded orange or lemon peel

1½ teaspoons bottled minced garlic or 3 cloves garlic, minced

2 cups chopped tomatoes or one 14½-ounce can diced tomatoes

2 tablespoons snipped fresh thyme Snipped fresh thyme (optional)

Dry white wine adds zest to fish soups, like this one, as well as to lobster bisque and creamy chowders. Be thrifty with salt in a soup to which wine is added; wine intensifies the saltiness.

Start to finish: 30 minutes

DIRECTIONS

1. Thaw fish, if frozen. Rinse fish; pat dry. Cut fish into 1-inch pieces; set aside.

2. Cut off and discard upper stalks of fennel. Remove any wilted outer layers; cut a thin slice from base. Wash fennel; cut in half lengthwise and thinly slice.

3. In a large saucepan combine fennel, broth, onion, squash, wine, orange peel, and garlic. Bring to boiling; reduce heat. Cover and simmer for 10 minutes. Stir in fish pieces, tomatoes, and the 2 tablespoons thyme. Cook about 3 minutes more or until fish flakes easily when tested with a fork. If desired, garnish with additional snipped thyme. Makes 4 servings.

NUTRITION FACTS PER SERVING:

 156 calories
3 g total fat
0 g saturated fat
18 mg cholesterol
752 mg sodium
15 g carbohydrate
8 g fiber
14 g protein

sherried salmon bisque

Salmon, shiitake mushrooms, leeks, and dry sherry come together to create this sophisticated soup.

INGREDIENTS

- ¾ pound fresh or frozen salmon steaks, cut ¾ inch thick
- 3 cups sliced fresh shiitake or other mushrooms
- ¾ cup thinly sliced leeks or ½ cup thinly sliced green onion
- 2 tablespoons margarine or butter
- 2 cups chicken broth or vegetable broth
- 1½ teaspoons snipped fresh dill or ½ teaspoon dried dillweed
- Dash pepper
- 2 cups half-and-half or light cream
- 2 tablespoons cornstarch
- 2 tablespoons dry sherry

Start to finish: 30 minutes

DIRECTIONS

1. Thaw salmon, if frozen. Rinse salmon; pat dry. Cut salmon into ¾-inch pieces. Discard skin and bones. In a large saucepan cook mushrooms and leeks or green onions in hot margarine or butter until tender. Stir in chicken broth or vegetable broth, fresh dill or dried dillweed, and pepper. Bring to boiling.

2. Combine half-and-half or light cream and cornstarch; stir into mushroom mixture. Cook and stir over medium heat until thickened and bubbly. Add salmon. Cover and simmer about 4 minutes or until fish flakes easily when tested with a fork. Gently stir in the dry sherry. Makes 4 servings.

NUTRITION FACTS PER SERVING:

365 calories
24 g total fat
11 g saturated fat
60 mg cholesterol
563 mg sodium
18 g carbohydrate
3 g fiber
20 g protein

Choose mushrooms that are

firm, fresh, and plump with no bruises. Store them, unwashed, in the refrigerator for up to 2 days. Store prepackaged mushrooms in the package. Loose mushrooms or those in an open package should be stored in a paper bag or in a damp cloth bag in the refrigerator. This allows them to breathe so they stay firmer longer. Don't store mushrooms in plastic bags because the mushrooms will deteriorate more quickly.

163

cream of shrimp soup

Cream, Dijon-style mustard, and nutmeg make this fancy seafood soup irresistible.

INGREDIENTS

- 3 cups vegetable broth or chicken broth
- 1½ cups frozen loose-pack peas and carrots
- 3 tablespoons thinly sliced green onions
- ⅛ teaspoon pepper
  Dash ground nutmeg
- 1 cup half-and-half or light cream
- 3 tablespoons all-purpose flour
- ½ pound cooked, peeled, and deveined shrimp, coarsely chopped
- 1 teaspoon Dijon-style mustard

The clean, sharp flavor of Dijon-style

mustard is ideal for shrimp dishes because it adds pizzazz without covering up the flavor of the shrimp. It is a light grayish lemon-colored mustard with a velvety texture that is made from brown or black mustard seeds, white wine, and a blend of spices.

Prep time: 10 minutes
Cooking time: 10 minutes

DIRECTIONS

1. In a large saucepan or Dutch oven combine vegetable broth or chicken broth, peas and carrots, green onions, pepper, and nutmeg. Bring to boiling; reduce heat. Cover and simmer about 5 minutes or until vegetables are tender.

2. Meanwhile, gradually stir half-and-half or light cream into flour until smooth. Stir flour mixture into vegetable mixture. Cook and stir over medium heat until bubbly; cook and stir for 1 minute more. Stir in shrimp and mustard; heat through. Makes 4 servings.

NUTRITION FACTS PER SERVING:

182 calories
9 g total fat
5 g saturated fat
133 mg cholesterol
914 mg sodium
15 g carbohydrate
2 g fiber
16 g protein

INGREDIENTS

2 medium onions, sliced

2 medium carrots, thinly sliced

1 tablespoon snipped fresh cilantro

2 teaspoons grated fresh ginger

1 teaspoon bottled minced garlic or 2 cloves garlic, minced

½ teaspoon ground allspice

2 tablespoons margarine or butter

1 14½-ounce can chicken broth

1 15-ounce can pumpkin

1 cup milk

1 8-ounce package frozen, peeled, and deveined cooked shrimp, thawed

Additional shrimp in shells, peeled, deveined, and cooked (optional)

Snipped fresh chives (optional)

spicy pumpkin and shrimp soup

During the week, convenience is key. Here's a way to turn a can of pumpkin into an exciting soup. Just the right blend of ginger, cilantro, allspice, and garlic complement the pumpkin for a terrific flavor.

3. In same saucepan combine pumpkin, milk, and remaining broth. Stir in blended vegetable mixture and shrimp; heat through. Ladle soup into bowls. If desired, thread additional cooked shrimp on small skewers; top each serving with snipped chives and skewered cooked shrimp. Makes 4 servings.

To devein shrimp for garnishing this soup, use a sharp knife to make shallow slits along the backs of the shrimp from the heads to the tails. Rinse under cold running water to remove the veins, using the tip of a knife, if necessary.

Start to finish: 30 minutes

DIRECTIONS

1. In a large covered saucepan cook onions, carrots, cilantro, fresh ginger, garlic, and allspice in hot margarine or butter for 10 to 12 minutes or until vegetables are tender, stirring once or twice.

2. Transfer the mixture to a blender container or food processor bowl. Add ½ cup of the chicken broth. Cover and blend or process until nearly smooth.

NUTRITION FACTS PER SERVING:

222 calories
9 g total fat
2 g saturated fat
116 mg cholesterol
579 mg sodium
19 g carbohydrate
5 g fiber
18 g protein

165

lemon and scallop soup

To create a complete Oriental-style meal, stop by your favorite Oriental fast-food restaurant and pick up some egg rolls to serve as an appetizer and some fortune cookies for dessert.

INGREDIENTS

- ¾ pound fresh or frozen bay scallops
- 5 cups reduced-sodium chicken broth
- ½ cup dry white wine or reduced-sodium chicken broth
- 3 tablespoons snipped fresh cilantro
- 2 teaspoons finely shredded lemon peel
- ¼ teaspoon pepper
- 1 pound fresh asparagus spears, trimmed and cut into bite-size pieces
- 1 cup fresh enoki mushrooms or shiitake mushrooms
- 4 green onions, sliced (½ cup)
- 1 tablespoon lemon juice

Long-stemmed, tiny-capped, and slightly crunchy, enoki mushrooms play an important role in Asian cooking. These elegant mushrooms have a light, fruity flavor. Toss a few into the soup at the last moment before serving, as they will toughen if heated.

Start to finish: 25 minutes

DIRECTIONS

1. Thaw scallops, if frozen. Rinse scallops; pat dry.

2. In a large saucepan combine the 5 cups chicken broth, wine or broth, cilantro, lemon peel, and pepper. Bring to boiling.

3. Add the scallops, asparagus, shiitake mushrooms (if using), and green onions. Return just to boiling; reduce heat.

4. Simmer, uncovered, about 5 minutes or until asparagus is tender and scallops are opaque. Remove from heat. Stir in the enoki mushrooms (if using) and lemon juice. Serve immediately. Makes 4 servings.

NUTRITION FACTS PER SERVING:

 153 calories
2 g total fat
0 g saturated fat
28 mg cholesterol
940 mg sodium
10 g carbohydrate
2 g fiber
20 g protein

oyster soup

Oyster soup is mildly seasoned so the delicate fish flavor comes through. If you like, float a small pat of margarine or butter on top of each serving.

INGREDIENTS

- ¼ cup finely chopped onion or sliced leek
- 2 teaspoons margarine or butter
- 1 pint shucked oysters
- ½ teaspoon salt
- 2 cups milk
- 1 cup half-and-half or light cream
- 1 tablespoon snipped fresh parsley
- ¼ teaspoon white pepper
- Margarine or butter (optional)
- Snipped fresh parsley (optional)

Start to finish: 15 minutes

DIRECTIONS

1. In a medium saucepan cook onion or leek in 2 teaspoons hot margarine or butter until tender. Add the undrained oysters and salt. Cook over medium heat about 5 minutes or until oysters curl around the edges, stirring occasionally.

2. Stir in the milk, half-and-half or light cream, the 1 tablespoon parsley, and white pepper. Heat through.

Ladle into soup bowls. If desired, top each serving with pat of margarine and sprinkle with additional parsley. Makes 4 servings.

When shopping for shucked

oysters, look for ones with no off-odor and that have clear, not cloudy, liquor (juice) around them. You can store them covered in their liquor for up to 5 days in the refrigerator, or freeze them for up to 3 months.

NUTRITION FACTS PER SERVING:

238 calories
14 g total fat
7 g saturated fat
93 mg cholesterol
502 mg sodium
14 g carbohydrate
0 g fiber
14 g protein

167

spicy seafood stew

Orange roughy, cod, or haddock make good choices for the fish in this full-bodied stew.

INGREDIENTS

- 1 pound fresh or frozen fish fillets and/or fresh or frozen peeled and deveined shrimp
- 2 cups chicken broth or vegetable broth
- 1 cup sliced fresh mushrooms
- 1 cup sliced zucchini or yellow summer squash
- 1 medium onion, chopped ($\frac{1}{2}$ cup)
- $\frac{1}{2}$ teaspoon bottled minced garlic or 1 clove garlic, minced
- $\frac{1}{8}$ teaspoon salt
- $\frac{1}{8}$ teaspoon crushed red pepper
- 1 bay leaf
- 2 14$\frac{1}{2}$-ounce cans Cajun-style stewed tomatoes
- 2 tablespoons snipped fresh parsley
- $\frac{1}{2}$ teaspoon finely shredded lemon peel

Look for bottled minced garlic in your supermarket's produce section. If you prefer to use fresh garlic, you can use a garlic press to crush the clove. Or, peel it quickly and easily by placing a flat side of a chef's knife over the clove and hitting it with the side of your fist; remove the peel and cut the garlic into tiny pieces using the chef's knife.

Start to finish: 25 minutes

DIRECTIONS

1. Thaw fish and/or shrimp, if frozen. Rinse fish and/or shrimp; pat dry. Cut fish into 1-inch pieces. In a large saucepan or Dutch oven combine chicken broth or vegetable broth, mushrooms, zucchini or yellow summer squash, onion, garlic, salt, crushed red pepper, and bay leaf. Bring to boiling; reduce heat. Cover and simmer for 5 to 8 minutes or until vegetables are tender.

2. Stir in undrained tomatoes, fish, and shrimp. Bring just to boiling; reduce heat. Cover and simmer for 2 to 3 minutes or until fish flakes easily when tested with a fork and shrimp turn pink. Discard bay leaf. Ladle into soup bowls.

3. In a small bowl combine parsley and lemon peel; sprinkle over stew. Makes 4 servings.

NUTRITION FACTS PER SERVING:

197 calories
2 g total fat
1 g saturated fat
61 mg cholesterol
1,300 mg sodium
19 g carbohydrate
4 g fiber
26 g protein

crab and cauliflower chowder

If you like, use broccoli flowerets instead of the cauliflower in this richly flavored chowder.

INGREDIENTS

6 ounces fresh or frozen crabmeat or one 6-ounce can crabmeat, drained, flaked, and cartilage removed
2½ cups small cauliflower flowerets
¼ cup margarine or butter
¼ cup all-purpose flour
¼ teaspoon white pepper
2 cups chicken broth or vegetable broth
2 cups milk
1 3-ounce package cream cheese with chives, softened and cut up
¼ cup dry white wine
2 tablespoons snipped fresh parsley

Start to finish: 20 minutes

DIRECTIONS

1. Thaw crabmeat, if frozen. In a large saucepan cook cauliflower flowerets in hot margarine or butter for 5 to 6 minutes or just until crisp-tender.

2. Stir in flour and white pepper. Add chicken broth or vegetable broth and milk all at once. Cook and stir until thickened and bubbly. Cook and stir for 1 minute more.

3. Gradually stir about 1 cup of the hot milk mixture into the softened cream cheese; return to saucepan. Cook and stir over low heat until cream cheese melts. Stir in crabmeat and wine; heat through. Ladle into soup bowls. Sprinkle each serving with parsley. Makes 4 servings.

NUTRITION FACTS PER SERVING:

353 calories
23 g total fat
9 g saturated fat
76 mg cholesterol
771 mg sodium
16 g carbohydrate
2 g fiber
19 g protein

For real convenience, stop

by your supermarket's salad bar or produce section and pick up some precut cauliflower flowerets. If you prefer to cut up your own, look for a solid heavy head with bright green leaves. Avoid heads that have brown bruises, a speckled appearance, or leaves that are yellowed or withered.

169

crab chowder

This creamy chowder features the prize of all seafood—crabmeat. It's even more enticing with bouquet garni seasoning and a small amount of cream cheese.

INGREDIENTS

1 6-ounce package frozen crabmeat or one 6-ounce can crabmeat, drained, flaked, and cartilage removed
1 medium zucchini, cut into 2-inch-long strips
1 medium red or green sweet pepper, chopped
2 tablespoons margarine or butter
2 tablespoons all-purpose flour
4 cups milk
1 green onion, sliced (2 tablespoons)
½ teaspoon bouquet garni seasoning

¼ teaspoon salt
⅛ teaspoon ground black pepper
1 3-ounce package cream cheese, cut up
1 teaspoon snipped fresh thyme
Fresh thyme sprigs (optional)

A traditional bouquet garni is a bundle of aromatic herbs—often thyme, parsley, and bay leaf—that's simmered in soups and stews to add flavor. Bouquet garni seasoning saves you the work of assembling a bundle on your own. Look for it in the spice aisle of your supermarket.

Start to finish: 25 minutes

DIRECTIONS

1. Thaw crabmeat, if frozen. In a medium saucepan cook zucchini and sweet pepper in hot margarine or butter until crisp-tender. Stir in the flour. Add the milk, green onion, bouquet garni seasoning, salt, and black pepper.

2. Cook and stir over medium-high heat until thickened and bubbly. Add the cream cheese; cook and stir until cream cheese melts. Stir in the crabmeat and snipped thyme; heat through. Ladle into soup bowls. If desired, garnish with fresh thyme sprigs. Makes 4 servings.

NUTRITION FACTS PER SERVING:

314 calories
19 g total fat
9 g saturated fat
64 mg cholesterol
844 mg sodium
18 g carbohydrate
1 g fiber
19 g protein

INGREDIENTS

- 1 cup packaged dried small shell macaroni or bow ties (4 ounces)
- 4 cups hot-style vegetable juice, chilled
- 1 tablespoon lime juice or lemon juice
- 6 ounces cooked lump crabmeat, flaked, or chopped cooked chicken (about 1¼ cups)
- 2 medium nectarines, chopped (about 1⅓ cups)
- 2 plum tomatoes, chopped (about ¾ cup)
- ¼ cup chopped, seeded cucumber
- 2 tablespoons snipped fresh basil
  Lime wedges (optional)

crab and pasta gazpacho

Gazpacho—the chilled tomato-and-vegetable soup—was created in Spain but reinvented in California, where it's a summer menu favorite. This fast, fresh version is full of sweet crab, juicy nectarines, and fragrant basil.

Start to finish: 25 minutes

DIRECTIONS

1. Cook pasta according to package directions; drain. Rinse pasta with cold water; drain again.

2. Meanwhile, in a large bowl stir together vegetable juice and lime juice. Stir in pasta, crabmeat, nectarines, tomatoes, cucumber, and basil. Ladle into soup bowls. If desired, garnish with lime wedges. Makes 6 servings.

NUTRITION FACTS PER SERVING:

162 calories
1 g total fat
0 g saturated fat
28 mg cholesterol
947 mg sodium
28 g carbohydrate
2 g fiber
11 g protein

Freshly squeezed lime or lemon juice adds tantalizing citrus flavor to all types of dishes. To get the most juice, purchase a fruit that is heavy for its size. Before squeezing, allow the lime or lemon to sit at room temperature for 30 minutes. Then roll it under the palm of your hand a few times so more juice will flow. A medium lime will yield about 2 tablespoons juice and a medium lemon will yield about 3 tablespoons juice.

171

borscht for busy people

This chill-banishing soup is ready in a jiffy thanks to coleslaw mix and canned broth and veggies.

INGREDIENTS

- 6 cups packaged shredded cabbage with carrot (coleslaw mix)
- 1 cup vegetable or beef broth
- 1 15-ounce can great northern beans, rinsed and drained
- 1 14½-ounce can tomatoes, cut up
- 1 14½-ounce can sliced beets
- 1 8-ounce can tomato sauce
- 1 large onion, sliced and separated into rings
- ¼ cup sugar
- 2 tablespoons vinegar
- ¼ teaspoon dried dillweed (optional)
- ¼ teaspoon pepper
- 6 tablespoons light dairy sour cream (optional)
- 6 fresh dill sprigs (optional)

Served either hot or cold,

borscht is an Eastern European favorite especially popular in Russia and Poland. Authentic borscht can include meat or be based on only vegetables. A dollop of sour cream on this magenta-colored soup is not only delicious but traditional.

Prep time: 10 minutes
Cooking time: 20 minutes

DIRECTIONS

1. In a large saucepan or Dutch oven stir together the cabbage with carrot, broth, beans, undrained tomatoes, undrained beets, tomato sauce, onion, sugar, vinegar, dillweed (if desired), and pepper. Bring to boiling; reduce heat. Cover and simmer for 20 minutes.

2. Ladle into soup bowls. If desired, garnish with sour cream and fresh dill. Makes 6 servings.

NUTRITION FACTS PER SERVING:

- 195 calories
- 2 g total fat
- 1 g saturated fat
- 2 mg cholesterol
- 758 mg sodium
- 41 g carbohydrate
- 6 g fiber
- 9 g protein

creamy carrot and pasta soup

Tricolor pasta adds a colorful touch to this nicely spiced soup, but you can use plain pasta in a pinch.

INGREDIENTS

- 2 14½-ounce cans chicken broth (3½ cups)
- 2 cups sliced carrots
- 1 large potato, peeled and diced
- 1 large onion, chopped (1 cup)
- 1 tablespoon grated fresh ginger
- ½ to 1 teaspoon Jamaican jerk seasoning or Homemade Jerk Seasoning (see recipe, page 88)
- 8 ounces packaged dried tricolor radiatore or rotini
- 1½ cups milk or one 12-ounce can evaporated fat-free milk

   Fresh chives (optional)

Start to finish: 30 minutes

DIRECTIONS

1. In a large saucepan combine chicken broth, carrots, potato, onion, fresh ginger, and Jamaican jerk seasoning. Bring to boiling; reduce heat. Cover and simmer for 15 to 20 minutes or until vegetables are very tender. Cool slightly.

2. Meanwhile, cook pasta according to package directions; drain.

3. Place one-fourth of the vegetable mixture in a food processor. Cover and process until smooth; pour into large bowl. Process remaining vegetable mixture one-fourth at a time. Return all to saucepan. Stir in pasta and milk; heat through. Ladle soup into bowls. If desired, garnish with chives. Makes 4 servings.

It's jerk seasoning that gives

this vegetable-and-pasta combo a tropical flair. This unique combination of spices, herbs, and fiery chilies is a Jamaican seasoning blend. Look for it with the herbs at the supermarket.

NUTRITION FACTS PER SERVING:

- 363 calories
- 4 g total fat
- 2 g saturated fat
- 8 mg cholesterol
- 750 mg sodium
- 65 g carbohydrate
- 3 g fiber
- 16 g protein

173

jalapeño corn chowder

Spectacular and rich, this chowder features the popular Southwestern flavors of corn, jalapeño peppers, and red sweet peppers.

INGREDIENTS

3   cups frozen loose-pack whole kernel corn or 3 cups fresh corn kernels (cut from 6 to 7 ears of corn)

1   14½-ounce can chicken broth

1¼ cups cooked small pasta (such as ditalini or tiny shell macaroni)

1   cup milk, half-and-half, or light cream

¼   of a 7-ounce jar roasted red sweet peppers, drained and chopped (¼ cup)

1   or 2 fresh jalapeño peppers, seeded and finely chopped

½   cup crumbled feta cheese (optional)

When using fresh corn, there are

two ways you can cut the corn kernels. To get whole kernels, cut the corn from the cobs at about three-quarters depth of kernels; do not scrape the cob. If you prefer cream-style corn, use a sharp knife to cut off just the kernel tips, then scrape the corn with a dull knife.

Start to finish: 20 minutes

DIRECTIONS

1. In a blender container or food processor bowl combine half of the corn and the chicken broth. Cover and blend or process until nearly smooth.

2. In a large saucepan combine the broth mixture and the remaining corn. If using fresh corn, bring to boiling; reduce heat. Cover and simmer for 2 to 3 minutes or until corn is crisp-tender.

3. Stir in cooked pasta; milk, half-and-half, or light cream; roasted peppers; and jalapeño peppers. Heat through. Ladle into soup mugs. If desired, top each serving with feta cheese. Makes 4 servings.

174

NUTRITION FACTS PER SERVING:

247 calories
3 g total fat
1 g saturated fat
5 mg cholesterol
363 mg sodium
47 g carbohydrate
1 g fiber
11 g protein

INGREDIENTS

- 1 14½-ounce can chicken broth
- 1 10-ounce package frozen whole kernel corn
- 1 4½-ounce can diced green chili peppers, drained
- ½ teaspoon chili powder
- 2 cups milk
- 3 tablespoons all-purpose flour
- 1 cup shredded American cheese (4 ounces)
-    Fresh parsley (optional)

cheesy corn chowder

American cheese gives this creamy soup its velvety texture.

Start to finish: 15 minutes

DIRECTIONS

1. In a large saucepan combine broth, corn, chili peppers, and chili powder. Bring to boiling; reduce heat. Cover and simmer 5 minutes.

2. Gradually stir the milk into the flour until combined. Stir milk mixture into hot mixture in the saucepan. Cook and stir over medium heat until mixture is slightly thickened and bubbly. Cook and stir for 1 minute more. Add cheese, stirring until melted. Ladle into soup bowls. If desired, garnish with parsley. Makes 4 servings.

NUTRITION FACTS PER SERVING:

273 calories
13 g total fat
7 g saturated fat
36 mg cholesterol
878 mg sodium
27 g carbohydrate
0 g fiber
16 g protein

Add a finishing touch to soups with any of these quick-as-a-wink ideas: Purchased bacon pieces, sour cream, yogurt, croutons, nuts, popcorn, crushed crackers, chow mein noodles, fresh herbs, sliced green onions or avocado, chopped hard-cooked eggs, shredded carrot or zucchini, sliced cucumber or olives, or bean sprouts.

175

quick corn chowder

Round out this ham-studded meal in a bowl with warm bread (see tip, below), a refreshing mixed fruit salad, and brownies from the bakery for dessert.

INGREDIENTS

- 2 cups chicken broth
- ¾ cup sliced celery
- 4 green onions, chopped (½ cup)
- ⅛ teaspoon pepper
- 1 16-ounce can whole kernel corn, drained
- 1 8¾-ounce can cream-style corn
- 5 ounces cooked ham, chopped (1 cup)
- 1 5-ounce can (⅔ cup) evaporated milk
- 1 tablespoon diced pimiento (optional)
- ½ cup packaged instant mashed potato flakes
- Pimiento strips (optional)

Pair a steaming bowl of this soup with a warm loaf of peppered bread. For bread, snip 8 to 10 refrigerated buttermilk or multigrain biscuits in half, and randomly arrange in a greased 7½×3½×2-inch loaf pan; brush with milk and generously sprinkle with pepper. Bake in a 350° oven about 20 minutes or until brown. Serve warm.

Start to finish: 25 minutes

DIRECTIONS

1. In a 2-quart saucepan combine the broth, celery, green onions, and pepper. Bring to boiling; reduce heat. Cover and simmer for 5 minutes.

2. Stir in whole kernel corn, undrained cream-style corn, ham, milk, and diced pimiento (if desired). Bring just to boiling; reduce heat. Stir in potato flakes; cook and stir until slightly thickened. Ladle into soup bowls. If desired, garnish with pimiento strips. Makes 4 servings.

NUTRITION FACTS PER SERVING:

453 calories
9 g total fat
3 g saturated fat
21 mg cholesterol
1,069 mg sodium
76 g carbohydrate
10 g fiber
21 g protein

INGREDIENTS

⅓ cup finely chopped onion

⅓ cup finely chopped celery

2 tablespoons finely chopped red
   sweet pepper

1 tablespoon margarine or butter

3 tablespoons all-purpose flour

1 tablespoon finely chopped
   lemongrass (white portion
   only) or 1 teaspoon finely
   shredded lemon peel

¼ teaspoon ground red pepper

1 14½-ounce can chicken broth

1 13½-ounce can purchased
   coconut milk (unsweetened)

½ cup creamy peanut butter

1 tablespoon soy sauce

½ cup chopped peanuts

   Snipped fresh cilantro (optional)

   Red sweet pepper strips
   (optional)

thai peanut soup

This creamy soup blends flavors that are popular in Thai recipes, including peanuts, coconut, lemongrass, and a bit of ground red pepper for "heat."

Start to finish: 25 minutes

DIRECTIONS

1. In a medium saucepan cook the onion, celery, and finely chopped red sweet pepper in hot margarine or butter about 4 minutes or until vegetables are tender, stirring occasionally. Stir in the flour, lemongrass or lemon peel, and ground red pepper. Add the chicken broth and coconut milk all at once. Cook and stir until the mixture is slightly thickened and bubbly. Cook and stir for 1 minute more.

2. Add peanut butter and soy sauce to the saucepan; stir until smooth and heated through. Ladle into soup bowls. Sprinkle with peanuts. If desired, garnish with cilantro and red sweet pepper strips. Makes 6 servings.

Serve this sophisticated soup with a sandwich as a full meal, or serve small portions as an appetizer course.

NUTRITION FACTS PER SERVING:

362 calories
31 g total fat
14 g saturated fat
0 mg cholesterol
635 mg sodium
14 g carbohydrate
3 g fiber
11 g protein

177

mushroom tortelloni in curry cream

Indonesian in flavor, this quick-cooking soup captures your attention with its wonderful aroma. Curry, coconut, and basil all add to the allure.

INGREDIENTS

1 shallot, finely chopped

1 fresh jalapeño pepper, seeded and finely chopped

½ teaspoon bottled minced garlic or 1 clove garlic, minced

2 teaspoons curry powder

1 tablespoon cooking oil

1 14½-ounce can chicken broth

1 13½-ounce can purchased coconut milk (unsweetened)

1 9-ounce package refrigerated mushroom tortelloni

1 tablespoon snipped fresh basil

1 medium tomato, chopped

Tortelloni is a large version of tortellini. If you're unable to find tortelloni, use tortellini instead.

Start to finish: 30 minutes

DIRECTIONS

1. In a medium saucepan cook shallot, jalapeño pepper, garlic, and curry powder in hot oil about 1 minute or until shallot is tender. Stir in chicken broth. Bring to boiling; reduce heat. Cover and simmer for 5 minutes.

2. Stir in the coconut milk, tortelloni, and basil. Cook and stir about 5 minutes more or until pasta is tender but still firm. Stir in the tomato. Cook and stir until heated through (do not boil). Makes 4 servings.

NUTRITION FACTS PER SERVING:

306 calories
14 g total fat
7 g saturated fat
24 mg cholesterol
649 mg sodium
35 g carbohydrate
3 g fiber
10 g protein

INGREDIENTS

- 4 cups reduced-sodium chicken broth
- 2 cups water
- 2 slightly beaten eggs
- 2 teaspoons cooking oil
- 4 ounces packaged dried angel hair pasta, broken into 2-inch-long pieces
- 2 medium leeks, sliced, or ⅔ cup sliced green onions
- 1 teaspoon bottled minced garlic or 2 cloves garlic, minced
- 4 ounces fresh sugar snap peas, cut in half crosswise (about 1 cup)
- 8 ounces fresh asparagus, cut into 1-inch-long pieces (about 1 cup)
- 2 tablespoons snipped fresh dill
- 2 teaspoons finely shredded lemon peel
  Fresh asparagus spears, cooked (optional)

spring green pasta soup

Thin strips of cooked egg, exquisite spring vegetables, and wispy threads of angel hair pasta compose this delicate soup with the airy lightness of a heavenly omelet.

Start to finish: 30 minutes

DIRECTIONS

1. In a large saucepan bring chicken broth and water to boiling.

2. Meanwhile, in a medium skillet cook eggs in hot oil over medium heat, without stirring, for 2 to 3 minutes or until eggs are set. To remove cooked eggs, loosen edge and invert skillet over a cutting board; cut eggs into thin, bite-size strips. Set aside.

3. Add pasta, leeks, and garlic to broth-water mixture. Boil gently, uncovered, about 3 minutes or until pasta is nearly tender. Add sugar snap peas, asparagus pieces, dill, and lemon peel. Return to boiling. Boil gently about 2 minutes more or until vegetables are crisp-tender; stir in egg strips. Ladle into soup bowls. If desired, garnish with asparagus spears. Makes 4 servings.

NUTRITION FACTS PER SERVING:

 235 calories
7 g total fat
1 g saturated fat
107 mg cholesterol
684 mg sodium
33 g carbohydrate
4 g fiber
12 g protein

Sugar snap peas

or sugar peas are one of two types of edible-pod peas. The other variety is the snow pea or Chinese pea pod. Sugar snap peas are sweet, tender pods that have fully developed, plump, round peas inside. Snow peas, on the other hand, are thin and crisp with small, flat peas inside. When shopping for sugar snap peas, look for crisp, brightly colored pods that are plump, but not bursting.

179

Angel Hair with Asparagus,
Tomatoes, and Fresh Basil
See recipe, page 190

meatless entrées

olive-potato frittata

Toss a fresh green salad to serve with this Spanish-style dinner omelet.

- 2 tablespoons olive oil or cooking oil
- 2 medium potatoes (such as long white, round white, round red, or yellow), thinly sliced (about 2 cups)
- 1 medium onion, cut into thin wedges
- 1 teaspoon bottled minced garlic or 2 cloves garlic, minced
- ¼ teaspoon salt
- ¼ teaspoon pepper
- 8 eggs
- 2 tablespoons snipped fresh oregano or 1 teaspoon dried oregano, crushed
- ¼ teaspoon salt
- ½ cup sliced pitted ripe olives
- ¼ cup finely shredded provolone or Parmesan cheese

Prep time: 15 minutes
Cooking time: 15 minutes

DIRECTIONS

1. In a 10-inch broiler-proof or regular skillet heat oil. Add the potatoes, onion, garlic, ¼ teaspoon salt, and pepper. Cover and cook over medium heat for 5 minutes. Turn potato mixture with a spatula. Cover and cook for 5 to 6 minutes more or until potatoes are tender, turning mixture once more.

2. In a medium mixing bowl beat together eggs, oregano, and ¼ teaspoon salt. Pour egg mixture over hot potato mixture. Sprinkle with olives. Cook over medium heat. As the mixture sets, run a spatula around the edge of the skillet, lifting egg mixture to allow the uncooked portion to flow underneath. Continue cooking and lifting edge until egg mixture is almost set (the surface will be moist).

3. Place the broiler-proof skillet under the broiler 4 to 5 inches from heat. Broil for 1 to 2 minutes or until top is set. (Or, if using a regular skillet, remove skillet from heat; cover and let stand for 3 to 4 minutes or until the top is set.) Sprinkle with cheese. Cut frittata into wedges and serve immediately. Makes 4 servings.

NUTRITION FACTS PER SERVING:

340 calories
21 g total fat
6 g saturated fat
431 mg cholesterol
671 mg sodium
21 g carbohydrate
2 g fiber
17 g protein

spinach-feta frittata

Whether you serve it for breakfast, brunch, or a light supper, this hearty skillet meal fits the bill. Complete the meal with some herb-seasoned cooked carrots and your favorite muffins from the bakery.

INGREDIENTS

- 6 slightly beaten eggs
- ¼ cup milk
- 1 teaspoon dried dillweed
- ¼ teaspoon salt
- ¼ teaspoon ground black pepper
- 1 medium onion, chopped (½ cup)
- ½ teaspoon bottled minced garlic or 1 clove garlic, minced
- 1 tablespoon margarine or butter
- ½ of a 10-ounce package frozen chopped spinach, thawed and well drained (see tip, page 42)
- ¼ teaspoon lemon-pepper seasoning
- ¼ cup crumbled feta cheese (1 ounce)
- Chopped red sweet pepper (optional)

Prep time: 10 minutes
Cooking time: 15 minutes

DIRECTIONS

1. In medium bowl combine eggs, milk, dillweed, salt, and ground black pepper. Set aside.

2. In a 10-inch broiler-proof or regular skillet cook onion and garlic in hot margarine or butter until tender. Stir in spinach and lemon-pepper seasoning.

3. Pour egg mixture into the skillet over spinach mixture. Cook over medium heat. As mixture sets, run a spatula around the edge of the skillet, lifting egg mixture to allow the uncooked portions to flow underneath. Continue cooking and lifting edge until egg mixture is almost set (surface will be moist).

4. Sprinkle with feta cheese. Place broiler-proof skillet under the broiler 4 to 5 inches from the heat. Broil for 1 to 2 minutes or until top is just set. (Or, if using a regular skillet, remove skillet from heat; cover and let stand for 3 to 4 minutes or until the top is set.) If desired, sprinkle with red sweet pepper. Cut into 8 wedges. Makes 4 servings.

Freeze any leftover feta cheese. Because it's a crumbly cheese, the texture changes little when frozen. Before freezing, wrap tightly in freezer wrap. Thaw in the refrigerator before using.

NUTRITION FACTS PER SERVING:

206 calories
14 g total fat
5 g saturated fat
335 mg cholesterol
536 mg sodium
6 g carbohydrate
0 g fiber
13 g protein

cheesy egg wedges

This dish is perfect just about any time. On weeknights, dish it up as a quick supper along with a tossed salad. For a leisurely weekend brunch, team it with a coffee cake and mixed fruit. When you're planning a party, cut it into 16 wedges and serve it as an appetizer.

INGREDIENTS

- 4 beaten eggs
- ⅓ cup milk
- ¼ cup all-purpose flour
- ½ teaspoon baking powder
- ⅛ teaspoon garlic powder
- 2 cups shredded cheddar or mozzarella cheese (8 ounces)
- 1 cup cream-style cottage cheese with chives
- 1 cup meatless spaghetti sauce or salsa
- Fresh basil (optional)

If cottage cheese with chives isn't available, stir some snipped fresh or dried chives into regular cottage cheese.

Start to finish: 30 minutes

DIRECTIONS

1. In medium bowl combine eggs, milk, flour, baking powder, and garlic powder. Beat with a rotary beater until combined. Stir in cheddar or mozzarella cheese and cottage cheese.

2. Pour into a greased 9-inch pie plate. Bake, uncovered, in a 375° oven for 25 to 30 minutes or until golden brown and a knife inserted near center comes out clean.

3. Meanwhile, in a small saucepan cook spaghetti sauce or salsa over medium-low heat about 5 minutes or until warm, stirring occasionally.

4. To serve, cut egg mixture into 6 wedges. Top with spaghetti sauce or salsa. If desired, garnish with fresh basil. Makes 6 servings.

NUTRITION FACTS PER SERVING:

273 calories
18 g total fat
10 g saturated fat
186 mg cholesterol
614 mg sodium
9 g carbohydrate
0 g fiber
20 g protein

rotini and sweet pepper primavera

Primavera means spring in Italian. This creamy pasta punctuated with tender asparagus, crisp sweet peppers, and tiny baby squash is the essence of that welcome season.

INGREDIENTS

- 14 ounces fresh asparagus spears
- 8 ounces packaged dried rotini or gemelli pasta (about 2½ cups)
- 1 cup mixed sweet pepper chunks from salad bar or 1 large red or yellow sweet pepper, cut into 1-inch pieces
- 1 cup halved baby pattypan squash or sliced yellow summer squash
- 1 10-ounce container refrigerated light alfredo sauce
- 2 tablespoons snipped fresh tarragon or thyme
- ¼ teaspoon crushed red pepper

Start to finish: 20 minutes

DIRECTIONS

1. Snap off and discard woody bases from asparagus. Bias-slice asparagus into 1-inch-long pieces (about 1½ cups).

2. Cook pasta according to package directions, adding asparagus, sweet pepper, and squash to pasta for the last 3 minutes of cooking; drain. Return pasta and vegetables to hot pan.

3. Meanwhile, in a small saucepan combine alfredo sauce, tarragon or thyme, and crushed red pepper. Cook and stir over medium heat about 5 minutes or until mixture is heated through. Pour over pasta and vegetables; toss gently to coat. Makes 4 servings.

Rotini and gemelli
are two types of spiral pasta. Rotini or corkscrew macaroni are about 1½-inch-long spirals and come in plain, whole wheat, or tricolor versions. Gemelli or rope macaroni are 1½-inch pieces that look like two ropes of spaghetti twisted together.

NUTRITION FACTS PER SERVING:

421 calories
12 g total fat
6 g saturated fat
31 mg cholesterol
622 mg sodium
66 g carbohydrate
2 g fiber
15 g protein

pasta with three cheeses

Cream cheese, Parmesan cheese, and your choice of Gouda, Edam, havarti, fontina, cheddar, or Swiss cheese make up the flavor-rich sauce.

INGREDIENTS

- 10 ounces packaged dried medium shell macaroni or rotini
- 2 cups frozen loose-pack cauliflower, broccoli, and carrots or other vegetable combination
- 1 cup milk
- 1 3-ounce package cream cheese, cut up
- ¼ teaspoon coarsely ground black pepper
- ¾ cup shredded Gouda, Edam, havarti, fontina, cheddar, or Swiss cheese (3 ounces)
- ¼ cup grated Parmesan cheese Grated Parmesan cheese (optional)

Start to finish: 30 minutes

Spend a few extra minutes putting away groceries, and you'll save a great deal of time before dinner.

Chill cans of fruits, vegetables, or meats for salads so they're ready when you need them.

Divide rolls, muffins, and breads into meal-size portions before freezing. At mealtime, simply thaw out as many as you need.

Stack individual ground meat patties, steaks, or chops between two layers of waxed paper. Slip them into a freezer bag. Seal, label, and freeze. To use, remove the number of pieces you need.

DIRECTIONS

1. In a large saucepan cook shell macaroni or rotini according to package directions, except add the frozen vegetables for the last 5 minutes of cooking. Drain.

2. In the hot saucepan combine milk, cream cheese, and pepper. Cook and stir over low heat until cheese is melted.

3. Return macaroni mixture to saucepan. Toss to coat with cream cheese mixture. Gently stir in the shredded cheese and the ¼ cup Parmesan cheese. Transfer to a serving bowl. If desired, sprinkle with additional Parmesan cheese. Makes 4 servings.

NUTRITION FACTS PER SERVING:

598 calories
25 g total fat
14 g saturated fat
86 mg cholesterol
596 mg sodium
66 g carbohydrate
3 g fiber
28 g protein

pasta and peas au gratin

Another time, try bite-size pieces of fresh asparagus instead of the peas. Simply add them to the pasta for the last 3 to 4 minutes of cooking time.

INGREDIENTS

- 1 9-ounce package refrigerated cheese-filled tortellini or cheese-filled ravioli
- 1 cup frozen peas
- 2 tablespoons all-purpose flour
- ⅛ teaspoon pepper
- 1 cup half-and-half, light cream, or milk
- 1 14-ounce can chunky tomatoes with garlic and spices
- 2 tablespoons shredded Parmesan cheese

Start to finish: 15 minutes

DIRECTIONS

1. In a large saucepan cook tortellini or ravioli according to package directions, except add peas for the last 1 minute of cooking. Drain. Return pasta mixture to the hot saucepan.

2. Meanwhile, in a medium saucepan stir together flour and pepper. Gradually stir in half-and-half, light cream, or milk. Cook and stir over medium heat until thickened and bubbly. Cook and stir for 1 minute more. Gradually stir in the undrained tomatoes. Pour over pasta. Toss to coat. Sprinkle with Parmesan cheese. Makes 4 servings.

This hearty main dish also makes a company-special side dish to serve with roasts, steaks, or chops. Simply dish up 8 servings instead of 4 and add an edible flower or a sprig of fresh herb for garnish.

NUTRITION FACTS PER SERVING:

433 calories
15 g total fat
5 g saturated fat
25 mg cholesterol
1,098 mg sodium
55 g carbohydrate
1 g fiber
18 g protein

187

spaghetti with vegetarian sauce bolognese

The cereal in the sauce creates a texture that is remarkably similar to ground meat. Serve it as you would regular spaghetti—with hot, crusty bread.

INGREDIENTS

- 8 ounces packaged dried spaghetti
- 1 tablespoon olive oil
- ½ cup finely chopped carrot
- ½ cup thinly sliced celery
- 1 medium onion, finely chopped (½ cup)
- ½ teaspoon dried oregano, crushed
- ¼ teaspoon pepper
- 1½ teaspoons bottled minced garlic or 3 cloves garlic, minced
- ¾ cup Grape Nuts cereal
- 1 14½-ounce can Italian-style stewed tomatoes
- 1 8-ounce can tomato sauce
- ¼ to ½ cup water

- 1 tablespoon olive oil
- Grated Parmesan or Romano cheese (optional)
- Fresh oregano (optional)

To make this sauce ahead,

prepare as directed, except cool completely. Transfer to a freezer container; seal, label, and freeze for up to 2 months. To serve, transfer the frozen sauce to a heavy saucepan. Add 1 to 2 tablespoons water. Cook, covered, over low heat 20 to 25 minutes or just until bubbly, stirring occasionally. Serve as directed.

Start to finish: 25 minutes

DIRECTIONS

1. Cook spaghetti according to package directions. Meanwhile, in a medium saucepan heat 1 tablespoon olive oil over medium-high heat. Add carrot, celery, onion, dried oregano, and pepper; cook until onion is tender. Add garlic; cook for 1 minute more. Stir in the cereal. Add the undrained tomatoes, tomato sauce, and desired amount of the water. Bring to boiling; reduce heat. Cover and simmer for 5 to 10 minutes or until desired consistency.

2. Drain the cooked pasta. Toss pasta with 1 tablespoon olive oil. Divide the hot pasta among 4 dinner plates. Spoon sauce over. If desired, sprinkle with the Parmesan or Romano cheese and garnish with fresh oregano. Makes 4 servings.

NUTRITION FACTS PER SERVING:

416 calories
8 g total fat
1 g saturated fat
0 mg cholesterol
907 mg sodium
76 g carbohydrate
3 g fiber
12 g protein

roasted red pepper sauce over tortellini

For leisurely dining, start in the fast lane by taking advantage of ready-to-use roasted peppers and tortellini. Then slow down and enjoy the delectable result.

INGREDIENTS

- 1   9-ounce package refrigerated or frozen cheese-filled tortellini or meat-filled tortellini
- 1   12-ounce jar roasted red sweet peppers, drained
- 1   medium onion, chopped (½ cup)
- 1½ teaspoons bottled minced garlic or 3 cloves garlic, minced
- 1   tablespoon margarine or butter
- 2   teaspoons snipped fresh thyme or ½ teaspoon dried thyme, crushed
- 2   teaspoons snipped fresh oregano or ¼ teaspoon dried oregano, crushed
- 1   teaspoon sugar
      Fresh herb sprigs (optional)

Start to finish: 20 minutes

DIRECTIONS

1. Cook tortellini according to package directions; drain. Return to saucepan.

2. Meanwhile, place roasted sweet peppers in a food processor bowl. Cover and process until smooth. Set aside.

3. For sauce, in a medium saucepan cook the onion and garlic in hot margarine or butter until tender. Add pureed peppers, thyme, oregano, and sugar. Cook and stir until heated through. Pour sauce over pasta; toss to coat. Transfer to a warm serving dish. If desired, garnish with fresh herbs. Makes 3 servings.

This herb-accented sauce is equally tasty spooned over grilled chicken or broiled fish. Sprinkle with a little crumbled farmer's or feta cheese for extra zing.

NUTRITION FACTS PER SERVING:

343 calories
15 g total fat
4 g saturated fat
75 mg cholesterol
298 mg sodium
40 g carbohydrate
2 g fiber
14 g protein

189

angel hair with asparagus, tomatoes, and fresh basil

This light and elegant dish goes from the grocery bag to the table in about 20 minutes.

INGREDIENTS

- 1 pound fresh asparagus spears
- 4 cloves garlic, thinly sliced
- ¼ teaspoon pepper
- 1 tablespoon olive oil
- 6 medium plum (Roma) tomatoes, seeded and chopped (2¼ cups)
- ¼ cup dry white wine
- ¼ teaspoon salt
- 1 tablespoon butter
- 1 9-ounce package refrigerated angel hair pasta
- ¼ cup shredded fresh basil

Butter helps to bind the sauce in this dish. Because margarine does not have all the same properties as butter, it isn't an effective substitute.

Start to finish: 20 minutes

DIRECTIONS

1. Snap off and discard woody bases from asparagus. Remove the tips; set aside. Bias-slice the remaining portions of asparagus spears into 1- to 1½-inch-long pieces; set aside.

2. In a large skillet cook and stir garlic and pepper in hot oil over medium heat for 1 minute. Add the tomatoes; cook for 2 minutes more, stirring often. Add the asparagus pieces, wine, and salt to the mixture in the skillet. Cook, uncovered, for 3 minutes. Add the asparagus tips; cook, uncovered, for 1 minute more. Add butter and stir until melted.

3. Meanwhile, cook the pasta according to package directions. Drain pasta; return to pan. Add asparagus mixture and basil to pasta, tossing to coat. Makes 3 servings.

NUTRITION FACTS PER SERVING:

- 484 calories
- 11 g total fat
- 3 g saturated fat
- 10 mg cholesterol
- 238 mg sodium
- 81 g carbohydrate
- 4 g fiber
- 15 g protein

INGREDIENTS

- 8 ounces packaged dried mostaccioli or penne pasta
- ¼ cup pine nuts or chopped almonds
- ¼ cup grated Parmesan cheese
- 1 teaspoon bottled minced garlic or 2 cloves garlic, minced
- 2 cups loosely packed fresh basil leaves, chopped
- ¼ cup olive oil
- 1½ pounds tomatoes, peeled, seeded, and cut into chunks
- ½ teaspoon salt
- ⅛ teaspoon pepper
  Fresh basil (optional)

pasta and sicilian tomato sauce

The no-cook convenience of this sauce, coupled with the tantalizing flavor blend of garlic, basil, Parmesan cheese, and pine nuts, makes this recipe one you'll want to serve time and again.

Start to finish: 20 minutes

DIRECTIONS

1. Cook the mostaccioli or penne pasta according to package directions. Drain and keep warm.

2. Meanwhile, for sauce, in a food processor bowl combine the pine nuts or almonds, cheese, and garlic. Cover and process until chopped. Add about half of the basil and all of the oil. Cover and process until the basil is chopped, stopping the machine occasionally to scrape the sides. Add the remaining basil and repeat. Add the tomatoes and process with several on/off turns. (The tomatoes should remain chunky. If the mixture is too smooth, add some chopped fresh tomato.) Stir in the salt and pepper.

3. Serve sauce over hot pasta. If desired, garnish with additional fresh basil. Makes 4 servings.

Be sure to use a food processor for this chunky sauce; a blender doesn't achieve the right consistency. If you prefer a warm sauce, pour it into a saucepan and heat through.

NUTRITION FACTS PER SERVING:

459 calories
22 g total fat
4 g saturated fat
5 mg cholesterol
400 mg sodium
55 g carbohydrate
3 g fiber
14 g protein

italian three-bean and rice skillet

Red beans, lima beans, and green beans are a tasty trio in this basil-accented skillet meal.

INGREDIENTS

1 15- to 15½-ounce can small red beans or red kidney beans, rinsed and drained

1 14½-ounce can Italian-style stewed tomatoes

1 cup vegetable broth or chicken broth

¾ cup quick-cooking brown rice

½ of a 10-ounce package frozen baby lima beans

½ of a 9-ounce package frozen cut green beans

½ teaspoon dried basil, crushed, or dried Italian seasoning, crushed

1 cup meatless spaghetti sauce

2 ounces thinly sliced mozzarella cheese or ¼ cup grated Parmesan cheese (optional)

Get meals on the table faster

by following these tips:

• Purchase food in the form called for (for example, shredded cheese or boned chicken breasts).

• Make turning on the oven or broiler (or starting the grill) your first cooking step.

• Overlap preparation steps. While waiting for water to boil, start chopping vegetables, opening cans, or mixing a filling.

• Measure liquids in an extra-large glass measuring cup. Then, rather than using a bowl, add the other ingredients to the cup and mix.

• Select a baking dish that doubles as a serving dish.

Prep time: 15 minutes
Cooking time: 15 minutes

DIRECTIONS

1. In a large skillet combine red beans or kidney beans, undrained tomatoes, broth, rice, lima beans, green beans, and basil or Italian seasoning. Bring to boiling; reduce heat. Cover and simmer about 15 minutes or until rice is tender.

2. Stir in spaghetti sauce. Heat through. If desired, top with mozzarella or Parmesan cheese. Makes 4 servings.

NUTRITION FACTS PER SERVING:

259 calories
4 g total fat
0 g saturated fat
0 mg cholesterol
1,103 mg sodium
50 g carbohydrate
10 g fiber
14 g protein

mixed bean and portobello ragoût

Ragoût is simply a thick, savory stew of French origin. This healthy, meatless ragoût features three kinds of beans, Cajun-style tomatoes, and mushrooms. Serve it with crusty bread.

INGREDIENTS

1   10-ounce package frozen baby lima beans

1   cup fresh green beans cut into 1-inch-long pieces

1½ cups sliced and halved fresh portobello mushrooms or sliced button mushrooms (about 4 ounces)

1   tablespoon olive oil

1   tablespoon cold water

2   teaspoons cornstarch

1   14½-ounce can Cajun- or Italian-style stewed tomatoes

1   cup canned garbanzo beans, rinsed and drained

Start to finish: 20 minutes

DIRECTIONS

1. Cook lima beans and green beans in lightly salted water according to lima bean package directions; drain.

2. Meanwhile, in a large skillet cook mushrooms in hot oil over medium heat for 5 minutes, stirring occasionally. Combine water and cornstarch; stir into mushrooms. Stir in undrained tomatoes and garbanzo beans. Cook and stir until thickened and bubbly. Cook and stir for 2 minutes more. Stir in lima and green beans; heat through. Makes 4 servings.

NUTRITION FACTS PER SERVING:

214 calories
5 g total fat
1 g saturated fat
0 mg cholesterol
528 mg sodium
36 g carbohydrate
10 g fiber
10 g protein

Portobellos are meaty, oversize brown mushrooms with an Italian-sounding name, rich flavor, and dense texture. You can use them sliced as in this recipe or grill or broil them whole to serve as an appetizer. To prepare the mushrooms, rinse them lightly, then gently dry them with paper towels. Never soak the mushrooms because soaking ruins their texture. Because the stems are woody, remove and discard them.

193

veggie skillet

For a zestier flavor, use 1 cup tomato sauce and 1 cup salsa in place of the spaghetti sauce.

INGREDIENTS

- 3 cups frozen loose-pack diced hash brown potatoes with onions and peppers
- 2 tablespoons cooking oil
- 2 cups meatless spaghetti sauce with mushrooms or Italian cooking sauce
- 1 cup frozen loose-pack peas and carrots
- 1 cup frozen loose-pack whole kernel corn
- ½ cup shredded cheddar cheese or mozzarella cheese (2 ounces)

Make kitchen chores a breeze with these timesaving utensils:

- Kitchen shears—to cut dried fruit, fresh herbs, canned tomatoes, and pizza.
- Vegetable peeler—to easily peel potatoes, apples, and cucumbers. It is also handy for cutting chocolate curls or strips of citrus peel for garnish.
- Egg slicer—to slice hard-cooked eggs, mushrooms, and small cooked potatoes.
- Melon baller—to hollow out vegetables and fruits for stuffing, to pit peaches or plums, as well as to make melon balls.

Start to finish: 20 minutes

DIRECTIONS

1. In a large skillet cook potatoes in hot oil over medium heat for 6 to 8 minutes or until nearly tender, stirring occasionally.

2. Stir spaghetti sauce or Italian cooking sauce, peas and carrots, and corn into the potatoes in the skillet. Bring to boiling; reduce heat. Cover and simmer for 5 to 7 minutes or until vegetables are tender. Sprinkle with cheese. Let stand, covered, about 1 minute or until cheese starts to melt. Makes 4 servings.

NUTRITION FACTS PER SERVING:

406 calories
21 g total fat
6 g saturated fat
20 mg cholesterol
742 mg sodium
49 g carbohydrate
5 g fiber
10 g protein

polenta with fresh tomato sauce

Making polenta the traditional way requires a strong stirring hand and plenty of time for cooking, chilling, and slicing. This easy version serves up medallions of polenta in just minutes. They're wonderfully crisp on the outside, creamy on the inside, and scrumptious served over a rosemary-olive tomato sauce.

INGREDIENTS

- 4 teaspoons olive oil
- ½ teaspoon bottled minced garlic or 1 clove garlic, minced
- 6 plum (Roma) tomatoes, coarsely chopped (about 2 cups)
- ¼ cup pitted halved kalamata olives or sliced pitted ripe olives
- 2 teaspoons snipped fresh rosemary or 2 tablespoons snipped fresh thyme
- Salt
- Pepper
- 1 16-ounce package prepared polenta
- ½ cup shredded smoked Gouda or Swiss cheese (2 ounces)

Start to finish: 20 minutes

DIRECTIONS

1. For sauce, in a medium saucepan heat 2 teaspoons of the oil and the garlic over medium heat. Add tomatoes; cook for 2 minutes. Stir in olives and rosemary or thyme. Bring to boiling; reduce heat. Simmer, uncovered, for 8 minutes, stirring occasionally. Season to taste with salt and pepper.

2. Meanwhile, cut polenta into 8 slices. In a large nonstick skillet or on a griddle heat the remaining oil over medium heat. Add polenta; cook about 6 minutes or until golden brown, turning once. Sprinkle with cheese. Spoon sauce onto 4 dinner plates. Serve polenta slices on sauce. Makes 4 servings.

NUTRITION FACTS PER SERVING:

- 226 calories
- 10 g total fat
- 3 g saturated fat
- 16 mg cholesterol
- 608 mg sodium
- 27 g carbohydrate
- 5 g fiber
- 8 g protein

Fresh herbs turn ordinary dishes into extraordinary ones. Some herbs—typically those with a sturdier constitution such as rosemary, bay leaf, and sage—are good for long-simmering or roasting. More delicate fresh herbs—such as basil, coriander, dill, and oregano—are best added shortly before the end of cooking. To substitute dried herbs for fresh, start by using one-third the amount of fresh herb called for in a recipe. (If a recipe uses 1 tablespoon fresh herb, add 1 teaspoon dried. Stronger herbs, such as rosemary or tarragon, may require only ½ teaspoon.)

pasta-fruit salad

This refreshing salad might surprise you as a main dish, but the pasta, cheese, and nuts team up to provide plenty of protein.

INGREDIENTS

- 4 ounces packaged dried ruffle pasta, medium shell macaroni, or rotini
- 1 16-ounce can apricot halves in light syrup or one 16-ounce can peach slices in light syrup, drained
- 1 8-ounce can pineapple tidbits (juice pack) or one 11-ounce can mandarin orange sections, drained
- 1 cup seedless red or green grapes, halved
- ¾ cup shredded cheddar cheese (3 ounces)
- ¼ cup broken pecans or walnuts
- ½ of an 8-ounce container vanilla yogurt
- 1 tablespoon frozen orange juice concentrate
- ⅛ teaspoon ground nutmeg
   Lettuce leaves

Keep cans of the apricot halves or peach slices and pineapple tidbits or mandarin orange sections on hand in the refrigerator to give the salad a head start on chilling. To quick-chill the salad, place the fruit-pasta mixture in the freezer while you prepare the dressing. (Don't leave it in the freezer longer than 30 minutes.)

Start to finish: 30 minutes

DIRECTIONS

1. Cook pasta according to package directions. Drain. Rinse with cold water. Drain again.

2. Meanwhile, cut up apricot halves or peach slices. In a large bowl toss together apricots or peaches, pineapple tidbits or orange sections, grapes, cheese, and pecans or walnuts. Add pasta. Toss to mix. Place in freezer until serving time (up to 30 minutes).

3. For dressing, stir together yogurt, orange juice concentrate, and nutmeg. Add dressing to pasta mixture; toss to coat. Line 4 salad plates with lettuce leaves. Divide salad among lettuce-lined plates. Makes 4 servings.

NUTRITION FACTS PER SERVING:

411 calories
13 g total fat
5 g saturated fat
24 mg cholesterol
163 mg sodium
65 g carbohydrate
3 g fiber
12 g protein

fontina and melon salad

Put the "lazy" back in Sundays. Organize brunch around this fruit-and-cheese pasta salad served in cantaloupe shells and made in a flash with bottled poppy seed dressing. Accompany with mimosas (equal parts champagne and orange juice), crisp bread sticks, creamy purchased pudding for dessert, and the Sunday paper.

INGREDIENTS

- 1½ cups packaged dried large bow ties (about 6 ounces)
- 2 cups cantaloupe and/or honeydew melon chunks
- 1 cup cubed fontina or Swiss cheese (4 ounces)
- ⅓ cup bottled fat-free poppy seed salad dressing
- 1 to 2 tablespoons snipped fresh mint
- 2 cups watercress, stems removed
- 4 cantaloupe shell halves (optional)
- Watercress (optional)

Start to finish: 25 minutes

DIRECTIONS

1. Cook pasta according to package directions; drain. Rinse with cold water. Drain again.

2. In a large bowl toss together pasta, 2 cups cantaloupe, and cheese. Combine salad dressing and mint; pour over pasta mixture, tossing gently to coat. (If desired, cover the salad and chill in the refrigerator for up to 24 hours.)

3. To serve, stir the 2 cups watercress into pasta mixture. If desired, serve salad in cantaloupe shell halves and garnish with additional watercress. Makes 4 servings.

Watercress has small, round, dark green leaves and a lively flavor with a peppery tang. It's usually sold in small bunches. Choose healthy-looking bright green leaves. When you get it home, wrap the watercress in a damp paper towel and refrigerate in a plastic bag for up to 2 days.

NUTRITION FACTS PER SERVING:

- 319 calories
- 11 g total fat
- 6 g saturated fat
- 73 mg cholesterol
- 309 mg sodium
- 41 g carbohydrate
- 1 g fiber
- 14 g protein

197

italian mozzarella salad

A simple stir-together dressing seasoned with basil, mustard, and garlic complements the vegetables and cheese in this refreshing salad. For variety, use whatever tomatoes you happen to have on hand. A combination of regular and cherry tomatoes is especially attractive.

INGREDIENTS

1   15-ounce can black beans or garbanzo beans, rinsed and drained

1   15-ounce can butter beans or great northern beans, rinsed and drained

1   small cucumber, quartered lengthwise and sliced (1 cup)

2   red and/or yellow tomatoes, cut into thin wedges

2   green onions, thinly sliced (¼ cup)

1   recipe Basil Dressing (see recipe, below) or ½ cup bottled oil and vinegar salad dressing

8   ounces round- or log-shaped fresh mozzarella or part-skim scamorze

Fresh basil (optional)

Start to finish: 20 minutes

It's worth seeking out

Italian markets, good cheese shops, and well-stocked gourmet delis to find fresh mozzarella. It is much softer, moister, and more elastic than the solid mozzarella used on pizza. In Italy, it's often served sliced in tomato salads or with fresh fruit for dessert. A similar Italian cheese is scamorze (also spelled scamorza or scamorzo) that's often aged and smoked, but also eaten fresh when young, like mozzarella.

DIRECTIONS

1. In large bowl combine beans, cucumber, tomatoes, and green onions. Add Basil Dressing; toss lightly to coat. Cut cheese into thin slices; gently toss with bean mixture. If desired, garnish with fresh basil. Makes 4 servings.

Basil Dressing: In a screw-top jar combine ¼ cup red wine vinegar; ¼ cup olive oil or salad oil; 1 tablespoon snipped fresh basil or 1 teaspoon dried basil, crushed; 1 teaspoon Dijon-style mustard; ¼ teaspoon crushed red pepper; and ½ teaspoon bottled minced garlic or 1 clove garlic, minced. Cover and shake well. If desired, chill in the refrigerator for up to 2 days.

NUTRITION FACTS PER SERVING:

434 calories
23 g total fat
8 g saturated fat
32 mg cholesterol
919 mg sodium
37 g carbohydrate
6 g fiber
27 g protein

198

mexican fiesta salad

Prepare this creamy chilled salad in the morning and look forward to a hearty, corn-and-bean-studded treat all day. Lime and cilantro infuse the sour cream dressing.

INGREDIENTS

- 2 cups packaged dried penne or rotini
- ½ cup frozen loose-pack whole kernel corn
- ½ cup light dairy sour cream
- ⅓ cup mild or medium chunky salsa
- 1 tablespoon snipped fresh cilantro
- 1 tablespoon lime juice
- 1 15-ounce can black beans, rinsed and drained
- 3 medium plum (Roma) tomatoes, chopped (about 1 cup)
- 1 medium zucchini, chopped (about 1 cup)
- ½ cup shredded sharp cheddar cheese (2 ounces)

Start to finish: 30 minutes

DIRECTIONS

1. Cook pasta according to package directions, adding the corn for the last 5 minutes of cooking. Drain pasta and corn. Rinse with cold water. Drain again.

2. Meanwhile, for dressing, in a small bowl stir together sour cream, salsa, cilantro, and lime juice. Set aside.

3. In a large bowl combine pasta mixture, black beans, tomatoes, zucchini, and cheese. Pour dressing over pasta mixture. Toss lightly to coat. Serve immediately or, if desired, cover and chill in the refrigerator for up to 24 hours. Makes 4 servings.

The dressing may stiffen up

when chilled. If it does, stir in a tablespoon or two of milk to make it the consistency you like.

NUTRITION FACTS PER SERVING:

- 373 calories
- 9 g total fat
- 4 g saturated fat
- 19 mg cholesterol
- 470 mg sodium
- 61 g carbohydrate
- 7 g fiber
- 20 g protein

199

grilled vegetable salad with garlic dressing

Vegetables, sweet and smoky from the grill, give pasta and cheese a jolt of flavor and color. To streamline the preparation even more, do the grilling ahead, and store the savory dressing in the refrigerator.

INGREDIENTS

2 red and/or yellow sweet peppers

2 Japanese eggplants, halved lengthwise

2 medium zucchini or yellow summer squash, halved lengthwise, or 8 to 10 yellow sunburst or pattypan squash

1 tablespoon olive oil

2 cups packaged dried tortiglioni or rigatoni

1 recipe Roasted Garlic Dressing (see recipe, below)

¾ cup cubed fontina cheese (3 ounces)

1 to 2 tablespoons snipped fresh Italian parsley or parsley

Fresh Italian parsley sprigs (optional)

If you're using sunburst or pattypan squash, precook the squash for 3 minutes in a small amount of boiling water before grilling.

Start to finish: 25 minutes

DIRECTIONS

1. Halve sweet peppers lengthwise; remove and discard stems, seeds, and membranes. Brush sweet peppers, eggplants, and zucchini with oil. To grill, place vegetables on the grill rack directly over medium-hot coals. Grill, uncovered, for 8 to 12 minutes or until vegetables are tender, turning occasionally. Remove vegetables from grill; cool slightly. Cut vegetables into 1-inch pieces.

2. Meanwhile, cook pasta according to package directions; drain. Rinse with cold water. Drain again.

3. In a large bowl combine pasta and grilled vegetables. Pour Roasted Garlic Dressing over salad. Toss lightly to coat. Stir in cheese; sprinkle with snipped parsley. If desired, garnish with parsley sprigs. Makes 4 servings.

Roasted Garlic Dressing: In a screw-top jar combine 3 tablespoons balsamic vinegar or red wine vinegar, 2 tablespoons olive oil, 1 tablespoon water, 1 teaspoon bottled roasted minced garlic, ¼ teaspoon salt, and ¼ teaspoon pepper. Cover and shake well.

NUTRITION FACTS PER SERVING:

369 calories
19 g total fat
6 g saturated fat
61 mg cholesterol
317 mg sodium
40 g carbohydrate
5 g fiber
12 g protein

rice 'n' bean tostadas

Quick-cooking brown rice, canned chili beans, shredded cheese, and a package of mixed salad greens make easy work of these tostadas.

INGREDIENTS

- 1½ cups water
- 1½ cups quick-cooking brown rice
- 1 medium onion, chopped (½ cup)
- 1 15-ounce can chili beans with chili gravy
- 1 8-ounce can whole kernel corn, drained
- 4 9- to 10-inch flour tortillas
- 3 cups torn mixed salad greens
- ½ cup shredded cheddar cheese (2 ounces)
- ¼ cup dairy sour cream
- 1 medium tomato, chopped (⅔ cup)

Quick-cooking brown rice is fast because it already has been cooked, then dehydrated. When you prepare it at home, you're really just putting the water back.

Prep time: 20 minutes
Baking time: 10 minutes

DIRECTIONS

1. In a large saucepan bring water to boiling. Stir in rice and onion. Return to boiling; reduce heat. Cover and simmer for 5 minutes. Remove from heat. Stir. Cover and let stand for 5 minutes. Stir undrained chili beans and corn into rice mixture. Heat through.

2. Meanwhile, place tortillas on a large baking sheet, overlapping as necessary. Bake in a 400° oven about 10 minutes or until tortillas begin to brown around the edges.

3. Place each tortilla on a dinner plate. Top tortillas with salad greens and the rice-bean mixture. Sprinkle with cheddar cheese. Serve with sour cream and chopped tomato. Makes 4 servings.

NUTRITION FACTS PER SERVING:

512 calories
14 g total fat
6 g saturated fat
21 mg cholesterol
735 mg sodium
81 g carbohydrate
9 g fiber
19 g protein

chickpea pita pockets

Packed in a pita, this grape, spinach, and garbanzo bean combo makes a satisfying meatless meal.

INGREDIENTS

1   15-ounce can garbanzo beans, rinsed and drained

1   cup shredded fresh spinach or lettuce

⅔   cup seedless grapes, halved

½   cup finely chopped red sweet pepper

⅓   cup thinly sliced celery

¼   cup finely chopped onion

¼   cup mayonnaise or salad dressing

2   tablespoons poppy seed salad dressing or desired creamy salad dressing

4   pita bread rounds, split in half crosswise

½   cup finely shredded Swiss cheese (2 ounces)

Garbanzo beans,

sometimes called chickpeas, are round, beige beans that stay slightly firm even when cooked. They have a mild, nutty flavor and often are used in Mediterranean and Mexican cooking. Look for them in the bean or Mexican food sections of your supermarket.

Start to finish: 20 minutes

DIRECTIONS

1. In a large bowl combine garbanzo beans, spinach or lettuce, grapes, red sweet pepper, celery, and onion.

2. In a small bowl stir together mayonnaise or salad dressing and poppy seed dressing or desired dressing. Add to garbanzo bean mixture, stirring until combined. Spoon into pita bread halves. Top with cheese. Makes 4 servings.

NUTRITION FACTS PER SERVING:

476 calories
21 g total fat
5 g saturated fat
21 mg cholesterol
857 mg sodium
58 g carbohydrate
6 g fiber
15 g protein

grilled vegetable sandwiches

A bun's worth of grilled veggies graduates from ho-hum to hurrah with a slathering of Easy Cumin Mayo.

INGREDIENTS

1   small eggplant, cut lengthwise into ½-inch slices

1   medium zucchini, cut lengthwise into ¼-inch slices

1   medium yellow summer squash, cut lengthwise into ¼-inch slices

1   medium red sweet pepper, seeded and cut into ½-inch strips

1   small onion, cut into ½-inch slices

⅓   cup olive oil

4   poppy seed kaiser rolls, split

¼   cup Easy Cumin Mayo (see recipe, below)

Start to finish: 30 minutes

DIRECTIONS

1. Brush the vegetables with some of the olive oil. Place onion slices on a long metal skewer. Grill the onion over medium coals for 5 minutes. Add remaining vegetables and grill for 12 to 15 minutes more or until vegetables are tender, turning once. (If some vegetables cook more quickly than others, remove and keep warm.) (Or, to broil, place half of the vegetables on the rack of a broiler pan. Broil 3 to 4 inches from heat 12 to 15 minutes or until vegetables are tender, turning once. Remove vegetables; keep warm. Repeat with remaining vegetables. Toast rolls under broiler about 1 minute.)

2. Brush split sides of rolls with remaining olive oil. Grill rolls, split sides down, 1 minute or until toasted. Layer vegetables on bottom halves of rolls. Top vegetables on each sandwich with 1 tablespoon Easy Cumin Mayo; cover with roll tops. Makes 4 servings.

Easy Cumin Mayo: In a bowl stir together 1 cup mayonnaise; 2 tablespoons lime juice; ½ teaspoon bottled minced garlic or 1 clove garlic, minced; and 1 teaspoon cumin seed, crushed.

NUTRITION FACTS PER SERVING:

465 calories
32 g total fat
4 g saturated fat
8 mg cholesterol
393 mg sodium
40 g carbohydrate
3 g fiber
7 g protein

italian vegetable melt

In the summertime, make this garden-fresh sandwich with just-picked vegetables. Try different vegetables, such as yellow summer squash, colorful sweet peppers, fennel, and kohlrabi.

INGREDIENTS

- 2 individual French or Italian loaves (6 to 7 inches long)
- 2 tablespoons clear Italian salad dressing
- ½ small onion, thinly sliced
- ½ small zucchini, halved lengthwise and sliced
- ½ small green sweet pepper, cut into thin strips
- ½ teaspoon bottled minced garlic or 1 clove garlic, minced
- 1 medium tomato, seeded and chopped
- 1½ cups shredded provolone or mozzarella cheese (6 ounces)
- 2 tablespoons grated Parmesan cheese

For a cool and carefree dessert, set up a sundae bar. Put out bowls of chopped nuts, fresh fruits, granola, chocolate topping, and whipped cream to spoon over vanilla or another favorite ice cream.

Start to finish: 15 minutes

DIRECTIONS

1. Split bread in half horizontally. Place halves on baking sheet, cut sides up. Set aside.

2. Pour salad dressing into a 10-inch skillet. Preheat the salad dressing. Add onion, zucchini, green pepper, and garlic. Stir-fry for 3 to 5 minutes or until crisp-tender. Stir in tomato. Sprinkle half of the provolone or mozzarella cheese on bread halves. Spoon vegetable mixture on cheese; sprinkle with remaining provolone or mozzarella cheese and the Parmesan cheese.

3. Broil 3 to 4 inches from the heat about 2 minutes or until cheese melts. Serve immediately. Makes 4 servings.

NUTRITION FACTS PER SERVING:

374 calories
18 g total fat
9 g saturated fat
32 mg cholesterol
836 mg sodium
35 g carbohydrate
1 g fiber
18 g protein

INGREDIENTS

- ¾ cup finely chopped broccoli
- ¼ cup shredded carrot
- 2 green onions, sliced (¼ cup)
- 2 tablespoons water
- 6 6-inch flour tortillas
- 1 teaspoon cooking oil
- 1 8-ounce package shredded
  cheddar or Monterey Jack
  cheese with jalapeño peppers
- Dairy sour cream (optional)
- Sliced green onion (optional)
- Sliced pitted ripe olives
  (optional)
- Salsa (optional)

vegetable quesadillas

The next time the occasion calls for a celebration, throw a Mexican fiesta. Serve these colorful tortilla fold-overs as appetizers instead of as a main dish. Simply cut quesadillas into wedges to make 6 servings.

Prep time: 20 minutes
Baking time: 6 minutes

DIRECTIONS

1. In a 1-quart microwave-safe casserole combine the broccoli, carrot, the 2 green onions, and water. Micro-cook, covered, on 100% power (high) for 2 to 4 minutes or until vegetables are crisp-tender. Drain.

2. Brush one side of 3 tortillas with some of the oil. Place tortillas, oiled side down, on a baking sheet. Top with the cheese, vegetable mixture, and remaining tortillas. Brush tops with remaining oil. Bake in a 450° oven about 6 minutes or until light brown.

3. To serve, cut each tortilla into wedges. If desired, serve with sour cream, additional green onion, olives, and salsa. Makes 3 servings.

NUTRITION FACTS PER SERVING:

499 calories
30 g total fat
17 g saturated fat
80 mg cholesterol
728 mg sodium
32 g carbohydrate
1 g fiber
24 g protein

Mix together a

Mock Tequila Sunrise to go along with the Southwest flavors of the quesadilla. In a small pitcher combine 2 cups orange juice, 1 cup apricot nectar, and 3 tablespoons lemon juice. Pour over ice in glasses. Slowly add 1 to 2 teaspoons grenadine syrup to each glass, then stir. Garnish with lime wedges.

Pizza Burgers
See recipe, page 214

kids'
favorites

introduce your kids to the kitchen

Kids who help cook are usually kids who eat well. Allowing children to help out in the kitchen encourages them to try new foods—especially those they help to make. Here are some hints for how kids can help with the recipes not only in this chapter but other favorites as well.

- **Encourage kids to help plan menus.** When you include their favorite foods, chances are your kids will be eager to help with the cooking.

- **Set guidelines.** Children as young as 3 years old can participate in cooking activities. Let them know you're glad to have their assistance. But also impress upon them that they always should have an adult around for safety's sake.

  Six-year-olds who can read may be able to use a microwave oven or toaster oven with your help. Start them with easy tasks such as defrosting hot dog buns and heating frankfurters or canned spaghetti.

  Once you're confident your youngsters can use appliances safely, store utensils within their easy reach. In the case of the microwave oven, keep aluminum foil and metal utensils away from young hands.

- **Stress organization.** Before cooking, pull out all the needed ingredients and keep a trash can and damp sponge nearby for easy cleanup.

- **Encourage good habits.** Start by washing hands with soap and water. Tie back long hair. Cover clothing with a large shirt or an apron. Then give kids their own work space. Give children a table knife for cutting, or for those 7 years old or older, your smallest paring knife.

- **Choose the best recipes.** Salads and sandwiches are fun dishes for kids to make. Young ones can tear the lettuce and toss the ingredients.

  Snack dips go together easily. At the same time, you can show your children how to cut up and enjoy vegetable and fruit dippers.

  Younger children (ages 5 and under) will enjoy stirring up a batter while you measure ingredients, so recipes for one-bowl cakes, muffins, cookies, or brownies work well. Later you can teach your children techniques such as separating eggs or kneading bread dough.

- **Work step by step.** To ensure their success, help your children follow recipes exactly. Go through each step, using the appropriate utensils.

INGREDIENTS

6 ounces packaged dried elbow macaroni or rotini (corkscrew macaroni) (about 1½ cups)

¾ pound lean ground beef, pork, or turkey

1 15-ounce can tomato sauce

1 14½-ounce can stewed tomatoes or Mexican-style stewed tomatoes

4 ounces American or sharp American cheese, cut into small cubes

1 tablespoon chili powder

Shredded Parmesan cheese

zippy beef, mac, and cheese

The whole family will love this fast-fixin' one-dish meal.

Prep time: 20 minutes
Cooking time: 6 minutes

DIRECTIONS

1. In a 3-quart saucepan cook pasta according to package directions, except do not add salt.

2. Meanwhile, in a 10-inch skillet cook ground meat until no pink remains. Drain off fat.

3. Drain pasta; return it to the saucepan. Stir in cooked meat, tomato sauce, undrained stewed tomatoes, American cheese, and chili powder. Heat and stir over medium heat about 6 to 8 minutes or until heated through. Sprinkle Parmesan cheese on top of each serving. Makes 4 servings.

For a fresh, pretty salad, peel and cut up oranges and cut jicama into strips; arrange on a lettuce leaf and drizzle with an oil-and-vinegar dressing.

NUTRITION FACTS PER SERVING:

342 calories
15 g total fat
7 g saturated fat
55 mg cholesterol
957 mg sodium
32 g carbohydrate
2 g fiber
20 g protein

easy shepherd's pie

Frozen mashed potatoes make this hearty skillet supper extra-easy.

INGREDIENTS

1   28-ounce package frozen mashed potatoes

1¾ cups milk

1   10-ounce package (2 cups) frozen mixed vegetables

1   pound ground beef, ground raw turkey, or ground raw chicken

¼   cup water

1   teaspoon dried minced onion

1   10¾-ounce can condensed tomato soup or one 10¾-ounce can reduced-sodium condensed tomato soup

1   teaspoon Worcestershire sauce

¼   teaspoon dried thyme, crushed

½   cup shredded cheddar cheese (2 ounces)

This skillet meal is so easy that older kids can prepare it with minimal help from you. If your kids aren't old enough to handle cooking on the range top, let them prepare a tossed salad using packaged salad greens and bottled dressing.

Start to finish: 25 minutes

DIRECTIONS

1. Prepare the potatoes according to package directions using 4 cups of the frozen potatoes and the milk. Meanwhile, run cold water over frozen mixed vegetables to separate.

2. In a large skillet cook ground beef, turkey, or chicken over medium-high heat until no pink remains. Drain off fat.

3. Stir in vegetables, water, and onion. Bring to boiling; reduce heat. Cover and simmer for 5 to 10 minutes or until vegetables are tender. Stir in soup, Worcestershire sauce, and thyme. Return to boiling. Drop potatoes in mounds on top of the hot mixture. Sprinkle with cheese. Reduce heat. Cover and simmer about 5 minutes more or until heated through. Makes 6 servings.

NUTRITION FACTS PER SERVING:

342 calories
16 g total fat
7 g saturated fat
62 mg cholesterol
541 mg sodium
30 g carbohydrate
1 g fiber
19 g protein

shapely sandwiches

The little ones at your house will love cutting out their favorite shapes and then eating them. Let them choose the type of cream cheese they prefer. Plain, flavored with pineapple, or flavored with chive and onion all work well.

INGREDIENTS

- 2 to 4 slices wheat and/or rye bread
- 1 or 2 slices lunch meat (bologna, ham, turkey, or turkey ham)
- 2 to 3 tablespoons tub cream cheese
- 1 or 2 tablespoons chopped walnuts, pecans, almonds, raisins, or mixed dried fruit
- Raisins (optional)
- Additional wheat or rye bread (optional)

Start to finish: 10 minutes

DIRECTIONS

1. Using 2½- or 3-inch cookie cutters, cut shapes from both the 2 to 4 slices bread and meat. Layer the bread shapes, cream cheese, 1 or 2 tablespoons nuts or fruit, and meat to form sandwiches.

2. If desired, decorate the sandwiches with additional raisins or bread cutouts, attaching with additional cream cheese. Makes 1 or 2 servings.

NUTRITION FACTS PER SERVING:

327 calories
20 g total fat
7 g saturated fat
31 mg cholesterol
627 mg sodium
28 g carbohydrate
3 g fiber
11 g protein

Use up the bread scraps by making Crunchy Treats:

Tear the remaining bread into bite-size pieces (about 1¾ cups). Melt 1 tablespoon butter in a small skillet. Remove from heat. Stir in 1 tablespoon grated Parmesan cheese and a dash of garlic powder. Spread the cubes in an 8×8×2-inch baking pan. Drizzle butter mixture over the bread; toss to coat. Bake, uncovered, in a 350° oven about 15 minutes or until browned and crisp, stirring the mixture once. Cool. Serve as a snack or sprinkle onto tossed salads or soups.

211

barbecued beef sandwiches

Slices of cheese top saucy beef strips in these robust sandwiches. Please a tender palate by using regular Monterey Jack cheese rather than cheese with jalapeños.

INGREDIENTS

¾ pound beef sirloin steak or beef top round steak, cut 1 inch thick

1 medium onion, sliced and separated into rings

1 tablespoon cooking oil

⅔ cup bottled barbecue sauce

1 teaspoon lemon juice or vinegar

4 hoagie buns, split and toasted

3 slices Monterey Jack cheese with jalapeño peppers or Monterey Jack cheese, quartered

If your family likes their barbecue really fiery, use a hot-style barbecue sauce.

Start to finish: 20 minutes

DIRECTIONS

1. Trim any separable fat from beef. Cut beef into bite-size strips.

2. In a large skillet cook onion in hot oil over medium-high heat about 3 minutes or until tender. Add beef strips. Cook and stir for 2 to 3 minutes or to desired doneness.

3. Stir in barbecue sauce and lemon juice or vinegar. Cook over medium heat until heated through, stirring occasionally. Spoon beef mixture onto hoagie bun bottoms. Top with cheese and then bun tops. Makes 4 servings.

NUTRITION FACTS PER SERVING:

689 calories
22 g total fat
9 g saturated fat
76 mg cholesterol
1,257 mg sodium
82 g carbohydrate
4 g fiber
37 g protein

INGREDIENTS

- 1 pound lean ground beef
- ½ cup chopped green sweet pepper
- 1 small onion, chopped
- 1 8-ounce can tomato sauce
- ½ cup bottled barbecue sauce
- 1 cup packaged shredded cabbage with carrot (coleslaw mix)
- 6 toasted hamburger buns, corn tortillas, or baked potatoes

snappy joes

This versatile beef-and-vegetable combo tastes equally good in hamburger buns, piled onto tortillas, or ladled over baked potatoes.

Prep time: 15 minutes
Cooking time: 10 minutes

DIRECTIONS

1. In a large skillet cook the ground beef, green pepper, and onion for 4 to 5 minutes or until no pink remains in beef. Drain off fat.

2. Stir in the tomato sauce, barbecue sauce, and cabbage with carrot. Bring to boiling; reduce heat. Simmer, uncovered, for 10 minutes. Spoon about ½ cup meat mixture onto each bun or over tortillas or potatoes. Makes 6 servings.

On the side,

serve baby carrots or crisp pasta chips. Serve the veggies and chips with this easy dip: Beat together equal amounts of reduced-fat cream cheese (Neufchâtel) and light dairy sour cream. Season with your favorite herb, such as basil, dill, or oregano.

NUTRITION FACTS PER SERVING:

277 calories
8 g total fat
3 g saturated fat
43 mg cholesterol
710 mg sodium
29 g carbohydrate
2 g fiber
21 g protein

213

pizza burgers

The beef is lean and the cheese is light, but the flavor comes on like a real heavyweight in the kid-pleasing burger arena.

INGREDIENTS

1 egg
¼ cup rolled oats
2 tablespoons catsup
¾ teaspoon dried Italian seasoning, crushed
¼ teaspoon garlic powder
¼ teaspoon onion powder
¼ teaspoon salt
¾ pound lean ground beef
4 ounces reduced-fat mozzarella cheese, sliced

Lettuce leaves (optional)
4 whole wheat buns or kaiser rolls, split and toasted
Tomato slices (optional)
Catsup or other condiments (optional)

To toast the buns for these juicy burgers, place bun halves, split sides up, on the unheated rack of a broiler pan. Broil 3 to 4 inches from heat just until golden (1 to 2 minutes). Check the buns frequently to prevent burning.

Prep time: 15 minutes
Broiling time: 13 minutes

DIRECTIONS

1. In a medium bowl stir together the egg, oats, 2 tablespoons catsup, dried Italian seasoning, garlic powder, onion powder, and salt. Add ground beef; mix well. Shape mixture into four ¾-inch-thick patties.

2. Place patties on the unheated rack of a broiler pan. Broil 3 to 4 inches from heat for 12 to 14 minutes or until well-done, turning once. Top with cheese; broil about 1 minute more or until cheese is melted.

3. If desired, place lettuce on bottoms of toasted buns or rolls. Top with hot pizza burgers. If desired, add tomato slices and additional catsup or other condiments. Makes 4 servings.

NUTRITION FACTS PER SERVING:

370 calories
15 g total fat
7 g saturated fat
122 mg cholesterol
711 mg sodium
28 g carbohydrate
3 g fiber
30 g protein

INGREDIENTS

- 1 green sweet pepper, cut into bite-size strips
- 1 small onion, sliced and separated into rings
- 1 tablespoon olive oil or cooking oil
- 1 tablespoon Dijon-style mustard or coarse brown mustard
- ½ teaspoon caraway seed, crushed
- 1 12-inch Italian bread shell (Boboli)
- 6 ounces cooked ham, cut into thin strips
- 1 cup cherry tomatoes, halved
- 1 cup shredded Swiss cheese (4 ounces)

ham and swiss pizza

In this simple recipe, traditional sandwich ingredients reconfigure into a family-pleasing pizza.

Prep time: 20 minutes
Baking time: 8 minutes

DIRECTIONS

1. In a large skillet cook green pepper and onion in hot oil for 2 to 3 minutes or until tender. Stir in mustard and caraway seed. Set aside.

2. Place bread shell on a lightly greased baking sheet. Top with pepper-onion mixture, ham, and cherry tomatoes. Sprinkle with Swiss cheese. Bake in a 400° oven about 8 minutes or until cheese melts and pizza is heated through. Makes 4 servings.

For bite-size pieces in no time, cut the pepper into strips about ¼ inch thick. Then gather the pepper strips together and cut them into lengths 1 to 1½ inches long.

NUTRITION FACTS PER SERVING:

- 529 calories
- 21 g total fat
- 6 g saturated fat
- 53 mg cholesterol
- 1,305 mg sodium
- 57 g carbohydrate
- 3 g fiber
- 31 g protein

easy sweet-and-sour chicken

Skip the hassle of deep-frying chicken pieces—use this recipe and start with frozen chicken chunks instead.

INGREDIENTS

- 1 10-ounce package frozen breaded cooked chicken chunks
- 1½ cups quick-cooking rice
- 1 8-ounce can pineapple tidbits (juice pack)
- 1 large red or green sweet pepper, cut into 1-inch pieces
- ¼ cup red wine vinegar or vinegar
- 3 tablespoons sugar
- 2 tablespoons cornstarch
- 2 tablespoons soy sauce
- ½ teaspoon instant chicken bouillon granules
- 1 8-ounce can sliced water chestnuts, drained
- Fresh parsley sprigs (optional)

Vegetables are crisp-tender

when they are still slightly firm to the bite. They shouldn't be soft or mushy.

Start to finish: 20 minutes

DIRECTIONS

1. Bake frozen chicken chunks according to package directions. Prepare quick-cooking rice according to package directions.

2. Meanwhile, drain pineapple, reserving juice. Add enough water to reserved juice to make 1½ cups liquid. Pour pineapple juice mixture into a medium saucepan. Add sweet pepper. Bring to boiling; reduce heat. Cover and simmer for 1 to 2 minutes or until pepper is crisp-tender.

3. Stir together vinegar, sugar, cornstarch, soy sauce, and bouillon granules. Stir into mixture in the saucepan. Cook and stir over medium heat until thickened and bubbly. Cook and stir for 2 minutes more. Gently stir in chicken chunks, pineapple tidbits, and water chestnuts. Heat through.

4. Serve chicken mixture over hot cooked rice. If desired, garnish with parsley sprigs. Makes 4 servings.

NUTRITION FACTS PER SERVING:

434 calories
10 g total fat
1 g saturated fat
67 mg cholesterol
1,142 mg sodium
68 g carbohydrate
1 g fiber
19 g protein

INGREDIENTS

- ¾ pound skinless, boneless chicken breasts
- 1 tablespoon cooking oil
- 1 15-ounce jar salsa
- ¾ cup chicken broth
- ½ cup chopped green sweet pepper
- ¼ cup sliced pitted ripe olives (optional)
- 1 cup quick-cooking rice
- ½ cup shredded cheddar cheese or Monterey Jack cheese (2 ounces)
- Green sweet pepper strips (optional)

southwest chicken skillet

Complete the meal with purchased or homemade corn muffins and a tossed salad.

Start to finish: 20 minutes

DIRECTIONS

1. Rinse chicken breasts; pat dry. Cut chicken into 1-inch pieces.

2. In a large skillet cook and stir chicken pieces in hot oil over medium heat for 2 to 3 minutes or until no longer pink.

3. Stir in salsa, chicken broth, chopped sweet pepper, and olives (if desired). Bring to boiling. Stir in rice. Remove from heat. Sprinkle with cheese. Cover and let stand about 5 minutes or until rice is tender. If desired, garnish with green pepper strips. Makes 4 servings.

To speed up this quick skillet dinner even more, look for frozen chopped green pepper in your supermarket's freezer case and buy a small can of sliced ripe olives instead of slicing your own.

NUTRITION FACTS PER SERVING:

344 calories
15 g total fat
4 g saturated fat
60 mg cholesterol
1,012 mg sodium
34 g carbohydrate
0 g fiber
25 g protein

217

easy salmon pasta

To save time, the pasta and vegetables cook together in the same saucepan.

INGREDIENTS

- 2 cups frozen loose-pack mixed vegetables or one 10-ounce package frozen mixed vegetables
- 1½ cups rotini (corkscrew macaroni)
- 2 green onions, sliced (¼ cup)
- 1 10¾-ounce can condensed cheddar cheese soup
- ½ cup milk
- ½ teaspoon dried dillweed
- ¼ teaspoon dry mustard
- ⅛ teaspoon pepper
- 2 6¾-ounce cans skinless, boneless salmon or two 6½-ounce cans tuna, drained
- Fresh dill (optional)

If you can't find skinless, boneless salmon, use regular salmon and remove the skin, bones, and cartilage.

Start to finish: 25 minutes

DIRECTIONS

1. In a large saucepan cook frozen vegetables, pasta, and green onions in boiling water for 10 to 12 minutes or until pasta is just tender. Drain and return to saucepan.

2. Stir the soup, milk, dillweed, dry mustard, and pepper into pasta mixture. Gently fold in salmon or tuna. Cook over low heat until heated through. If desired, garnish with fresh dill. Makes 5 servings.

NUTRITION FACTS PER SERVING:

347 calories
9 g total fat
4 g saturated fat
56 mg cholesterol
827 mg sodium
41 g carbohydrate
1 g fiber
22 g protein

baked potato with santa fe chicken topper

Pricking the potatoes allows the steam that builds up during baking to escape and keeps the potatoes from bursting.

INGREDIENTS

- 4   6- to 8-ounce baking potatoes
- ¾   cup tomato sauce
- ½   cup salsa
- 1   cup cubed cooked chicken
- 1   8-ounce can whole kernel corn, drained
- 2   green onions, thinly sliced (¼ cup)
- ¼   cup shredded Colby and Monterey Jack cheese or Monterey Jack cheese with jalapeño peppers (2 ounces)

Start to finish: 20 minutes

DIRECTIONS

1. Scrub potatoes; pat dry. Prick potatoes with a fork. On a microwave-safe plate arrange potatoes in a spoke fashion. Microwave, uncovered, on 100% power (high) for 14 to 17 minutes or until tender, rearranging potatoes once. Let stand for 5 minutes. Using a hot pad, roll each potato on a hard surface to loosen skin. Cut a crisscross in top of each with a knife. Press in and up on ends.

2. Meanwhile, in a 1-quart saucepan combine tomato sauce and salsa; bring to boiling. In another saucepan combine chicken, corn, and green onions. Cook and stir until heated through.

3. Spoon the chicken mixture onto baked potatoes. Top with tomato sauce mixture and cheese. Makes 4 servings.

If you have more time, bake the potatoes in the oven. Prick potatoes with a fork. If desired, for soft skins, rub potatoes with shortening. Bake potatoes in a 425° oven for 40 to 60 minutes or until tender. Using a hot pad, roll each potato on a hard surface to loosen skin. Cut a crisscross in top of each with a knife. Press in and up on potato ends. Serve as directed at left.

NUTRITION FACTS PER SERVING:

377 calories
10 g total fat
4 g saturated fat
48 mg cholesterol
732 mg sodium
55 g carbohydrate
3 g fiber
21 g protein

219

parmesan-turkey sandwiches

A light crumb-and-cheese coating complements the turkey in this tantalizing sandwich.

INGREDIENTS

½ cup cornflake crumbs or crushed rich round crackers (about 12 crackers)

¼ cup grated Parmesan cheese

⅛ teaspoon garlic powder

⅛ teaspoon pepper

1 beaten egg

1 tablespoon water

4 turkey breast tenderloin steaks (about 1 pound total)

2 tablespoons margarine or butter

4 lettuce leaves

4 hoagie buns, split and toasted

¼ cup creamy Parmesan or creamy buttermilk ranch salad dressing

2 tomatoes, thinly sliced

Measure stick margarine

or butter the easy way by using the markings right on the wrapper. If your brand doesn't have the markings, simply remember that 1 stick is ½ cup, a half-stick is ¼ cup, and a quarter-stick is 2 tablespoons.

Prep time: 15 minutes
Cooking time: 8 minutes

DIRECTIONS

1. In a shallow dish stir together cornflake crumbs or crushed crackers, Parmesan cheese, garlic powder, and pepper. In another shallow dish beat together egg and water. Dip turkey steaks into egg mixture. Coat with the crumbs.

2. In a large skillet cook turkey in hot margarine or butter over medium heat for 8 to 10 minutes or until no longer pink, turning once.

3. Place lettuce on bottom halves of hoagie buns. Top with turkey, salad dressing, and tomato slices. Add bun tops. Makes 4 servings.

NUTRITION FACTS PER SERVING:

686 calories
21 g total fat
5 g saturated fat
112 mg cholesterol
1,177 mg sodium
83 g carbohydrate
5 g fiber
39 g protein

hot turkey sub sandwiches

Pair these hefty sandwiches with bowls of tomato soup.

INGREDIENTS

- 1 tablespoon olive oil
- 1 teaspoon dried basil, crushed
- ½ teaspoon bottled minced garlic or 1 clove garlic, minced, or ⅛ teaspoon garlic powder
- 1 8-ounce loaf or ½ of a 16-ounce loaf unsliced French bread
- 6 ounces sliced mozzarella cheese
- ¼ pound sliced smoked turkey
- 2 tablespoons sliced pitted ripe olives
- 2 tomatoes, thinly sliced
- ⅛ teaspoon coarsely ground black pepper

Prep time: 15 minutes
Baking time: 10 minutes

DIRECTIONS

1. In a small bowl stir together the olive oil, basil, and garlic or garlic powder. Split the French bread lengthwise. Use a spoon to hollow out the top half, leaving a ¾-inch-thick shell. Brush the cut sides of both bread halves with the olive oil mixture.

2. On the bottom half of the French bread, layer half of the mozzarella cheese, all of the smoked turkey, the olives, the remaining cheese, and the tomato slices. Sprinkle with pepper. Top with the bread top. Wrap in heavy-duty foil.

3. Bake in a 375° oven about 10 minutes or until heated through. Cut into 4 portions. Makes 4 servings.

NUTRITION FACTS PER SERVING:

335 calories
13 g total fat
5 g saturated fat
36 mg cholesterol
849 mg sodium
33 g carbohydrate
1 g fiber
22 g protein

221

fish sandwiches

When those hectic Saturdays roll around, serve the family these easy and economical sandwiches for lunch.

INGREDIENTS

- 4 frozen breaded fish fillets or patties (10 to 12 ounces total)
- 4 thin tomato slices
- ½ teaspoon dried basil, crushed
- ⅛ teaspoon pepper
- 4 ounces mozzarella, cheddar, Swiss, or American cheese, thinly sliced
- 2 tablespoons buttermilk ranch, creamy cucumber, or creamy Parmesan salad dressing
- 4 hamburger buns, split and toasted

Have the kids mix up coleslaw while you make the sandwiches. Use packaged shredded cabbage with carrot (coleslaw mix) and combine it with bottled coleslaw salad dressing.

Start to finish: 25 minutes

DIRECTIONS

1. Bake fish fillets or patties according to the package directions.

2. Top each fillet or patty with a tomato slice. Sprinkle each with basil and pepper. Top each with cheese. Return to the oven for 2 to 3 minutes or until cheese is melted.

3. Spread the salad dressing over the bottom halves of the buns. Top with fish and bun tops. Makes 4 servings.

NUTRITION FACTS PER SERVING:

444 calories
20 g total fat
6 g saturated fat
108 mg cholesterol
854 mg sodium
43 g carbohydrate
3 g fiber
23 g protein

INGREDIENTS

- 1   18-ounce roll refrigerated peanut butter cookie dough
- ½ cup semisweet chocolate pieces
- ½ cup peanut butter pieces
- ¾ cup tiny marshmallows
- ⅔ cup peanuts
- ½ cup miniature candy-coated semisweet chocolate pieces

peanut butter pizza

Is there a kid alive who doesn't wish to live on pizza? True, it's hard to improve on the pie's perfection, but adding peanut butter, another juvenile favorite, just might push pizza off the chart.

Prep time: 5 minutes
Baking time: 23 minutes

DIRECTIONS

1. Pat the refrigerated cookie dough evenly in ungreased 12- to 13-inch pizza pan. Bake in a 350° oven for 18 to 20 minutes or until golden brown. Remove from oven.

2. Sprinkle with chocolate pieces and peanut butter pieces. Let stand for 1 to 2 minutes or until softened. With spatula, spread melted pieces over crust.

3. Top with marshmallows, peanuts, and miniature candy pieces. Bake about 5 minutes more or until marshmallows are golden brown. Cool in pan on wire rack. Makes 12 servings.

NUTRITION FACTS PER SERVING:

355 calories
20 g total fat
4 g saturated fat
11 mg cholesterol
253 mg sodium
39 g carbohydrate
1 g fiber
8 g protein

To keep active little fingers occupied at a party or on a rainy day, let the children help you pat the dough into place.

saddlebag trail mix

Let the kids stir together a batch of this high-energy snack mix. It's perfect for hiking, biking, and anytime munching.

INGREDIENTS

- 2 cups raisins
- 2 cups dried banana chips
- 2 cups unsalted dry roasted peanuts
- 1 6-ounce package mixed dried fruit bits (1⅓ cups)

Whether it's a birthday party, holiday gathering, or a Valentine celebration, this easy-to-munch mix makes an ideal party favor. Simply pour some into decorated paper cups next to each guest's place at the table.

Start to finish: 5 minutes

DIRECTIONS

1. In a storage container combine the raisins, banana chips, peanuts, and fruit. Store in a cool, dry place for up to 1 week. (To tote, take the container or divide among small resealable plastic bags.) Makes about 7 cups (twenty-eight ¼-cup servings).

NUTRITION FACTS PER SERVING:

172 calories
9 g total fat
4 g saturated fat
0 mg cholesterol
6 mg sodium
22 g carbohydrate
1 g fiber
3 g protein

soda fountain favorites

Just like saddle shoes, the jukebox, and your favorite after-school hangout, these golden oldies are just too good to forget. What's more, your youngsters will enjoy them as much as you did. If they're thirsty, choose a fizzy cooler with a splash of flavored syrup. But when the kids are hungry for ice cream, let them hop on the fountain stool for a float, a soda, or a creamy malt.

- **Red River:** A stream of cherry syrup* flows through this classic fountain drink. In a tall glass stir a 12-ounce can of carbonated water or club soda into a couple of spoonfuls of cherry-flavored syrup. Cool it with ice cubes.

- **Cherry Phosphate:** A phosphate is like a Red River, only with a tart flavoring added, usually citric acid or lemon juice. In a tall glass stir a can of carbonated water or club soda into a spoonful or two of cherry syrup* and lemon juice. Plunk in some ice cubes.

- **Cherry Cola:** In a tall glass stir a can of cola into a splash of cherry syrup.* Add a few ice cubes and a couple of bright red maraschino cherries.

- **Root Beer Float:** Plop vanilla ice cream into root beer and watch it float. Start with a tall glass, and figure on 2 scoops of ice cream to a 12-ounce can of root beer.

- **Chocolate Soda:** A soda is a cross between a fizzy drink, a float, and a milk shake. In a tall, wide-mouthed glass stir some carbonated water or club soda into a couple of spoonfuls of chocolate-flavored syrup. Add a scoop of vanilla ice cream. Stir until the ice cream is almost melted. Add the rest of the can of soda to almost fill glass. Top with another scoop of ice cream.

- **Chocolate Malt:** This malt is so thick, you'll need a spoon to eat it. The malt flavor comes from malted milk powder. In a blender container combine 2 scoops of vanilla ice cream, ½ cup milk, a couple of spoonfuls of chocolate-flavored syrup, and a spoonful of malted milk powder. Cover and blend until smooth. Serve it in a tall glass.

*Note: Look for the cherry syrup needed for the Red River, Cherry Phosphate, and Cherry Cola near the ice-cream toppings or with the flavored syrups for coffee in your local supermarket.

Summer Vegetable Paella
See recipe, page 239

side dishes

seven-spice rice pilaf

The flavors of spinach, almonds, onions, and raisins are enhanced by a blend of sweet and savory spices.

INGREDIENTS

1 small onion, chopped (⅓ cup)
1 tablespoon cooking oil or olive oil
1 cup long grain rice
½ teaspoon ground cardamom
½ teaspoon paprika
¼ teaspoon ground coriander
¼ teaspoon ground cinnamon
¼ teaspoon ground cumin
¼ teaspoon pepper
⅛ teaspoon ground nutmeg
1 14½-ounce can vegetable broth
¼ cup water
1 cup chopped fresh spinach
¼ cup golden raisins
¼ cup sliced almonds
¼ to ½ teaspoon rose water (optional)
Small fresh spinach leaves (optional)

Rose water, a flavoring
made from rose petals, has both the taste and smell of the flower. It is often used in Middle Eastern, Indian, and Chinese cooking. Ask for it at your local pharmacy.

Prep time: 10 minutes
Cooking time: 20 minutes

DIRECTIONS

1. In a medium saucepan cook and stir onion in hot oil until tender. Stir in uncooked rice, cardamom, paprika, coriander, cinnamon, cumin, pepper, and nutmeg. Cook and stir over medium heat about 5 minutes or until rice is golden. Carefully add the vegetable broth and water. Bring to boiling; reduce heat. Cover and simmer for 15 minutes.

2. Remove from heat; let stand, covered, for 5 minutes. Stir in chopped spinach, golden raisins, and almonds. If desired, sprinkle with rose water and garnish with small spinach leaves. Makes 4 to 6 servings.

NUTRITION FACTS PER SERVING:

290 calories
9 g total fat
1 g saturated fat
0 mg cholesterol
437 mg sodium
51 g carbohydrate
2 g fiber
6 g protein

INGREDIENTS

- ¾ cup packaged dried orzo (rosamarina) pasta
- 1 pound fresh mushrooms (such as button, chanterelle, and/or shiitake), sliced
- ½ teaspoon bottled minced garlic or 1 clove garlic, minced
- 1 tablespoon margarine or butter
- 1 teaspoon cornstarch
- ¼ teaspoon salt
- ⅛ teaspoon pepper
- ½ of a 12-ounce can (¾ cup) evaporated fat-free milk
- ½ cup shredded fontina cheese (2 ounces)
- ¼ cup slivered almonds
- ¼ to ½ teaspoon dried tarragon, crushed
- 1 tablespoon snipped fresh chives

mushroom risotto

Quick-cooking orzo, also called rosamarina, makes this a speedy side dish. Serve it with poultry for a fast and flavorful meal.

Start to finish: 30 minutes

DIRECTIONS

1. Cook pasta according to package directions. Drain and keep warm.

2. Meanwhile, in a large skillet cook and stir mushrooms and garlic in hot margarine or butter over medium-high heat about 5 minutes or until tender and most of the liquid has evaporated; stir occasionally.

3. Stir in cornstarch, salt, and pepper. Stir in evaporated milk all at once. Cook and stir over medium heat until thickened and bubbly. Cook and stir for 1 minute more. Add fontina cheese, almonds, and tarragon; cook and stir until cheese is melted. Stir in cooked orzo.

4. Transfer to a serving bowl; sprinkle with snipped chives. Makes 4 to 6 servings.

NUTRITION FACTS PER SERVING:

322 calories
13 g total fat
4 g saturated fat
18 mg cholesterol
340 mg sodium
39 g carbohydrate
2 g fiber
16 g protein

spring herb rice

This recipe brings out the best in short grain rice by cooking it quickly, keeping ingredients simple, and pairing the rice with the freshest of the season's herbs.

INGREDIENTS

- 1¾   cups water
- 1   cup short grain rice
- 1   cup chopped onion
- 1   tablespoon olive oil
- 1   tablespoon margarine or butter
- 1   cup sliced celery
- 1   cup sliced fresh mushrooms
- ½   teaspoon salt
- ¼   teaspoon pepper
- 2   tablespoons snipped fresh herbs (such as basil, oregano, parsley, thyme, verbena, and/or lemon thyme)
- 1   teaspoon snipped fresh rosemary

Keep olive oil at its peak by storing it in a cool, dark place—it will stay fresh for up to a year. When you use it in a salad dressing that is chilled, the olive oil may solidify and the dressing may be too thick to pour immediately. This won't affect the flavor. Simply let the dressing stand at room temperature for 10 to 15 minutes, shake or mix it, and serve.

Start to finish: 30 minutes

DIRECTIONS

1. In a saucepan bring the water to boiling; stir in uncooked rice. Return to boiling; reduce heat. Cover and simmer about 15 minutes or until liquid is absorbed. Remove saucepan from heat; let rice stand, covered, for 5 minutes.

2. Meanwhile, in a large skillet cook and stir onion in hot oil and margarine or butter over medium heat for 3 minutes. Add celery, mushrooms, salt, and pepper. Cook and stir for 1 minute more or until vegetables are tender. Remove skillet from heat. Stir in cooked rice, desired fresh herbs, and rosemary just until combined. Makes 6 servings.

230

NUTRITION FACTS PER SERVING:

173 calories
4 g total fat
1 g saturated fat
0 mg cholesterol
224 mg sodium
30 g carbohydrate
1 g fiber
3 g protein

garden risotto

Slow cooking is the key to producing the creamy results in this classic Italian dish.

INGREDIENTS

- 1 cup Arborio rice or other short grain rice
- 2 tablespoons olive oil or cooking oil
- 1 teaspoon bottled minced garlic or 2 cloves garlic, minced
- 3¼ to 3½ cups reduced-sodium chicken broth or vegetable broth
- 1 cup shredded carrot
- ¼ cup thinly sliced green onions
- ¼ to ½ cup shredded Parmesan or Romano cheese
- 2 tablespoons snipped fresh basil
  Long, thin carrot curls (optional)
  Basil leaves (optional)

Start to finish: 30 minutes

DIRECTIONS

1. In a large saucepan cook and stir uncooked rice in hot oil over medium heat for 5 minutes. Add garlic; cook and stir 1 minute more.

2. Meanwhile, in a medium saucepan bring broth to boiling; reduce heat so broth is simmering. Slowly add 1 cup of the broth to the rice mixture (be careful of spattering); stir constantly. Cook and stir over medium heat until broth is absorbed (about 5 minutes).

3. Add 2 more cups of the broth, ½ cup at a time, stirring constantly until broth is absorbed. Stir in remaining broth, shredded carrot, and green onions. Cook and stir until rice is creamy and just tender. Stir in Parmesan or Romano cheese and snipped basil.

4. If desired, garnish with carrot curls and basil leaves. Makes 4 servings.

Short grain rices,
such as Arborio rice, have almost round grains and a high starch content that causes the rice to stick together. This quality makes short grain rice ideal for Oriental dishes that are eaten with chopsticks and for creamy risottos such as this one.

NUTRITION FACTS PER SERVING:

289 calories
10 g total fat
1 g saturated fat
5 mg cholesterol
611 mg sodium
42 g carbohydrate
1 g fiber
8 g protein

farfalle with spinach and mushrooms

If you're using spinach that hasn't been washed, be sure to rinse it well because very often it is sandy.

INGREDIENTS

- 6 ounces packaged dried farfalle pasta (bow ties) (3 cups)
- ¾ cup chopped onion
- 1 cup sliced fresh mushrooms (such as portobello, chanterelle, shiitake, and/or crimini)
- 1 teaspoon bottled minced garlic or 2 cloves garlic, minced
- 1 tablespoon margarine or butter
- 4 cups thinly sliced fresh spinach, or 2 cups thinly sliced fresh sorrel and 2 cups thinly sliced fresh spinach
- 1 teaspoon snipped fresh thyme
- ⅛ teaspoon pepper
- 1 tablespoon licorice liqueur (optional)
- 2 tablespoons finely shredded Parmesan cheese

How much pasta is enough?

When preparing pasta, plan on 1 to 1½ ounces of dried pasta per serving for a side-dish portion. As a main-dish serving, 2 to 3 ounces dried pasta (or about 4 ounces fresh) served with a hearty sauce provides a satisfying serving. A 4-ounce bundle of dried spaghetti is about the same diameter as a quarter.

Start to finish: 25 minutes

DIRECTIONS

1. Cook pasta according to package directions. Drain.

2. Meanwhile, in a large skillet cook and stir onion, mushrooms, and garlic in hot margarine or butter over medium heat for 2 to 3 minutes or until mushrooms are nearly tender. Stir in spinach or sorrel and spinach, thyme, and pepper; cook about 1 minute or until heated through and spinach is slightly wilted.

3. Stir in cooked pasta and, if desired, liqueur; toss gently to mix. Sprinkle with Parmesan cheese. Makes 4 servings.

NUTRITION FACTS PER SERVING:

214 calories
6 g total fat
1 g saturated fat
39 mg cholesterol
127 mg sodium
33 g carbohydrate
2 g fiber
9 g protein

INGREDIENTS

- 8 ounces assorted packaged dried pastas
- 2 tablespoons walnut oil or olive oil
- 2 tablespoons coarsely snipped mixed fresh herbs (such as sage, rosemary, and basil)
- ¼ teaspoon salt
- ¼ teaspoon coarsely ground black pepper

mixed pastas with fresh herbs

Use interesting pasta shapes in this simple recipe. Try shapes that have similar cooking times so you can cook them together. The pastas shown in the photo are trenne (*tren-NAY*) and red-pepper quadrelle (*kwah-DRELL-e*).

Start to finish: 20 minutes

DIRECTIONS

1. Cook pasta according to package directions. Drain. Toss the hot pasta with the oil, herbs, salt, and pepper. Makes 8 servings.

NUTRITION FACTS PER SERVING:

170 calories
7 g total fat
1 g saturated fat
0 mg cholesterol
67 mg sodium
22 g carbohydrate
0 g fiber
4 g protein

The distinctively nutty flavor of walnut oil is delicious in this simple pasta side dish, as well as in oil-and-vinegar salad dressings. Look for walnut oil in large supermarkets or specialty food shops.

linguine with mixed nuts and gorgonzola

When cooks say nuts are as good as gold, they aren't kidding. Early American settlers considered them to be such a valuable delicacy that they exchanged nuts for tools. Today nuts still add delicious crunch and flavor to everything from soups to desserts to pasta dishes like this one.

Refrigerated fresh pastas

are increasingly available in supermarket deli cases. Fresh pastas go better with lighter sauces (such as wine- or broth-based sauces) that don't overpower their subtle flavors. Use dried pastas for heavier sauces, such as cream-, meat-, or tomato-based sauces.

INGREDIENTS

1   9-ounce package refrigerated linguine or fettuccine
¾   cup chopped hazelnuts (filberts), pecans, and/or pine nuts
1   tablespoon butter
1   tablespoon olive oil
½   cup crumbled Gorgonzola or blue cheese (2 ounces)
¼   cup shredded Parmesan cheese (1 ounce)
2   tablespoons snipped fresh basil
    Fresh basil (optional)

Start to finish: 15 minutes

DIRECTIONS

1. Cook pasta according to package directions. Drain. Return to pan; keep warm.

2. Meanwhile, in a medium skillet cook the hazelnuts, pecans, or pine nuts in hot butter and olive oil until toasted and butter begins to brown, stirring frequently. Add nut mixture to pasta. Add the Gorgonzola or blue cheese, Parmesan cheese, and the snipped basil; toss gently to coat. If desired, garnish with fresh basil leaves. Makes 6 servings.

NUTRITION FACTS PER SERVING:

298 calories
19 g total fat
4 g saturated fat
23 mg cholesterol
212 mg sodium
25 g carbohydrate
1 g fiber
9 g protein

INGREDIENTS

- ¾ cup packaged dried orzo (rosamarina) pasta
- 4 ounces assorted fresh mushrooms (such as crimini, chanterelle, shiitake, or button), sliced or quartered
- 1 leek or 2 large green onions, chopped (about ⅓ cup)
- ½ teaspoon bottled minced garlic or 1 clove garlic, minced
- ¼ teaspoon pepper
- ⅛ teaspoon salt
- 1 tablespoon margarine or butter
- ¼ cup water

- ½ to 1 teaspoon snipped fresh marjoram or ¼ teaspoon dried marjoram, crushed
- ½ teaspoon instant beef or chicken bouillon granules
- Grated Romano cheese (optional)
- Fresh marjoram sprigs (optional)

orzo pasta with mushrooms and leeks

Enjoy this simple side dish with grilled or roasted beef or chicken.

Start to finish: 20 minutes

DIRECTIONS

1. Cook pasta according to package directions. Drain.

2. Meanwhile, in a large skillet cook mushrooms, leek or green onions, garlic, pepper, and salt in hot margarine or butter over medium-high heat for 5 minutes. Add water, snipped fresh or dried marjoram, and bouillon. Reduce heat; cook about 6 minutes or until liquid is almost absorbed. Toss the mushroom mixture with pasta. If desired, sprinkle with Romano cheese and garnish with marjoram sprigs. Makes 4 to 6 servings.

NUTRITION FACTS PER SERVING:

  167 calories
  4 g total fat
  2 g saturated fat
  8 mg cholesterol
  209 mg sodium
  29 g carbohydrate
  2 g fiber
  5 g protein

Many varieties of wild and cultivated

mushrooms—in all shapes, sizes, and flavors—are sold today. In Italy, crimini mushrooms (alias Italian brown or Roman mushrooms) are especially popular. They have the same shape as button mushrooms, but are light tan to dark brown in color. They also have a deeper, earthier flavor than button mushrooms.

235

moroccan-style stuffing

Take a stuffing mix from simple to sensational by adding flavor-packed dried fruits.

- 1 6-ounce package chicken-flavored stuffing mix
- 1 to 1¼ cups chicken broth
- 2 tablespoons margarine or butter
- ¾ cup snipped pitted prunes
- ¾ cup snipped dried apricots
- ½ cup dried cranberries
- ⅓ cup pine nuts or chopped almonds, toasted
- 2 tablespoons lemon juice
- 1 tablespoon snipped fresh mint or ½ teaspoon dried mint, crushed

You'll find dried cranberries in your supermarket's produce section. A 6-ounce package will yield about 1½ cups of berries. You can use them in all sorts of dishes as you would raisins. Once you've opened the package, wrap the fruit securely in an airtight plastic bag and store it in the refrigerator. Or, place the cranberries in a freezer bag and freeze for up to 6 months.

Start to finish: 20 minutes

DIRECTIONS

1. In a 2-quart saucepan combine the seasoning packet from stuffing mix, 1 cup of the broth, margarine or butter, prunes, apricots, and cranberries. Bring to boiling; reduce heat. Cover and simmer for 6 minutes. Remove from heat.

2. Stir in the stuffing mix, pine nuts or almonds, lemon juice, and mint. If necessary, stir in the remaining broth to moisten. Cover and let stand for 5 minutes. Before serving, fluff with fork. Makes 8 servings.

NUTRITION FACTS PER SERVING:

234 calories
7 g total fat
1 g saturated fat
11 mg cholesterol
499 mg sodium
40 g carbohydrate
2 g fiber
6 g protein

INGREDIENTS

¾ cup chopped onion

1 teaspoon bottled minced garlic
or 2 cloves garlic, minced

1 tablespoon cooking oil

½ teaspoon ground cumin

1 cup reduced-sodium chicken
broth

¾ cup frozen loose-pack peas

¾ cup coarsely chopped tomato or
¾ cup canned diced
tomatoes

2 tablespoons snipped fresh
cilantro or 2 teaspoons dried
cilantro, crushed

¾ cup quick-cooking couscous
Fresh cilantro sprigs (optional)

mexicana couscous

Quick couscous helps put this dish, reminiscent of
Spanish rice, on the table in no time.

Start to finish: 15 minutes

DIRECTIONS

1. In a medium saucepan
cook and stir onion and garlic
in hot oil over medium heat
until tender. Stir in cumin;
cook for 30 seconds.

2. Carefully add the broth,
peas, tomato, and snipped
fresh or dried cilantro. Bring
mixture to boiling. Stir in
couscous; remove from heat.
Cover and let stand for
5 minutes. Fluff with a fork.
If desired, garnish with
cilantro sprigs. Makes
6 servings.

NUTRITION FACTS PER SERVING:

134 calories
3 g total fat
0 g saturated fat
0 mg cholesterol
124 mg sodium
23 g carbohydrate
6 g fiber
4 g protein

**Couscous
is a** commercially produced
grain product that's shaped in tiny
beads. It's a staple of North African
cooking and can be used in recipes
or served as a side dish in place of
rice. You'll find it in the rice or
pasta section of the supermarket
or at specialty food stores.

237

caramelized sweet potatoes

Just like other potatoes, sweet potatoes can be baked, mashed, or hashed, but are sweetly sublime when sautéed with onions and brown sugar, as in this side dish.

INGREDIENTS

2 large red or white onions, cut into ¾-inch chunks

4 teaspoons margarine or butter

2 large sweet potatoes or yams, peeled and sliced ½ inch thick (about 1 pound)

¼ cup water

2 tablespoons brown sugar

¾ teaspoon snipped fresh rosemary or ¼ teaspoon dried rosemary, crushed

Fresh rosemary sprigs (optional)

Sweet potatoes and yams can be used interchangeably in most recipes. Yams are a tropically grown tuber with brownish skin and yellow to white starchy flesh. They are not widely available in the United States and many times, the vegetables labeled yams in supermarkets are a type of sweet potato.

Start to finish: 30 minutes

DIRECTIONS

1. In a large skillet cook onions in hot margarine or butter over medium-high heat for 3 to 4 minutes or until onions are nearly tender; stir frequently. Stir in sweet potatoes and water. Cover and cook over medium heat for 10 to 12 minutes or until sweet potatoes are nearly tender, stirring occasionally.

2. Uncover skillet; add brown sugar and the snipped fresh or dried rosemary. Cook, stirring gently, over medium-low heat for 4 to 5 minutes or until onions and sweet potatoes are glazed. If desired, garnish with fresh rosemary sprigs. Makes 4 servings.

NUTRITION FACTS PER SERVING:

 173 calories
4 g total fat
1 g saturated fat
0 mg cholesterol
57 mg sodium
33 g carbohydrate
4 g fiber
2 g protein

INGREDIENTS

- 1 6-ounce jar marinated artichoke hearts
- 1 large onion, cut into wedges
- 2 teaspoons bottled minced garlic or 4 cloves garlic, minced
- 2 14½-ounce cans (3½ cups total) reduced-sodium chicken broth or vegetable broth
- ⅓ cup water
- ½ teaspoon ground black pepper
- ¼ teaspoon ground saffron
- 2 cups green beans cut into 1-inch pieces
- 1 cup Arborio or long grain rice

- 2 fresh ears of corn, husked and cut crosswise into 2-inch pieces
- 2 medium zucchini, cut into ½-inch slices
- 1 medium red sweet pepper, cut into strips
- ½ teaspoon finely shredded lemon peel
- 1 15-ounce can garbanzo beans, drained

summer vegetable paella

Fresh corn, green beans, zucchini, and red sweet pepper add both color and flavor to this hearty rice and vegetable side dish.

Start to finish: 30 minutes

DIRECTIONS

1. Drain marinade from the artichokes into a 12-inch skillet; set artichokes aside. Heat marinade over medium heat. Add onion and garlic. Cook, stirring frequently, for 5 minutes. Add chicken or vegetable broth, water, black pepper, and saffron. Bring to boiling. Stir in green beans and uncooked rice. Return to boiling; reduce heat. Cover and simmer for 8 minutes.

2. Add corn, zucchini, sweet pepper, and lemon peel. Cover and cook for 7 to 8 minutes more or until vegetables and rice are tender. Stir in garbanzo beans and artichoke hearts; heat through. Makes 8 servings.

NUTRITION FACTS PER SERVING:

409 calories
6 g total fat
0 g saturated fat
1 mg cholesterol
1,125 mg sodium
79 g carbohydrate
8 g fiber
14 g protein

up-and-down biscuits

To eat these fun biscuits, peel away the cinnamon-spiced up-and-down layers one at a time.

INGREDIENTS

2   cups all-purpose flour
3   tablespoons sugar
4   teaspoons baking powder
½   teaspoon cream of tartar
½   teaspoon salt
½   cup shortening
⅔   cup milk
¼   cup margarine or butter, melted
¼   cup sugar
2   to 3 teaspoons ground cinnamon

Prep time: 20 minutes
Baking time: 10 minutes

DIRECTIONS

1. Grease twelve 2½-inch muffin cups; set aside. In a medium bowl mix flour, the 3 tablespoons sugar, baking powder, cream of tartar, and salt. Using a pastry blender, cut in shortening until mixture resembles coarse crumbs. Make a well in the center; add milk all at once. Stir just until the dough clings together.

2. On a lightly floured surface, knead dough gently 10 to 12 strokes. Divide dough in half. Roll out half of the dough to a 12×10-inch rectangle. Brush with half of the melted margarine or butter. Combine the ¼ cup sugar and cinnamon; sprinkle half over dough. Cut rectangle into five 12×2-inch strips. Stack the 5 strips on top of one another. Cut into six 2-inch squares. Place squares, cut sides down, in prepared muffin cups. Repeat with remaining dough, margarine or butter, and sugar mixture.

3. Bake in a 450° oven 10 to 12 minutes or until golden brown. Serve warm. Makes 12.

NUTRITION FACTS PER SERVING:

216 calories
13 g total fat
3 g saturated fat
1 mg cholesterol
262 mg sodium
23 g carbohydrate
1 g fiber
2 g protein

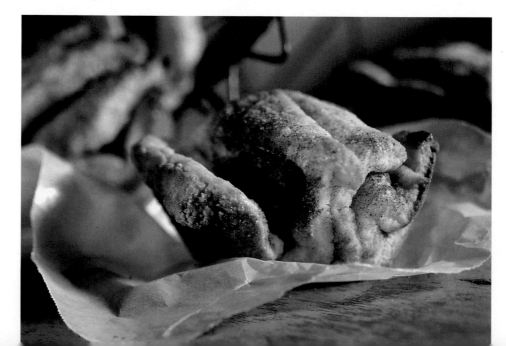

INGREDIENTS

- 1   cup all-purpose flour
- 1   cup yellow cornmeal
- ¼   cup sugar
- 1   tablespoon baking powder
- ¼   teaspoon salt
- ¼   to ½ teaspoon ground red pepper
- 2   eggs
- 1   cup milk
- ¼   cup margarine or butter, melted

- 1   cup shredded smoked cheddar cheese (4 ounces)
- Desired toppings (such as sunflower seed, poppy seed, sesame seed, pine nuts, thin strips of roasted red sweet peppers, or additional shredded smoked cheddar cheese)

smoked cheddar muffins

These savory corn-breadlike muffins pair perfectly with hearty soups and stews—especially chili.

Prep time: 10 minutes
Baking time: 12 minutes

DIRECTIONS

1. Grease twelve 2½-inch muffin cups; set aside. In a medium bowl combine the flour, cornmeal, sugar, baking powder, salt, and red pepper. In another bowl beat together eggs, milk, and melted margarine or butter. Add to flour mixture. Add the 1 cup shredded cheese and stir just until batter is smooth (do not overmix).

2. Spoon batter into prepared muffin cups, filling each almost full. Top with desired toppings. Bake in a 425° oven for 12 to 15 minutes or until golden brown. Cool in pan on a wire rack for 5 minutes. Remove from cups. Serve warm. Makes 12 muffins.

To tell when muffins are perfectly baked, check them after the minimum baking time listed in the recipe. They should have golden brown tops and a wooden toothpick inserted near the centers should come out clean.

NUTRITION FACTS PER SERVING:

193 calories
9 g total fat
3 g saturated fat
47 mg cholesterol
260 mg sodium
22 g carbohydrate
1 g fiber
6 g protein

241

green chili muffins

For a hearty breakfast or brunch, serve these tender muffins with Skillet Sausage and Potatoes (see recipe, page 44).

INGREDIENTS

- 2 cups all-purpose flour
- ¼ cup sugar
- 2 teaspoons baking powder
- ¼ to ½ teaspoon salt
- 2 slightly beaten eggs
- 1 cup milk
- ¼ cup margarine or butter, melted
- 1 4-ounce can diced green chili peppers, rinsed and drained

Ledges on the edges are those
unwanted rims around the edges of muffins. To get nicely rounded muffins without ledges, grease the muffin cups on the bottoms and only halfway up the sides, or use paper bake cups.

Prep time: 10 minutes
Baking time: 20 minutes

DIRECTIONS

1. Lightly grease ten to twelve 2½-inch muffin cups; set aside. In a small bowl combine the flour, sugar, baking powder, and salt. In another bowl combine the eggs, milk, melted margarine or butter, and green chili peppers. Add the flour mixture all at once to the egg mixture. Stir just until moistened (the batter will be lumpy).

2. Spoon batter into prepared muffin cups, filling each two-thirds full. Bake in a 400° oven for 20 to 25 minutes or until golden brown. Cool in pan on a wire rack for 5 minutes. Remove from cups. Serve warm. Makes 10 to 12 muffins.

Green Chili Muffins and Skillet Sausage and Potatoes (see recipe, page 44)

NUTRITION FACTS PER SERVING:

173 calories
6 g total fat
3 g saturated fat
57 mg cholesterol
229 mg sodium
24 g carbohydrate
1 g fiber
5 g protein

INGREDIENTS

- 2 cups torn romaine
- 2 cups coarsely shredded radicchio and/or Belgian endive
- 2 cups torn escarole
- 1 medium onion, thinly sliced and separated into rings
- 1 tablespoon sugar
- 3 tablespoons olive oil or salad oil
- 2 tablespoons pine nuts or slivered almonds
- 1 teaspoon bottled minced garlic or 2 cloves garlic, minced
- ¼ teaspoon dried tarragon, crushed

Toasted baguette slices (optional)
Freshly ground black pepper
Lemon wedges

warm winter salad

Serve this easy wilted salad as a companion to broiled fish and chicken. Keep your cooked entrée warm while you quickly toss together this fanciful medley.

Start to finish: 20 minutes

DIRECTIONS

1. In a large bowl toss together the romaine, radicchio and/or Belgian endive, and escarole; set aside. In a 10-inch skillet cook and stir onion and sugar in hot oil about 5 minutes or until onion is tender. Add pine nuts or almonds. Cook and stir for 1 to 2 minutes more or until nuts are toasted.

2. Add garlic, tarragon, and greens to skillet. Toss 30 to 60 seconds or just until greens are wilted (do not overcook). If desired, serve over baguette slices. Sprinkle with pepper. Pass lemon to squeeze over salad. Makes 4 servings.

NUTRITION FACTS PER SERVING:

151 calories
13 g total fat
2 g saturated fat
0 mg cholesterol
13 mg sodium
9 g carbohydrate
1 g fiber
3 g protein

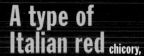

A type of Italian red chicory, radicchio is most commonly used in salads. Its brilliant ruby-red leaves have thick, white veins. When eaten alone, the leaves are quite bitter and peppery, but when mixed with other greens, they add a zesty accent. Choose heads with fresh, crisp leaves. The white core at the base should be firm and unblemished. To use, cut out and discard the core. Separate the leaves; rinse and dry well.

243

crimson greens and papaya salad

Coarsely ground papaya seeds add a peppery kick to the dressing in contrast to the soothing sweetness of the fresh fruit.

INGREDIENTS

- 1 large papaya
- 7 cups torn red-tip leaf lettuce and/or mixed salad greens
- 1 cup shredded radicchio
- 1 small red onion, thinly sliced and separated into rings
- ¼ cup snipped fresh cilantro
- 3 tablespoons salad oil
- 1 tablespoon toasted sesame oil*
- 2 tablespoons lemon juice
- 2 tablespoons rice wine vinegar or white wine vinegar
- 1 tablespoon sugar
- ⅛ teaspoon salt

Mixed baby greens are sometimes labeled mesclun in the store. This combination is a medley of young salad greens. The number and proportion of lettuces is seasonal and varied, but the mixture always features a variety of flavors, textures, and colors. Often mesclun includes arugula, dandelion greens, frisee, oak leaf, radicchio, and/or sorrel.

Start to finish: 25 minutes

DIRECTIONS

1. Peel, seed, and slice the papaya, reserving 1 tablespoon of the seeds for the dressing.

2. In a large salad bowl combine the papaya, leaf lettuce or mixed salad greens, radicchio, red onion, and cilantro; toss gently to mix.

3. For dressing, in a blender container or food processor bowl combine salad oil, sesame oil, lemon juice, vinegar, sugar, and salt. Cover and blend or process until smooth. Add the reserved papaya seeds and blend or process until the seeds are the consistency of coarsely ground pepper. Pour dressing over salad. Toss lightly to coat. Makes 8 servings.

*Note: If toasted sesame oil is unavailable, increase the salad oil to ¼ cup.

NUTRITION FACTS PER SERVING:

87 calories
7 g total fat
1 g saturated fat
0 mg cholesterol
40 mg sodium
6 g carbohydrate
1 g fiber
1 g protein

244

INGREDIENTS

- **3** cups packaged dried small pasta (such as penne, radiatore, corkscrew macaroni, and/or wagon wheel)
- **¼** cup olive oil
- **2** tablespoons balsamic vinegar or wine vinegar
- **½** teaspoon finely shredded lemon peel
- **2** tablespoons lemon juice
- **1** to 2 tablespoons sugar (optional)
- **1** tablespoon Dijon-style mustard
- **1** teaspoon snipped fresh basil or ¼ to ½ teaspoon dried basil, crushed
- **1** teaspoon snipped fresh thyme or ¼ to ½ teaspoon dried thyme, crushed
- **½** teaspoon snipped fresh marjoram or ¼ to ½ teaspoon dried marjoram, crushed
- **¼** teaspoon ground black pepper
- **2** yellow, red, and/or green sweet peppers, cut into thin strips
- **½** cup pitted green olives, drained and halved
- **½** cup thinly sliced green onions

pepper-olive pasta salad

A collage of shapes turns simple pasta salad into something extraordinary. Penne and radiatore pasta make a pleasing combination, but you can use whatever small pastas you happen to have in the pantry.

Start to finish: 25 minutes

DIRECTIONS

1. In a large saucepan cook the desired pasta according to package directions. Drain. Rinse with cold water; drain again. Set aside.

2. For dressing, in a screw-top jar combine olive oil, balsamic or wine vinegar, lemon peel, lemon juice, sugar (if desired), mustard, basil, thyme, marjoram, and black pepper. Cover and shake well to mix.

3. In a large salad bowl combine the pepper strips, olives, green onions, and pasta. Add dressing; toss gently to coat. Makes 8 to 10 servings.

The elegant yet simple lemon-mustard dressing used in this pasta salad is equally delicious served on mixed greens. Purchase your favorite combination of packaged salad greens, toss with the dressing, and sprinkle with a few toasted pecans. Enjoy!

NUTRITION FACTS PER SERVING:

193 calories
8 g total fat
1 g saturated fat
0 mg cholesterol
211 mg sodium
26 g carbohydrate
1 g fiber
4 g protein

crisp apple-rice salad

Next time you serve brown rice with a stir-fry, cook enough extra to chill for this intriguing salad.

INGREDIENTS

- 2 cups cooked brown and/or wild rice, chilled
- 2 cups chopped apple (about 2 medium)
- 1 cup thinly sliced celery
- ¼ cup shelled sunflower seeds
- ¼ cup dried currants
- 2 tablespoons balsamic vinegar
- 1 tablespoon olive oil
- 2 teaspoons honey
- 2 teaspoons brown mustard or Dijon-style mustard
- 2 teaspoons finely shredded orange peel
- ½ teaspoon bottled minced garlic or 1 clove garlic, minced
- ¼ teaspoon salt
- Radicchio (optional)
- Curly leaf lettuce (optional)

You can change the flavor of this salad

by the variety of apple you choose. Gala, Red Delicious, Golden Delicious, Fuji, and Jonagold apples all will add a rich, sweet accent. Cortland, Granny Smith, Jonathan, McIntosh, and Winesap will give the salad a hint of tangy tartness.

Start to finish: 20 minutes

DIRECTIONS

1. In a large salad bowl combine chilled rice, apple, celery, sunflower seeds, and currants. Set aside.

2. Stir together vinegar, oil, honey, mustard, orange peel, garlic, and salt. Drizzle over rice mixture, tossing to coat. If desired, serve on top of radicchio and curly leaf lettuce. Makes 6 servings.

Note: To make the salad ahead, prepare as directed, except do not add apple. Cover and chill in refrigerator up to 24 hours. Just before serving, chop apple and add to salad; toss. Serve as directed.

NUTRITION FACTS PER SERVING:

183 calories
6 g total fat
1 g saturated fat
0 mg cholesterol
133 mg sodium
30 g carbohydrate
3 g fiber
4 g protein

246

INGREDIENTS

- 1 **pink or red grapefruit**
- 1 **blood or navel orange**
- ¼ **cup salad oil**
- ½ **teaspoon finely shredded lemon peel**
- 2 **tablespoons lemon juice**
- 1 **teaspoon sugar**
- 2 **teaspoons Dijon-style mustard**
- ¼ **teaspoon pepper**
- 2 **cups thinly sliced Belgian endive**
- 2 **cups torn escarole**
- ½ **of a small jicama, peeled and cut into thin bite-size strips (about 1 cup)**

mixed citrus salad

Grapefruits, oranges, and lemons by the crateful shine in produce departments. While you're there, pick up fresh Belgian endive, escarole, and jicama to create this light and crisp side salad. Never tried jicama? It's crisp like a carrot and mildly sweet.

Start to finish: 20 minutes

DIRECTIONS

1. Peel and section grapefruit and orange, reserving any juices. Cover and set aside or chill in refrigerator until needed.

2. In a screw-top jar combine oil, lemon peel, lemon juice, sugar, mustard, pepper, and grapefruit and orange juices. Cover and shake well.

3. Place Belgian endive and escarole on salad plates.

Arrange grapefruit sections, orange sections, and jicama over greens; drizzle with dressing. Makes 4 to 6 servings.

NUTRITION FACTS PER SERVING:

191 calories
14 g total fat
2 g saturated fat
0 mg cholesterol
70 mg sodium
17 g carbohydrate
2 g fiber
2 g protein

To prepare the Belgian endive, pull apart the leaves to reveal the core. Use a knife to remove this bitter core. Thinly slice the remaining cone-shaped bunch of leaves crosswise.

caribbean slaw

As the temperature heats up, cool down with this refreshing fruit-and-vegetable slaw and one of your grilled poultry or fish favorites.

INGREDIENTS

2 tablespoons snipped fresh basil or 1 teaspoon dried basil, crushed

2 tablespoons snipped fresh mint or 1 teaspoon dried mint, crushed

2 tablespoons olive oil

2 tablespoons rice vinegar or white wine vinegar

2 teaspoons soy sauce

4 cups thinly sliced Napa cabbage (about ½ of a small head)

1 mango, peeled, pitted, and sliced; or 2 peaches or nectarines, pitted and sliced

1 large cucumber, peeled, seeded, and cut into pieces

1 small red sweet pepper, cut into thin bite-size strips

½ of a small red onion, quartered and thinly sliced

When ripe, mangoes should be fully colored (yellow or green with a tinge of red), smell fruity, and feel fairly firm when pressed. Since the meat holds tightly to the seed, remove the meat by cutting through the mango and sliding a sharp knife next to the seed along one side of the mango. Repeat on the other side of the seed, resulting in two large pieces. Then cut away any meat that remains around the seed. Remove the peel and slice.

Start to finish: 30 minutes

DIRECTIONS

1. For dressing, in a screw-top jar combine basil, mint, olive oil, vinegar, and soy sauce. Cover and shake dressing well. Set aside.

2. In a large bowl combine the cabbage; mango, peaches, or nectarines; cucumber; sweet pepper; and red onion. Add the dressing; toss gently to combine. Serve immediately. Makes 5 servings.

NUTRITION FACTS PER SERVING:

98 calories
6 g total fat
1 g saturated fat
0 mg cholesterol
145 mg sodium
12 g carbohydrate
2 g fiber
2 g protein

quick bread salad

In Italy, day-old bread is put to good use as a replacement for croutons. The large cubes of sourdough bread hold the dressing as croutons only wish they could.

INGREDIENTS

- ¼ cup olive oil
- 3 tablespoons red wine vinegar
- 3 tablespoons snipped fresh oregano
- ½ teaspoon sugar
- ¼ teaspoon salt
- ¼ teaspoon ground black pepper
- 4 ounces whole wheat sourdough or other country-style bread, cut into 1½-inch cubes
- ½ of a 10-ounce package (about 5 cups) purchased torn Italian-style mixed salad greens
- 1 medium tomato, cut into thin wedges
- ¼ cup halved yellow cherry tomatoes or yellow sweet pepper, cut into ½-inch pieces
- ½ cup Greek black olives or other olives

Start to finish: 20 minutes

DIRECTIONS

1. In a screw-top jar combine the olive oil, wine vinegar, oregano, sugar, salt, and black pepper. Cover tightly and shake well.

2. In a large salad bowl combine bread cubes, mixed greens, tomato wedges, yellow cherry tomatoes or sweet pepper, and olives. Add dressing; toss gently to combine. Serve immediately. Makes 6 servings.

Although Italian-style mixed greens may vary by brand, they usually are a combination of romaine lettuce and radicchio.

NUTRITION FACTS PER SERVING:

151 calories
11 g total fat
1 g saturated fat
0 mg cholesterol
238 mg sodium
13 g carbohydrate
1 g fiber
2 g protein

fresh vegetable-pasta salad

Serve this colorful pasta salad alongside broiled fish or chicken.

INGREDIENTS

- ¼ cup loosely packed fresh parsley sprigs
- 2 tablespoons salad oil
- 2 tablespoons wine vinegar
- 2 tablespoons water
- 1 to 2 cloves garlic
- ½ teaspoon dry mustard
- ¼ teaspoon salt
- ¼ teaspoon ground black pepper
- 4 ounces refrigerated linguine, cut into 4-inch-long pieces
- 1 large carrot, cut into thin bite-size strips
- 1 small turnip, cut into thin bite-size strips
- 1 small zucchini, cut into thin bite-size strips
- ½ cup chopped red sweet pepper
- ½ cup frozen loose-pack peas, thawed
- 2 ounces part-skim mozzarella, Gruyère, or Swiss cheese, cubed

If you prefer, substitute 2 ounces of dried linguine broken into pieces for the refrigerated linguine. Cook the dried linguine according to package directions, adding the carrot and turnip the last 3 to 4 minutes of cooking. Drain, rinse, and serve as at right.

Start to finish: 20 minutes

DIRECTIONS

1. For dressing, in a blender container or food processor bowl combine the parsley sprigs, salad oil, wine vinegar, water, garlic cloves, dry mustard, salt, and black pepper. Cover and blend or process until combined. Set aside.

2. In a large saucepan cook the linguine, carrot, and turnip in a large amount of boiling water for 3 to 4 minutes or until pasta and vegetables are tender. Drain. Rinse with cold water; drain again.

3. In a large salad bowl combine cooked pasta mixture, zucchini, sweet pepper, peas, and cheese. Add the dressing; toss gently to combine. Makes 6 servings.

NUTRITION FACTS PER SERVING:

155 calories
7 g total fat
1 g saturated fat
27 mg cholesterol
166 mg sodium
18 g carbohydrate
2 g fiber
6 g protein

INGREDIENTS

- 3 medium tomatoes, cut into wedges
- 1 medium cucumber, halved lengthwise and thinly sliced
- 1 small red onion, cut into thin wedges
- 2 tablespoons olive oil or salad oil
- 2 tablespoons lemon juice
- 2 teaspoons snipped fresh oregano or ½ teaspoon dried oregano, crushed
- ⅛ teaspoon salt
- ⅛ teaspoon pepper
- 8 to 10 Greek black olives
- ½ cup crumbled feta cheese (2 ounces)

greek salad

Feta cheese—a key ingredient in Greek cooking—gets its sharp, salty flavor from the brine in which it is cured.

Start to finish: 15 minutes

DIRECTIONS

1. In a salad bowl combine the tomatoes, cucumber, and red onion. Set aside.

2. For dressing, in a screw-top jar combine olive or salad oil, lemon juice, oregano, salt, and pepper. Cover and shake well.

3. Pour dressing over tomato mixture; toss gently to combine. Sprinkle with Greek olives and feta cheese. Makes 4 servings.

Greek olives

are ripe Kalamata olives that are imported from Greece. They have a saltier, more intense flavor than the more commonly available black or Mission olive.

NUTRITION FACTS PER SERVING:

143 calories
12 g total fat
3 g saturated fat
12 mg cholesterol
273 mg sodium
9 g carbohydrate
2 g fiber
4 g protein

Fruit Brûlée
See recipe, page 256

desserts

fruit sundaes

This fresh fruit snack is fast, fun, and nutritious.

INGREDIENTS

1½ cups fresh or frozen
strawberries, cut up

3 cups cut-up fresh fruits (such as
apples, bananas, cherries,
seedless red grapes,
kiwifruit, and/or peaches)

5 large waffle cones

2 tablespoons finely shredded
jicama (optional)

Cherries with stems (optional)

For a flavor variation, try different fresh berries or berry combinations in place of the blended strawberries. Or, stir your favorite yogurt into the fresh fruit mixture or combine the yogurt with the blended strawberries. As a final touch, sprinkle on a few chopped nuts or a little toasted coconut.

Start to finish: 10 minutes

DIRECTIONS

1. In a blender container place strawberries. Cover and blend until smooth.

2. In a mixing bowl gently combine cut-up fruits. Spoon into waffle cones.

3. Drizzle fruit with blended strawberries. If desired, top with jicama and cherries with stems. Makes 5 servings.

NUTRITION FACTS PER SERVING:

160 calories
1 g total fat
0 g saturated fat
0 mg cholesterol
27 mg sodium
38 g carbohydrate
3 g fiber
3 g protein

caramel oranges

Another time try this caramel sauce drizzled over ice cream or slices of pound cake.

INGREDIENTS

- **1 cup sugar**
- **½ cup hot orange-flavored tea**
- **1 to 2 drops oil of orange or ¼ teaspoon vanilla**
- **4 medium oranges, peeled and sliced crosswise**
- **4 teaspoons finely snipped crystallized ginger (optional)**
- **Orange peel curl (optional)**

Start to finish: 30 minutes

DIRECTIONS

1. To caramelize sugar, in a small heavy saucepan cook sugar over medium-high heat until sugar begins to melt, shaking pan occasionally to heat sugar evenly. Do not stir. Once the sugar starts to melt, reduce heat to low. Cook about 5 minutes more or until all of the sugar is melted and golden, stirring as needed with a wooden spoon.

2. Very slowly and carefully stir hot tea into caramelized sugar. If necessary, return to heat; cook until any hard sugar particles dissolve. Cool. Stir in the oil of orange or the vanilla.

3. To serve, pour the syrup onto 6 dessert plates. Arrange orange slices in syrup. If desired, sprinkle each serving with ginger and garnish with an orange peel curl. Makes 6 servings.

Ask for oil of orange at your
pharmacy or at a food specialty shop. If you have some orange flavoring on hand, it also can be substituted for the oil. Use about ¼ teaspoon.

NUTRITION FACTS PER SERVING:

- 170 calories
- 0 g total fat
- 0 g saturated fat
- 0 mg cholesterol
- 1 mg sodium
- 44 g carbohydrate
- 2 g fiber
- 1 g protein

fruit brûlée

When watermelon and nectarines are out of season, try this creamy topper on apple and pear slices.

INGREDIENTS

- 4 cups seeded watermelon balls
- 1 cup sliced nectarines
- 1 banana, bias-sliced
- ¼ cup orange liqueur or orange juice
- 1 8-ounce carton light dairy sour cream
- 2 teaspoons finely shredded lime peel
- ½ cup sugar

For ease in making

watermelon balls, purchase one of the newer varieties of seedless watermelon. That way you won't have to remove those pesky seeds.

Start to finish: 30 minutes

DIRECTIONS

1. Arrange fruit in 4 dessert bowls. Drizzle with orange liqueur or orange juice. Combine sour cream and lime peel; spoon ¼ cup mixture onto each serving.

2. To caramelize sugar, in a small heavy saucepan cook sugar over medium-high heat until sugar begins to melt, shaking pan occasionally to heat sugar evenly. Do not stir. Once the sugar starts to melt, reduce heat to low. Cook about 5 minutes more or until all of the sugar is melted and golden, stirring as needed with a wooden spoon.

3. Quickly and carefully drizzle caramelized sugar over each serving. Serve immediately. Makes 4 servings.

NUTRITION FACTS PER SERVING:

294 calories
5 g total fat
2 g saturated fat
7 mg cholesterol
68 mg sodium
57 g carbohydrate
1 g fiber
5 g protein

INGREDIENTS

- 2 cups chilled, seeded, and cubed watermelon
- 2 cups chilled, seeded, and cubed cantaloupe
- 1 to 2 teaspoons sugar
- ¼ cup balsamic vinegar
- 1 teaspoon freshly ground black pepper (optional)

Desserts

bella melone

It simply means "beautiful melon," but the Italians say it best. The secret is in the vinegar, and not just any kind will do. Balsamic vinegar boasts a rich, mellow note that wakes up summer's lazy taste buds.

Start to finish: 10 minutes

DIRECTIONS

1. Divide chilled watermelon cubes and cantaloupe cubes among 4 dessert dishes.

2. Stir sugar into vinegar until dissolved. Drizzle some of the vinegar mixture over each serving. If desired, sprinkle with pepper. Makes 4 servings.

NUTRITION FACTS PER SERVING:

73 calories
1 g total fat
0 g saturated fat
0 mg cholesterol
11 mg sodium
17 g carbohydrate
1 g fiber
1 g protein

To choose a cantaloupe

at the peak of perfection, press the blossom end with your index finger. It should give to gentle pressure. Then smell the melon; it should have a sweetly aromatic scent. A strong smell indicates over-ripeness. If you're buying a cut melon, look for deep apricot-colored meat inside— the deeper the color the sweeter the taste.

257

glazed nectarines with chocolate sauce

Celebrate the sweet arrival of nectarines with this luscious dessert. Indulging is easy because it goes together in just minutes. Serve it with a frosty mug of sun-brewed tea.

INGREDIENTS

4 medium nectarines or peaches, peeled (about 1½ pounds total)

¼ cup orange marmalade or apricot or peach preserves

1 tablespoon margarine or butter

1 tablespoon orange liqueur, apricot brandy, or orange juice

Chocolate ice-cream topping

To glaze the nectarines in the microwave oven, pit fruit as directed. For glaze, in a 1½-quart microwave-safe casserole, microwave margarine or butter, uncovered, on 100% power (high) for 30 to 40 seconds or until melted. Stir in marmalade or preserves and liqueur. Add fruit; spoon glaze over fruit. Cover and micro-cook on high for 3 to 4 minutes or until the fruit is tender, gently stirring once or twice. Serve as at right.

Prep time: 15 minutes
Cooking time: 7 minutes

DIRECTIONS

1. Carefully remove and discard the pits from nectarines or peaches, leaving fruit whole. Set aside.

2. For glaze, in a medium skillet combine the marmalade or preserves, margarine or butter, and liqueur; heat over medium heat just until margarine and marmalade are melted.

3. Add fruit. Spoon glaze over fruit. Bring to boiling; reduce heat. Cover and simmer for 7 to 9 minutes or until fruit is tender, gently stirring once.

4. To serve, divide fruit among 4 dessert dishes. Spoon glaze and chocolate topping over fruit. Makes 4 servings.

NUTRITION FACTS PER SERVING:

144 calories
3 g total fat
1 g saturated fat
0 mg cholesterol
41 mg sodium
30 g carbohydrate
2 g fiber
1 g protein

apricot-glazed pears

The sweetness of apricot jam brings out the juicy best in succulent fresh pears. Serve this simple, yet sophisticated, dessert as a fitting finale to a special meal.

INGREDIENTS

- ⅓ cup apricot jam
- ¼ cup orange juice
- 4 small pears, halved, peeled, and cored
  Whipped cream (optional)

Start to finish: 30 minutes

DIRECTIONS

1. In a 2-quart rectangular baking dish stir together jam and orange juice. Place pears in dish, cut sides down; spoon sauce over top. Bake, covered, in a 350° oven about 25 minutes or until pears are tender.

2. Serve warm pears in individual dessert dishes. Spoon sauce over pears. If desired, serve with whipped cream. Makes 4 servings.

NUTRITION FACTS PER SERVING:

178 calories
1 g total fat
0 g saturated fat
0 mg cholesterol
3 mg sodium
45 g carbohydrate
5 g fiber
1 g protein

Keep the kitchen

cool by preparing this refreshing dessert in the microwave oven. Prepare fruit as directed, except decrease orange juice to 3 tablespoons. Stir together jam and juice; arrange pear halves in a 2-quart microwave-safe baking dish. Cover with plastic wrap; turn back a corner to vent steam. Microwave on 100% power (high) for 6 to 9 minutes or until pears are tender, rearranging pears once during cooking. Serve as directed.

sweet and spicy peaches

Frozen peaches make it possible for you to enjoy this dessert year-round. Top it with yogurt as suggested, or spoon over a scoop of light ice cream.

INGREDIENTS

    2   tablespoons brown sugar
    1   tablespoon lime juice or lemon
          juice
    ½   teaspoon vanilla
    ¼   teaspoon ground allspice
    1   pound peaches, peeled, pitted,
          and sliced (3 cups), or 3 cups
          frozen unsweetened peach
          slices
    ¼   cup vanilla low-fat yogurt or
          fat-free dairy sour cream
        Lime peel strips (optional)

Prep time: 10 minutes
Cooking time: 15 minutes

Micro-cook these juicy peaches by combining the brown sugar, lime or lemon juice, vanilla, and allspice in a 1-quart microwave-safe casserole. Stir in the peaches. Cover and microwave on 100% power (high) for 2 to 5 minutes (4 to 7 minutes if using frozen peaches) or until the peaches are tender and heated through, stirring once. Serve as directed.

DIRECTIONS

1. In a medium saucepan combine the brown sugar, lime or lemon juice, vanilla, and allspice. Stir in the peaches.

2. Bring to boiling; reduce heat. Cover and simmer about 10 minutes or until peaches are tender and hot. Serve warm, topped with the yogurt or sour cream. If desired, garnish with lime peel strips. Makes 4 servings.

NUTRITION FACTS PER SERVING:

 93 calories
0 g total fat
0 g saturated fat
1 mg cholesterol
11 mg sodium
23 g carbohydrate
2 g fiber
2 g protein

fresh fruit with creamy sauce

Fresh fruit desserts can satisfy your sweet tooth yet still supply important vitamins. The best part—they're generally low in calories.

INGREDIENTS

½ cup vanilla low-fat yogurt
¼ cup unsweetened applesauce
1 teaspoon honey
1 cup sliced nectarines; sliced, peeled peaches; orange sections; or sliced strawberries
1 cup sliced apple or pear
1 small banana, sliced
½ cup seedless grapes
   Ground cinnamon or ground nutmeg

Start to finish: 10 minutes

DIRECTIONS

1. For sauce, stir together the yogurt, applesauce, and the honey.

2. In a medium bowl stir together the nectarines, peaches, oranges, or strawberries; the apple or pear; the banana; and grapes.

3. Divide the fruit mixture among 6 dessert dishes. Spoon some of the sauce over each serving. Sprinkle with cinnamon or nutmeg. Makes 6 servings.

NUTRITION FACTS PER SERVING:

75 calories
1 g total fat
0 g saturated fat
1 mg cholesterol
12 mg sodium
17 g carbohydrate
1 g fiber
1 g protein

For the best-tasting

dessert, choose peaches or nectarines carefully. The fruits should be plump, tender, brightly colored, and heavy for their size (this indicates juiciness). Avoid fruits with mold, mildew, bruises, cuts, or other blemishes. To ripen peaches or nectarines, place them in a paper bag and let them stand at room temperature for a few days until desired ripeness, checking the fruit every day. Once the fruit is ripe, store it in the refrigerator.

sweet-topped raspberries

Yogurt lends a livelier flavor to frozen dessert topping by adding a slight tang. Top other desserts with this slimming combination instead of fat-laden whipped cream.

INGREDIENTS

- ½ teaspoon finely shredded orange peel
- 2 tablespoons orange juice
- 2 cups fresh raspberries, blueberries, or sliced strawberries
- ½ cup thawed frozen light or fat-free whipped dessert topping
- ¼ cup vanilla low-fat yogurt
  Finely shredded orange peel (optional)

When choosing fresh berries, look for berries with healthy color for the particular variety. Once you have them home, spread them in a single layer, loosely cover, and store in the refrigerator until you're ready to use them. Because berries are highly perishable, they need to be used within 1 to 2 days. Just before you're ready to eat them, wash them.

Start to finish: 10 minutes

DIRECTIONS

1. In a medium bowl stir together the ½ teaspoon orange peel and the orange juice. Add the berries; toss to coat.

2. For topping, in a small bowl stir together the dessert topping and yogurt.

3. Divide berry mixture among 4 dessert dishes. Spoon some of the topping over each serving. If desired, sprinkle with additional finely shredded orange peel. Serve immediately. Makes 4 servings.

NUTRITION FACTS PER SERVING:

57 calories
1 g total fat
1 g saturated fat
1 mg cholesterol
12 mg sodium
11 g carbohydrate
3 g fiber
1 g protein

autumn apple fritters

You won't fritter away your time in the kitchen, creating these batter-covered fruit slices. Simply leave the apple peels on (but do remove the core) to produce this homey treat perfect for dessert or a snack.

INGREDIENTS

- 2 tart medium cooking apples (such as Jonathan or Granny Smith)
- ⅔ cup all-purpose flour
- 1 tablespoon powdered sugar
- ½ teaspoon finely shredded lemon peel
- ¼ teaspoon baking powder
- 1 egg
- ½ cup milk
- 1 teaspoon cooking oil
  Shortening or cooking oil for deep-fat frying
  Powdered sugar (optional)

Start to finish: 20 minutes

DIRECTIONS

1. Core apples and cut each crosswise into 6 rings. In a medium bowl combine flour, the 1 tablespoon powdered sugar, the lemon peel, and baking powder.

2. In a bowl use a wire whisk to combine egg, milk, and the 1 teaspoon cooking oil. Add egg mixture all at once to flour mixture; beat until smooth.

3. Using a fork, dip apple rings into batter; drain off excess batter. Fry 2 to 3 fritters at a time in deep hot fat (365°) about 2 minutes or until golden, turning once with a slotted spoon. Drain on paper towels. Repeat with remaining apple rings. If desired, sprinkle fritters with powdered sugar. Cool on wire racks. Makes 12 fritters.

When deep-fat frying, don't overheat the melted shortening or cooking oil to the point that it smokes. By that time, it is already breaking down. Instead invest in a deep-fat-frying thermometer and heat the fat or oil to the temperature called for in a recipe. For these fritters, the temperature is 365°.

NUTRITION FACTS PER SERVING:

91 calories
6 g total fat
1 g saturated fat
19 mg cholesterol
18 mg sodium
9 g carbohydrate
1 g fiber
2 g protein

263

apples with cinnamon-cider dip

Once cut, the apple slices brown quickly. Sprinkle them with lemon juice mixed with a little water, or treat them with an ascorbic acid color keeper.

INGREDIENTS

- 2 tablespoons cornstarch
- 1 tablespoon brown sugar
- 1¼ cups apple cider or apple juice
- 3 tablespoons honey
- 2 teaspoons lemon juice
- ½ teaspoon ground cinnamon
- ⅛ teaspoon salt (optional)
- Dash ground cloves
- Dash ground allspice
- 1 tablespoon butter or margarine
- 4 apples, cored and sliced

This spicy dip
tastes great with pears, too. Or, try it as a sauce over vanilla ice cream or pound cake.

Start to finish: 15 minutes

DIRECTIONS

1. For dip, in a medium saucepan combine cornstarch and brown sugar. Stir in apple cider, honey, lemon juice, cinnamon, salt (if desired), cloves, and allspice. Cook and stir until thickened and bubbly. Cook and stir for 2 minutes more. Remove from heat. Add butter or margarine; stir until melted.

2. Serve dip warm with sliced apples. Makes 4 to 6 servings.

NUTRITION FACTS PER SERVING:

221 calories
3 g total fat
2 g saturated fat
8 mg cholesterol
34 mg sodium
51 g carbohydrate
3 g fiber
0 g protein

fresh fruit with mocha fondue

Dessert fondues encourage lingering over the dinner table with good conversation. For a truly memorable dessert, we added coffee crystals and coffee liqueur to a rich chocolate fondue.

INGREDIENTS

- 1 4-ounce package sweet baking chocolate, broken up
- 4 ounces semisweet chocolate, chopped
- ⅔ cup half-and-half, light cream, or milk
- ½ cup sifted powdered sugar
- 1 teaspoon instant coffee crystals
- 2 tablespoons coffee liqueur
   Assorted fresh fruit (such as apricot wedges, pear wedges, plum wedges, strawberries, pineapple chunks, kiwifruit wedges, and/or banana slices)

Start to finish: 15 minutes

DIRECTIONS

1. In a heavy medium saucepan combine sweet baking chocolate; semisweet chocolate; half-and-half, light cream, or milk; powdered sugar; and coffee crystals. Heat and stir over low heat until melted and smooth. Remove from heat; stir in liqueur.

2. Pour into a fondue pot; keep warm over low heat. Serve with fresh fruit as dippers. Makes 6 to 8 servings.

NUTRITION FACTS PER SERVING:

305 calories
16 g total fat
10 g saturated fat
10 mg cholesterol
13 mg sodium
43 g carbohydrate
2 g fiber
3 g protein

For attractive fruit pieces, dip the pear wedges and banana slices in a little lemon juice to keep them from turning brown.

265

fresh fruit with honey-lime sauce

Sweet and juicy, fresh pineapple makes a wonderful addition to all kinds of fruit desserts. To simplify preparation, look for peeled and cored fresh pineapple in the produce section of your supermarket.

INGREDIENTS

- 2 cups cut-up fresh pineapple
- 3 kiwifruit, peeled, halved lengthwise, and sliced
- 1 medium papaya, peeled, seeded, and sliced
- 1 medium banana, sliced
- ¼ of a small watermelon, sliced and cut into wedges
- 2 tablespoons lime juice
- 1 8-ounce carton vanilla low-fat yogurt
- 4 teaspoons honey
- ½ teaspoon finely shredded lime peel
- 1 tablespoon lime juice

Why throw away limes, lemons, or oranges when you can still use the peel? After squeezing out the juice, store the halved rinds in a storage container in the freezer. When a recipe calls for finely shredded peel, simply grate the frozen rind. That way, you get the fresh citrus flavor without having to keep the fresh fruits on hand.

Start to finish: 25 minutes

DIRECTIONS

1. Arrange pineapple, kiwifruit, papaya, banana, and watermelon on 6 dessert plates. Sprinkle with the 2 tablespoons lime juice.

2. For sauce, in a medium bowl stir together vanilla yogurt, honey, lime peel, and the 1 tablespoon lime juice.

3. Spoon sauce over fruit. Serve immediately. Makes 6 servings.

NUTRITION FACTS PER SERVING:

144 calories
1 g total fat
1 g saturated fat
2 mg cholesterol
26 mg sodium
33 g carbohydrate
3 g fiber
3 g protein

INGREDIENTS

- 1 cup ricotta cheese
- ⅓ cup sifted powdered sugar
- 1 tablespoon unsweetened cocoa powder
- ¼ teaspoon vanilla
- 2 tablespoons miniature semisweet chocolate pieces
- 1 teaspoon finely shredded orange peel
- 3 large ripe Bosc, Anjou, or Bartlett pears
- 2 tablespoons orange juice

- 2 tablespoons slivered or sliced almonds, toasted
- Orange peel curls (optional)

chocolate ricotta-filled pears

Discover the wonderful flavors of the classic Sicilian ricotta-chocolate-fruit-filled cake called cassata—without turning on your oven or chopping a thing.

Start to finish: 20 minutes

DIRECTIONS

1. In a medium bowl beat the ricotta cheese, powdered sugar, cocoa powder, and vanilla with an electric mixer on medium speed until combined. Stir in chocolate pieces and the 1 teaspoon orange peel. Set aside.

2. Peel the pears; cut in half lengthwise and remove the cores. Remove a thin slice from the rounded side of each half so it will sit flat. Brush the pears all over with orange juice.

3. Place the pears on dessert plates. Spoon the ricotta mixture on top of the pears and sprinkle with almonds. If desired, garnish with orange peel curls. Makes 6 servings.

Toasting the almonds gives
them a deeper, richer flavor and helps them stay crisp. To toast the almonds, spread them in a single layer in a shallow baking pan. Bake in a 350° oven for 5 to 10 minutes or until golden. Watch the nuts carefully and stir them once or twice so they don't burn.

NUTRITION FACTS PER SERVING:

  166 calories
6 g total fat
2 g saturated fat
13 mg cholesterol
52 mg sodium
24 g carbohydrate
3 g fiber
6 g protein

caramel crunch ice-cream sauce

Surprise—cereal adds crunch to this sauce, which is ready in 15 minutes.

INGREDIENTS

- ¼ cup margarine or butter
- ⅓ cup chopped or sliced almonds
- ⅓ cup light-colored corn syrup
- ⅓ cup packed brown sugar
- 1 tablespoon water
- ⅓ cup crisp rice cereal, coarsely crushed

  Ice cream

For an extra-special sundae, top ice cream with sliced bananas and drizzle with some of this easy caramel sauce. It's equally delicious over pound cake or fruit.

Start to finish: 15 minutes

DIRECTIONS

1. In a medium skillet melt margarine or butter. Add the almonds; cook and stir over medium-low heat about 5 minutes or until almonds are browned.

2. Add the corn syrup, brown sugar, and water to the skillet. Cook and stir until bubbly and the brown sugar is dissolved (about 4 minutes). Stir in the rice cereal. Serve immediately over ice cream. Makes about 1 cup sauce.

NUTRITION FACTS PER SERVING:

159 calories
9 g total fat
1 g saturated fat
0 mg cholesterol
92 mg sodium
21 g carbohydrate
1 g fiber
1 g protein

268

peachy cherry sauce

This luscious fruit dessert boasts only 2 grams of fat per serving.

INGREDIENTS

- ¼ cup low-calorie orange marmalade spread
- ¼ cup orange juice
- 2 teaspoons cornstarch
- 1 teaspoon margarine or butter
- ¼ teaspoon ground cardamom or ground cinnamon
- 2 cups sliced, peeled peaches or nectarines or frozen unsweetened peach slices
- 1 cup pitted dark sweet cherries or frozen unsweetened pitted dark sweet cherries
- ½ cup frozen yogurt or low-fat or light ice cream

Prep time: 20 minutes
Cooking time: 10 minutes

DIRECTIONS

1. In a medium saucepan combine the marmalade spread, orange juice, cornstarch, margarine or butter, and cardamom or cinnamon. Cook and stir until thickened and bubbly. Stir in the peaches and cherries. Cover and cook over medium heat for 10 to 12 minutes or until fruits are just tender, stirring once. Cool slightly.

2. To serve, spoon sauce into dessert dishes. Top each serving with a small spoonful of the frozen yogurt. Makes 5 servings.

NUTRITION FACTS PER SERVING:

117 calories
2 g total fat
1 g saturated fat
2 mg cholesterol
21 mg sodium
24 g carbohydrate
2 g fiber
2 g protein

To remove the peel from a peach, dip the peach into boiling water for 20 seconds. Then use a paring knife to remove the skin. If the skin doesn't peel easily, return the peach to the boiling water for a few more seconds.

cinnamon-spiked mocha sundaes

Summer and sundaes go together like peanut butter and jelly. When temperatures soar, let your ice-cream-loving crowd create these sundaes.

INGREDIENTS

¾ cup fudge ice-cream topping
1½ to 2 teaspoons instant coffee crystals
1 pint (2 cups) cinnamon ice cream, (see tip, below)
Whipped cream
Almond brickle pieces
Cinnamon sticks (optional)

If you can't find cinnamon ice cream, stir ¾ teaspoon ground cinnamon into 1 pint (2 cups) softened vanilla ice cream. Freeze until firm.

Start to finish: 10 minutes

DIRECTIONS

1. In a microwave-safe bowl combine ice-cream topping and coffee crystals. Cover. Microwave on 100% power (high) until warm, stirring often.

2. In each of 4 sundae glasses layer cinnamon ice cream and sauce. Top with whipped cream and almond brickle pieces. If desired, garnish with cinnamon sticks. Makes 4 servings.

NUTRITION FACTS PER SERVING:

410 calories
23 g total fat
13 g saturated fat
52 mg cholesterol
139 mg sodium
50 g carbohydrate
0 g fiber
6 g protein

270

rum-sauced bananas

Shop for the best nutritional bargain when selecting low-fat or light ice cream. Compare the nutrition content of several brands and choose the one that's lowest in calories and fat.

INGREDIENTS

- ¼ cup apple cider or apple juice
- 4 teaspoons brown sugar
- 1 teaspoon margarine or butter
  Dash ground nutmeg
- 2 large bananas, sliced (about 1¾ cups)
- 1 tablespoon rum
- 1 cup vanilla or coffee low-fat or light ice cream or frozen yogurt

Start to finish: 10 minutes

DIRECTIONS

1. In a medium saucepan combine the apple cider or apple juice, brown sugar, margarine or butter, and nutmeg. Heat just to boiling.

2. Add sliced bananas; toss to coat. Heat through. Stir in the rum.

3. Serve banana mixture over the ice cream. Makes 4 servings.

NUTRITION FACTS PER SERVING:

163 calories
3 g total fat
1 g saturated fat
5 mg cholesterol
41 mg sodium
33 g carbohydrate
2 g fiber
2 g protein

If you prefer, prepare the banana mixture in the microwave oven. In a 1-quart microwave-safe bowl combine the apple cider, brown sugar, margarine or butter, and nutmeg. Microwave, uncovered, on 100% power (high) for 1 minute. Add the sliced bananas; toss to coat. Micro-cook on 100% power (high) for 1½ to 2 minutes or until the bananas are heated through; stir in the rum. Serve over the ice cream.

271

grilled banana sundaes

Even if you can't vacation in the tropics, you can enjoy the taste of the tropics. Cook bananas and a quick caramel sauce on the grill, then spoon over ice cream.

INGREDIENTS

- 3 large firm bananas
- 1 tablespoon margarine or butter, melted
- 2 teaspoons lime juice or orange juice
- ½ cup caramel ice-cream topping
- ¼ teaspoon ground cinnamon
- 1 pint vanilla ice cream
- Toasted coconut (optional)
- Sliced almonds, toasted (optional)

Start to finish: 20 minutes

DIRECTIONS

1. Cut bananas in half lengthwise, then cut each piece in half crosswise. (You should have 12 pieces.) Stir together margarine or butter and 1 teaspoon of the lime or orange juice. Brush mixture on all sides of banana pieces.

2. Place bananas directly on the grill rack over medium-hot coals. Grill, uncovered, for 2 minutes; turn over and grill for 2 minutes more or until heated through.

3. Meanwhile, in a heavy, medium skillet or saucepan combine the caramel topping and the remaining lime or orange juice. Heat on the grill rack alongside bananas directly over the coals until bubbly, stirring frequently. (Or, heat on range top over medium heat until bubbly, stirring frequently.) Stir in cinnamon. Add bananas and stir gently to coat.

4. To serve, scoop ice cream into 4 dessert dishes. Spoon sauce and bananas over ice cream. If desired, sprinkle with the coconut and/or almonds. Makes 4 servings.

NUTRITION FACTS PER SERVING:

367 calories
11 g total fat
5 g saturated fat
29 mg cholesterol
231 mg sodium
70 g carbohydrate
2 g fiber
4 g protein

INGREDIENTS

- 1 12-ounce jar caramel ice-cream topping
- 1/3 cup pure maple syrup or maple-flavored syrup
- 1 quart (4 cups) macadamia brittle, butter brickle, or butter-pecan ice cream
- 2 cups sliced mango or papaya or fresh pineapple chunks
  Shredded coconut, toasted (optional)

tropicana delight

Indulge in this irresistible sundae topped with mango, papaya, or pineapple and experience the romance of the tropics.

Start to finish: 10 minutes

DIRECTIONS

1. Stir together caramel ice-cream topping and maple syrup.

2. Layer scoops of ice cream and caramel mixture into 8 sundae glasses. Top with sliced mango, papaya, or pineapple chunks. If desired, sprinkle with toasted coconut. Makes 8 servings.

NUTRITION FACTS PER SERVING:

343 calories
9 g total fat
5 g saturated fat
30 mg cholesterol
211 mg sodium
63 g carbohydrate
2 g fiber
2 g protein

For a raspberry delight, combine some unsweetened raspberries (thawed, if frozen) and a few spoonfuls of sugar. Mash some of the raspberries slightly. Let stand at room temperature until syrupy. Layer scoops of raspberry sherbet and the raspberries in sundae glasses. Sprinkle generously with white chocolate shavings. If desired, garnish with fresh mint.

273

chocolate malt-peppermint cooler

Create your own diner at home—serve this fun-to-slurp shake with hamburgers and fries.

INGREDIENTS

- 3 cups chocolate milk
- 1 quart (4 cups) vanilla or chocolate ice cream
- ¼ cup malted milk powder
- ½ teaspoon peppermint extract
- ⅛ teaspoon ground cinnamon
  Coarsely crushed hard peppermint candies
- 6 peppermint sticks

To clean your blender in a jiffy, fill the blender container two-thirds full with lukewarm water and a small amount of detergent. Cover and blend a few seconds until the container is clean. Rinse, dry, and return to base.

Start to finish: 15 minutes

DIRECTIONS

1. In a blender container place the chocolate milk, half of the ice cream, the malted milk powder, peppermint extract, and ground cinnamon. Cover and blend until mixture is smooth. Pour into 6 large, chilled glasses.

2. Top each drink with a scoop of the remaining ice cream. Sprinkle with the crushed candy pieces. Place a peppermint stick in each glass. Makes 6 servings.

NUTRITION FACTS PER SERVING:

329 calories
13 g total fat
8 g saturated fat
49 mg cholesterol
199 mg sodium
46 g carbohydrate
0 g fiber
8 g protein

just peachy shake

Because you have the choice of fresh or frozen peaches, you can enjoy this fruit-and-peanut-butter treat any time you like.

INGREDIENTS

1   pint (2 cups) vanilla frozen
        yogurt
1   medium peach, peeled, pitted,
        and cut up, or ½ cup frozen
        unsweetened peach slices
1   tablespoon honey
1   tablespoon creamy peanut
        butter
    Chopped peaches (optional)
    Finely chopped peanuts
        (optional)

Start to finish: 10 minutes

DIRECTIONS

1. In a blender container combine frozen yogurt, cut-up fresh or frozen peach pieces, honey, and peanut butter. Cover and blend until smooth.

2. Pour into 2 glasses. If desired, garnish each serving with chopped peaches and finely chopped peanuts. Makes 2 servings.

NUTRITION FACTS PER SERVING:

326 calories
12 g total fat
6 g saturated fat
4 mg cholesterol
165 mg sodium
50 g carbohydrate
1 g fiber
8 g protein

Your blender does a lot more than

make shakes. At the flick of a switch, you can use it to make short work of chopping parsley or other fresh herbs. You also can chop hard-cooked eggs for egg salad, and crush graham crackers for piecrusts. Rely on it to speed up preparing fruit juice concentrates. And, when it comes to grating hard cheeses, such as Parmesan cheese, your blender can save you lots of time and effort.

275

berry-banana sipper

This refreshing dessert in a glass is the perfect windup for just about any dinner.

INGREDIENTS

1 small banana, peeled, cut up, and frozen (see tip, below)

¼ cup fresh or frozen assorted berries (such as strawberries, blackberries, and/or raspberries)

1 cup orange juice

3 tablespoons vanilla low-fat yogurt

Fresh strawberries, sliced (optional)

Peel and cut up the banana

before freezing. Place the cut-up banana in a freezer container or plastic bag, then use the pieces straight from the freezer.

Start to finish: 10 minutes

DIRECTIONS

1. In a blender container combine banana pieces, desired berries, orange juice, and yogurt. Cover and blend until smooth.

2. To serve, pour into tall glasses. If desired, garnish with strawberries. Makes 2 servings.

NUTRITION FACTS PER SERVING:

132 calories
0 g total fat
0 g saturated fat
1 mg cholesterol
14 mg sodium
29 g carbohydrate
2 g fiber
2 g protein

Berry-Banana Sipper (front) and
Coffee-Banana Smoothie (back)

INGREDIENTS

  2 small bananas, peeled, cut up,
       and frozen (see tip, opposite
       page)
1½ cups fat-free milk
  1 8-ounce carton coffee
       low-fat yogurt
  ¼ teaspoon ground cinnamon
      Dash ground nutmeg
      Banana slices (optional)
      Fresh mint (optional)

coffee-banana smoothie

Be sure to start with frozen bananas; this makes the drink taste rich and icy like a milk shake. (See photograph, opposite page.)

Start to finish: 10 minutes

DIRECTIONS

1. In a blender container combine bananas, milk, yogurt, cinnamon, and nutmeg. Cover and blend until smooth.

2. To serve, pour into glasses. If desired, garnish with banana slices and mint. Makes 2 servings.

NUTRITION FACTS PER SERVING:

280 calories
2 g total fat
1 g saturated fat
9 mg cholesterol
165 mg sodium
52 g carbohydrate
4 g fiber
13 g protein

Be creative— make smoothies

with different combinations of fruits and yogurts. Try these ideas and then branch out—almost anything goes.

• Pineapple-Orange Smoothie: In blender container combine 1 medium banana, peeled and cut up; one 8-ounce can crushed pineapple (juice pack); one 8-ounce carton vanilla yogurt; and 1 cup orange juice. Cover and blend until smooth. Makes 4 servings.

• Strawberry-Banana Smoothie: In blender container combine 2 small bananas, peeled and cut up; 1 cup frozen unsweetened whole strawberries; one 8-ounce carton vanilla low-fat yogurt; and ¾ cup milk. Cover and blend until smooth. Makes 2 servings.

• Peach Smoothie: Peel, pit, and cut up 2 medium peaches. In a blender container combine peaches, 1½ cups milk, one 8-ounce carton vanilla yogurt, and 1 to 2 tablespoons powdered sugar. Cover and blend until smooth. With blender running, add ½ cup ice cubes, one at a time, through lid opening. Blend until smooth. Makes 4 servings.

towering brownie sundaes

The smaller the brownies, the quicker they bake. The individual mini brownies used in this recipe bake in just 15 minutes.

INGREDIENTS

Nonstick cooking spray
¼ cup butter
1 ounce unsweetened chocolate, cut up
½ cup sugar
1 egg
½ teaspoon vanilla
⅓ cup all-purpose flour
¼ cup coarsely chopped peanuts
1 cup chocolate-fudge ice-cream topping
2 tablespoons peanut butter
1 quart (4 cups) tin roof sundae ice cream or vanilla ice cream
Banana slices (optional)

Chocolate-covered peanut butter cups, chopped (optional)
Peanuts (optional)

Start to finish: 30 minutes

DIRECTIONS

1. Lightly coat twelve 1¾-inch muffin cups with nonstick spray; set aside.

2. In a medium saucepan melt butter and unsweetened chocolate over low heat. Remove from heat. Cool 3 minutes. Stir in sugar. Add egg and vanilla, beating lightly with a spoon just until combined. (Don't overbeat.) Stir in flour and the ¼ cup peanuts.

3. Divide batter evenly among prepared muffin cups, filling each nearly full. Bake in a 350° oven 15 minutes or until set (toothpick will not come out clean, nor will brownies spring back). Cool brownies 3 minutes in pan; remove to a wire rack to cool.

4. Meanwhile, in a small heavy saucepan heat and stir ice-cream topping and peanut butter over medium-low heat until smooth. Remove saucepan from heat.

5. Spoon ice cream into 6 dessert dishes. Top each serving with 2 brownies and, if desired, banana slices. Drizzle with the warm peanut butter mixture. If desired, top with peanut butter cups and additional peanuts. Makes 6 servings.

NUTRITION FACTS PER SERVING:

640 calories
36 g total fat
18 g saturated fat
95 mg cholesterol
299 mg sodium
77 g carbohydrate
1 g fiber
12 g protein

278

INGREDIENTS

- 1 9½-inch tart-shaped sponge cake or 8 individual sponge cakes or shortcakes
- ½ cup cherry juice or orange juice
- ½ of a 4-ounce container frozen whipped dessert topping, thawed
- 1 6-ounce carton cherry-vanilla yogurt or desired flavor yogurt
- 2 cups fresh light or dark sweet cherries (such as Rainier or Bing)

cherry trifle cake

Sliced strawberries or fresh raspberries also make a delicious company-special trifle.

Start to finish: 20 minutes

DIRECTIONS

1. Place cake(s) on a serving platter. Sprinkle cherry juice or orange juice over cake(s). Set aside.

2. For topping, in a small bowl stir together whipped topping and yogurt. Spread topping onto cake(s). Cover and store in refrigerator while preparing cherries.

3. Remove stems from cherries. Halve the cherries and remove seeds. Arrange the cherries, cut sides down, on top of the yogurt mixture. Makes 8 servings.

If you like, substitute 2 to 4 tablespoons cream sherry for an equal amount of the cherry juice or orange juice.

NUTRITION FACTS PER SERVING:

- 146 calories
- 3 g total fat
- 2 g saturated fat
- 27 mg cholesterol
- 76 mg sodium
- 28 g carbohydrate
- 1 g fiber
- 3 g protein

crunch-topped peach pizza

Starting with an Italian bread shell takes most of the work out of this peachy dessert-style pizza.

INGREDIENTS

1   16-ounce (12-inch) Italian bread shell (Boboli)

1   21-ounce can peach or apple pie filling

⅓   cup quick-cooking rolled oats

¼   cup packed brown sugar

3   tablespoons all-purpose flour

3   tablespoons butter or margarine, melted

Supermarkets often stock summer fruits in the dead of winter. That's because on the other side of the equator (especially in Chile) these fruits are picked and shipped north during our winter. Because these fruits are harvested when mature but still unripe, they need ripening at room temperature in a paper bag. Save these imported gems for fresh fruit bowls or lunch-box treats. For baked desserts that require cupfuls of fruit, use frozen fruits or canned pie filling as in this recipe.

Prep time: 15 minutes
Baking time: 12 minutes

DIRECTIONS

1. Place the Italian bread shell on a pizza pan or large baking sheet. Top with the peach or apple pie filling, spreading evenly.

2. In a small bowl stir together rolled oats, brown sugar, and flour. Stir in the melted butter or margarine until well mixed. Sprinkle over pie filling. Bake in a 400° oven for 12 to 15 minutes or until heated through. Makes 8 servings.

NUTRITION FACTS PER SERVING:

   334 calories
8 g total fat
1 g saturated fat
8 mg cholesterol
389 mg sodium
61 g carbohydrate
1 g fiber
8 g protein

INGREDIENTS

- 1 16-ounce can peach slices (juice-pack), drained and cut up
- 1 16-ounce can pear halves (juice-pack), drained and cut up
- 1 teaspoon grated fresh ginger
- ½ cup finely crushed gingersnaps
- ½ cup quick-cooking rolled oats
- 2 tablespoons brown sugar

gingered peach and pear crisp

You get a double dose of ginger with each bite of this luscious dessert. Fresh grated ginger flavors the fruit filling, and gingersnaps—combined with rolled oats—form the crumb topping.

Prep time: 15 minutes
Baking time: 15 minutes

DIRECTIONS

1. In an 8-inch quiche dish or 8×1½-inch round baking pan place the peaches, pears, and fresh ginger. Toss to mix.

2. In a small bowl stir together the gingersnaps, oats, and brown sugar. Sprinkle evenly over fruit. Bake in a 425° oven for 15 to 20 minutes or until heated through. Makes 6 servings.

Keep fresh ginger stored in the freezer. When frozen, it grates easily and there are no messy juices.

NUTRITION FACTS PER SERVING:

♥ 138 calories
1 g total fat
1 g saturated fat
0 mg cholesterol
48 mg sodium
32 g carbohydrate
2 g fiber
2 g protein

283

Metric Cooking Hints

By making a few conversions, cooks in Australia, Canada, and the United Kingdom can use the recipes in this book with confidence. The charts on this page provide a guide for converting measurements from the U.S. customary system, which is used throughout this book, to the imperial and metric systems. There also is a conversion table for oven temperatures to accommodate the differences in oven calibrations.

Product Differences: Most of the ingredients called for in the recipes in this book are available in English-speaking countries. However, some are known by different names. Here are some common U.S. American ingredients and their possible counterparts:
• Sugar is granulated or castor sugar.
• Powdered sugar is icing sugar.
• All-purpose flour is plain household flour or white four. When self-rising flour is used in place of all-purpose flour in a recipe that calls for leavening, omit the leavening agent (baking soda or baking powder) and salt.
• Light-colored corn syrup is golden syrup.
• Cornstarch is cornflour.
• Baking soda is bicarbonate of soda.
• Vanilla is vanilla essence.
• Green, red, or yellow sweet peppers are capsicums.
• Golden raisins are sultanas.

Volume and Weight: U.S. Americans traditionally use cup measures for liquid and solid ingredients. The chart, below, shows the approximate imperial and metric equivalents. If you are accustomed to weighing solid ingredients, the following approximate equivalents will help.
• 1 cup butter, castor sugar, or rice = 8 ounces = about 230 grams
• 1 cup flour = 4 ounces = about 115 grams
• 1 cup icing sugar = 5 ounces = about 140 grams

Spoon measures are used for smaller amounts of ingredients. Although the size of the tablespoon varies slightly in different countries, for practical purposes and for recipes in this book, a straight substitution is all that's necessary.
Measurements made using cups or spoons always should be level unless stated otherwise.

Equivalents: U.S. = Australia/U.K.

⅛ teaspoon = 0.6 ml
¼ teaspoon = 1.25 ml
½ teaspoon = 2.5 ml
1 teaspoon = 5 ml
1 tablespoon = 1 tablespoon = 15 ml
¼ cup = 4 tablespoons = 2 fluid ounces = 60 ml
⅓ cup = ¼ cup = 5 tablespoons + 1 teaspoon = 3 fluid ounces = 80 ml
½ cup = ⅓ cup = 4 fluid ounces = 120 ml
⅔ cup = ½ cup = 10 tablespoons + 2 teaspoons = 6 fluid ounces = 160 ml
¾ cup = ⅔ cup = 6 fluid ounces = 180 ml
1 cup = ¾ cup = 8 fluid ounces = 240 ml
1¼ cup = 1 cup
2 cups = 1 pint = 16 fluid ounces
1 quart = 1 liter
½ inch = 1.27 cm
1 inch = 2.54 cm

Baking Pan Sizes

American	Metric
8×1½-inch round baking pan	20×4-cm cake tin
9×1½-inch round baking pan	23×4-cm cake tin
11×7×1½-inch baking pan	28×18×4-cm baking tin
13×9×2-inch baking pan	32×23×5-cm baking tin
2-quart rectangular baking dish	28×18×4-cm baking tin
15×10×1-inch baking pan	38×25.5×2.5-cm baking tin (Swiss roll tin)
9-inch pie plate	22×4- or 23×4-cm pie plate
7- or 8-inch springform pan	18- or 20-cm springform or loose-bottom cake tin
9×5×3-inch loaf pan	23×13×8-cm or 2-pound narrow loaf tin or pâté tin
1½-quart casserole	1.5-liter casserole
2-quart casserole	2-liter casserole

Oven Temperature Equivalents

Fahrenheit Setting	Celsius Setting*	Gas Setting
300°F	150°C	Gas Mark 2 (slow)
325°F	160°C	Gas Mark 3 (moderately slow)
350°F	180°C	Gas Mark 4 (moderate)
375°F	190°C	Gas Mark 5 (moderately hot)
400°F	200°C	Gas Mark 6 (hot)
425°F	220°C	Gas Mark 73.859
450°F	230°C	Gas Mark 8 (very hot)
Broil		Grill

*Electric and gas ovens may be calibrated using Celsius. However, for an electric oven, increase the Celsius setting 10 to 20 degrees when cooking above 160°C. For convection or forced-air ovens (gas or electric), lower the temperature setting 10°C when cooking at all heat levels.